3/26/11
#18.95

A Government Ill Executed

A Government Ill Executed:

∾ THE DECLINE OF THE FEDERAL SERVICE
AND HOW TO REVERSE IT

PAUL C. LIGHT

HARVARD UNIVERSITY PRESS

Cambridge, Massachusetts, and London, England

First Harvard University Press paperback edition, 2009

Library of Congress Cataloging-in-Publication Data

Light, Paul Charles.
  A government ill executed : the decline of the federal service and how to reverse it /
Paul C. Light.
    p. cm.
  Includes bibliographical references and index.
  ISBN 978-0-674-02808-1 (cloth : alk. paper)
  ISBN 978-0-674-03478-5 (pbk.)
  1. Civil service—United States. 2. Public administration—United States. I. Title.
  JK692.L534 2008
  351.73—dc22   2007044648

Contents

Foreword

by Paul A. Volcker

Nothing is more certain in American political life than complaints about the performance of the federal government. At the same time, there are insistent demands for government to do more—to provide more security, personal, national, and financial; to improve health care; to protect the environment; to build transport systems; not least to build a strong and independent judiciary.

But somehow, the contradiction between the two discordant opinions is never really understood or addressed. The challenge for public administration—what it takes to improve performance—is hardly addressed.

Universities vie to nurture schools of *business* administration, and students covet the MBA. Prestigious schools of law and medicine attract many of our best young people, including those eager to "make a difference." But with some significant exceptions, schools of *public* administration wither on the vine without needed financial support, academic priority, prestige, or public interest.

Paul Light's important new book irrefutably documents the challenge that so many of us sense—that government performance at all levels has deteriorated over these recent decades and too little is being done to change the picture.

For all of us interested in government, it is not a pretty picture— really not tolerable for a strong democracy that purports to be the benign world leader, with unique responsibilities as the one and only superpower.

In that sense, the book is a call to action—action beyond campaign rhetoric or popular catchphrases that typically lack substance or fail to sustain effort. Paul Light goes further. Drawing from decades of experience and analysis, he sets out the substance of what is required for real and lasting reform. As he argues, the problems exist at every level of the federal hierarchy.

There is much to be done to repair this damage, but action must start with the call to service that framed the recommendations of the 1989 National Commission on the Public Service, which I chaired. As the very first paragraph of the 1989 report argued:

> The central message of this report of the Commission on the Public Service is both simple and profound, both urgent and timeless. In essence, we [call] for a renewed sense of commitment to the highest traditions of the public service—to a public service responsive to the political will of the people and also protective of our constitutional values; to a public service able to cope with complexity and conflict and also able to maintain the highest ethical standards; to a public service attractive to the young and talented from all parts of our society and also capable of earning the respect of all our citizens.

This call to service has become Light's passion. It frames this book and its forceful program for reform—reform not in the sense of one all-encompassing program but rather an analysis of the many steps necessary to make a real difference.

It has also created a book that should be required reading for every member of Congress and the president. It outlines the key issues they must address if the federal government is to meet its responsibility to faithfully execute all the laws. If Congress and presidents do not act soon, they can expect more breakdowns and disappointments.

Government reform may not be an exciting issue on Capitol Hill and in the White House, but I believe over time it will arguably be the most important. The crisis in competence was at the root of the failure to respond quickly to Hurricane Katrina, the flawed intelligence that led to the war in Iraq, the Space Shuttle Columbia disaster, and a host of other recent federal disappointments. This is not the time for further incremental reform that Congress and presidents so often throw at federal management problems. It is the time for bold action. Paul Light provides an accessible agenda for rebuilding the public service.

A Government Ill Executed

Introduction

This book is based on Alexander Hamilton's warning about the dangers of a government ill executed. As he argued in *Federalist No. 70*, "A feeble execution is but another phrase for a bad execution; and a government ill executed, whatever it may be in theory must be in practice, a bad government."[1] A government well executed was essential to virtually every challenge that faced the new republic.

More than two hundred years later, however, the federal government seems plagued by bad execution.

The stories are all too familiar: taxpayer abuse by the Internal Revenue Service, security breaches at the nation's nuclear laboratories, missing laptops at the Federal Bureau of Investigation, the Challenger and Columbia space shuttle disasters, breakdowns in policing everything from toys to cattle, the sluggish response to Hurricane Katrina, miscalculations about the war in Iraq, a cascade of wasteful government contracts, continued struggles to unite the nation's intelligence services, agonizing backlogs at the Social Security Administration and the Passport Bureau, near misses on airport runways, staff shortages across the government, porous borders, mistakes on airline passenger screening lines, the subprime mortgage meltdown, destruction of the CIA interrogation tapes, and negligent medical care of veterans. As the stories have accumulated, the federal government's customer service ratings have plummeted, and now rank with those of the airlines and cable TV.

This is not to suggest that the federal government is a wasteland of failure. To the contrary, the federal government accomplishes the impossible every day. Yet, if the federal government is still far from being ill executed, it is not uniformly well executed, either.

Hamilton's warning reflected more than his own experience with a government ill executed during the Revolutionary War.[2] He also recognized that the new government would fail unless it could execute the laws. After all, the Constitution said almost nothing about the administrative state beyond giving the president a role, checked and balanced, in appointing and overseeing the officers of government. Otherwise, it was up to the president to decide how to "take care" that the laws would be faithfully executed. According to Hamilton, that required an energetic executive and a federal service to match.[3] And he soon began setting precedents for both.

A Government Ill Executed

Imagine for a moment the worst possible circumstances for creating and sustaining that energetic federal service.

First, the federal service would have an agenda of staggering reach that would barely keep pace with the resources for faithful execution. Carved from the hopes and dreams of a great society, the federal service would be asked to convert dozens of great endeavors into lasting achievements—from guaranteeing voting rights to building interstate highways, from reducing disease to helping the homeless, from protecting endangered species to waging war on terrorism, from protecting retirement security to providing humanitarian relief when crisis strikes.

The federal service would not just have a long list of responsibilities, however. It would also have a long list of frustrations. After all, it is one thing to launch a great endeavor, and quite another to produce a great achievement. Even as Congress and the president would continue adding new missions to the list, they would belittle the federal service in their campaigns for office, starve the government of needed resources, and expect more for less with each passing year.

Second, the federal service would be governed by a chain of command that would vitiate accountability. Built on the notion that more leaders somehow equals more leadership, the chain of command would have needless layers of management and increasing numbers of leaders in each layer. Guidance would flow downward through a patchwork of political and career executives, each of whom would hold the guidance just long enough to produce a cascade of delay. In turn, information would flow upward at a glacial pace in a bureaucratic version of the childhood game of gossip.

Third, the federal service would be led by presidential appointees selected through a process that guarantees delays, vacancies, and exhaustion. It would assume the very worst, treating them as "innocent until nominated."[4] To prevent yet another embarrassment, it would ask nominees to fill out sixty pages of forms, some with a typewriter, looking back fifteen years at every job they had held, every address at which they had lived, every article and book they had published, every medical crisis they had endured, every domestic employee they had hired, every foreign trip they had taken, including short trips to Canada and Mexico, and every traffic fine over $150 they had received.[5]

Fourth, the federal service would employ a workforce motivated more by pay, benefits, and security than by the chance to make a difference, help people, and pursue meaningful work. It would also create a civil service system that fails at virtually every task it is designed to do. The system would be slow and confusing in hiring, permissive in promoting and rewarding, reluctant in disciplining, and unwilling to provide the technology, information, employees, and training to do jobs well. Created to celebrate merit, the civil service system would tolerate favoritism, foment labor-management conflict, stifle whistle-blowing, and deny civil servants the chance to accomplish something worthwhile.

Fifth, government would discourage young Americans from imagining the federal service as a career of choice. Although the federal government would be seen as the place to serve the country during times of patriotic need, even its most committed recruits would see nonprofit agencies as the destination of choice for meaningful work. Moreover, instead of acknowledging the changing nature of careers, the federal government would require its employees to enter the system early in their career, advance through the decades, and exit upon retirement.

Sixth, the federal service would be battered by one administrative reform after another, all in search of higher performance, but few sharing the same direction. Instead, the tides of reform would represent every philosophy of change, from the scientific management that Hamilton brought into office with him as secretary of the treasury to the war on waste that soon followed with Thomas Jefferson, from the liberation management that marks efforts to free federal employees from onerous rules to new efforts to expose government to the sunshine. These reforms would force the federal service to invest resources and attention in the passing fads favored by each Congress and the president. Instead of offering steadiness in administration, the federal service would be asked to implement one contradictory reform after another, including yet another management agenda from each new president.

Finally, the federal service would share accountability with a vast, growing, and mostly hidden workforce of contractors, grantees, and state and local government employees who work for the federal government under mandates. This blended workforce would often be unaccountable for what goes right or wrong in the execution of the laws. It would grow larger with the expanding government mission, but be nearly impossible to measure because of resistance from those who want to hide the true size of government while promising to deliver more for less. Although this hidden workforce would include the networks of public, private, and nonprofit employees that must work together to execute many of the laws designed to protect the nation in the post-9/11 world, its primary purpose would be to disguise the true cost of the federal agenda.

Unfortunately, this is not just the worst case for creating a government well executed. It is the reality in the federal government today. Bluntly put, the federal service is suffering its greatest crisis since it was founded in the first moments of the republic. At best, it is running out of energy at what seems to be an accelerating rate. At worst, it is already unable to faithfully execute all the laws.

An Energetic Executive

Hamilton believed that energy in the executive was a "leading character" in good government. "It is essential to the protection of the community against foreign attacks," he wrote in *Federalist No. 70;* "it is not less essential to the steady administration of the laws; to the protection of property against those irregular and high-handed combinations which sometimes interrupt the ordinary course of justice; to the security of liberty against the enterprises and assaults of ambition, of faction, and of anarchy."[6]

Having declared the great value of energy in the executive, Hamilton spent *Federalist Nos. 70–77* defining the term. Although the federal service and faithful execution of the laws were always implied, Hamilton focused on the four ingredients of that provided energy: unity in the executive, duration in office, adequate provision of support, and competent powers.

He defined unity in *Federalist No. 70* as a single executive. "That unity is conducive to energy will not be disputed," Hamilton wrote. "Decision, activity, secrecy, and dispatch will generally characterize the proceedings of one man in a much more eminent degree than the proceedings of any greater number; and in proportion as the number is increased, these qualities will be diminished."[7] Yet, even as he focused on the single executive, Hamilton also wrote of the operations of government, extending unity to clarity of command:

> Wherever two or more persons are engaged in any common enterprise or pursuit, there is always danger of difference of opinion. If it be a public trust or office, in which they are clothed with equal dignity and authority, there is peculiar danger of personal emulation and even animosity. From either, and especially from all these causes, the most bitter dissensions are apt to spring. Whenever these happen, they lessen the respectability, weaken the authority, and distract the plans and operation of those whom they divide.[8]

He defined duration in office in *Federalist Nos. 71–72* as a four-year term and unlimited "re-eligibility" for election. "The first is necessary to give the officer himself the inclination and the resolution to act his part well," Hamilton wrote in *Federalist No. 72*, "and to the community time and leisure to observe the tendency of his measures, and thence to form an experimental estimate of their merits. The last is necessary to enable the people, when they see reason to approve his conduct, to continue him in his station, in order to prolong the utility of his talents and virtues, and to secure to the government the wise advantage of permanency in a wise system of administration."[9]

Hamilton defined adequate provision of support as a presidential salary that cannot be raised or lowered during a president's term of office. "The legislature, with a discretionary power over the salary and emoluments of the Chief Magistrate, could render him as obsequious to their will as they might think proper to make him," Hamilton wrote in *Federalist No. 73*. "They might, in most cases, either reduce him to famine, or tempt him by largesse, to surrender at discretion his judgment to their inclinations."[10] Hence, the president's salary cannot be raised or lowered during the term of office.

Finally, he defined competent powers as the authority to veto legislation, command the military, require the written opinions of the principal officers of government, grant pardons, make treaties, and make appointments. He clearly understood that the president's greatest powers would come to be exercised during war. "The propriety of this provision is so evident in itself, and it is, at the same time, so consonant to the precedents of the States constitutions in general, that little need be said to explain or enforce it."[11]

An Energetic Federal Service

Energy in the executive also required an energetic federal service. Although Hamilton's contributions to the *Federalist Papers* are often characterized as a narrow defense of the single executive, his writings hide a much broader vision of the administrative state as a whole, a vision he pursued once in office himself. A unified executive required a unified federal service; duration in government required duration in service; adequate support included a competent federal service; and a due diligence for the people required accountability from the top to the bottom of government.

As Hamilton wrote in *Federalist No. 68*, "the true test of a good government is its aptitude and tendency to produce a good administration."[12] Note Hamilton's use of the word "it," not "his." Energy in the executive was useless without an energetic federal service to execute the laws. As such, an energetic federal service was also a leading character in good government.[13]

Hamilton emphasized this point later in *Federalist No. 70*. Even as differences of opinion and party conflict promoted deliberation in Congress, they had no place in the executive:

> When a resolution too is once taken, the opposition must be at an end. That resolution is a law, and resistance to it punishable. But no favorable circumstances palliate or atone for the disadvantages of dissention in the executive department. Here they are pure and unmixed. There is no point at which they cease to operate. They constantly counteract those qualities in the Executive which are the most necessary ingredients in its composition—vigor and expedition, and this without any counterbalancing good."[14]

Even as he helped create an inventory of missions that mattered to the nation's survival, Hamilton used his position as secretary of the treasury to set the administrative state in order. He pursued a tight chain of command from the top of his department to the bottom, placed experienced officers at key intersections in the hierarchy, recruited federal employees with the competence to do their jobs well, tried to establish a pipeline of future recruits, argued for steadiness in administration, and endorsed the need for transparency and competence as a guarantee of responsibility to the public.

Once his model was in place, Hamilton fought the inevitable attacks on his creation, which soon provoked the first presidential campaign built around an attack on government waste. "Nothing is more easy than to reduce the number of agents employed in any business, and yet for the business to go on," he wrote in 1802 as Jefferson cut government employment, "but before the reduction is applauded, it ought to be ascertained that the business is as well done as it was before."[15]

The Seven Characteristics of an Energetic Federal Service

Hamilton's precedents were based on a set of implied attributes of an energetic federal service. As Leonard White argued in 1926, "The Federalists not only organized a continental system of administration, but impressed upon it high ideals of competence, impartiality, integrity and responsibility."

Despite efforts to inject partisanship into the appointments process, White concluded that the first forty years of public administration at the national level "rested firmly on impressively high ideals."[16] Hamilton's basic vision of an energetic federal service survived the Jefferson administration largely intact and shapes the debate about reform to this day.

Hamilton and the Federalists were hardly angels, of course, a point well made in detailed histories of the civil service.[17] Nevertheless, Hamilton's energetic federal service had at least seven characteristics that he believed were central to its success:

1. *Missions that matter for the public benefit.* As Hamilton argued in *Federalist No. 72*, government exists to pursue "extensive and arduous enterprise for the public benefit."[18] He did not see government as a passive instrument that would only react to threats, but as a force for strengthening the nation's economic, political, and social infrastructure. Although government only grew slightly under the Federalists, the federal service was given a long list of great missions and responsibilities, including everything from building postal roads to restoring the nation's beleaguered currency.

2. *Clarity of command.* Hamilton saw clear links between the chief executive and officers of government as essential for both effective administration and accountability to the public, and believed that these officers should be subject to the president's direct control, or "subservience." In turn, the federal service would, by implication, also be subject to the direct control of the senior officers of government. The president would not only have the appointment power, albeit subject to Senate confirmation, but would supervise the day-to-day activities of

the executive branch as part of what Hamilton defined as "execution in detail." This concept was part of Hamilton's belief in a science of management and produced an ever-growing chain of command.

3. *Posts of honor.* Hamilton repeatedly referred to the officers of government as the extension of an energetic executive. He did not believe such officers would be perfect, but did believe that the president's appointees would have the "moderation, firmness, and liberality with exactness" to assure a government well executed.[19] Although George Washington did pay attention to political loyalty in recruiting appointees, the primary focus was on persons with merit and expertise who would be drawn from the highest ranks of society. These occupants of what Benjamin Franklin called "posts of honor" were to be an integral part of the character of an administration, too.[20]

4. *Vigor and expedition.* Executive control involved more than clear direction from the top; it also involved a commitment to effective execution of the laws down the hierarchy. However, Hamilton did not believe that civic duty would supply the needed incentive for faithful execution of the laws. Instead, he argued that adequate compensation and the opportunity for promotion would do so. Yet, he also believed that pay, benefits, and security would produce the vigor and expedition to execute the laws, which was his ultimate purpose in building an energetic federal service in the first place.[21]

5. *A spirit of service.* Unlike Jefferson, who often talked about the duty of every citizen to answer the call to service no matter how low the salary or great the drudgery, Hamilton rarely, if ever, mentioned future public servants in his writings. Nevertheless, he was a strong advocate of a national military academy and a national university, both of which would have provided the training to fill the top posts of government. Given the general belief in a federal service of well-trained elites, and the role of education in producing them, there is at least some evidence that Hamilton cared about building institutions that would produce enough talent to fill the federal service of the future.

6. *Steadiness in administration.* Hamilton's general belief in giving members of the federal service tenure in office was based on his notion that the chief executive should be allowed to serve long enough to pursue extensive and arduous enterprises to their completion. But he also wrote in *Federalist No. 72* that change rooted in the natural human desire to "reverse and undo what has been done by a predecessor, is very often considered by a successor as the best proof he can give of his own capacity and desert . . ." But such change cannot fail to "occasion a disgraceful and

ruinous mutability in the administration of the government."[22] Although obviously linked to the duration of the presidential term, Hamilton's concern appears to extend to the stability of the whole system of administration, and its change with each passing administration and Congress.

7. *Safety in the executive.* Hamilton believed that a government well executed had to provide safety through transparency of results. Having defined safety in "the republican sense" as a due dependence on and responsibility to the people, Hamilton defined accountability as the public's ability to detect, censure, and punish "national miscarriage or misfortune," which would be infinitely easier to prevent in a tightly connected hierarchy. Acknowledging that there could be many actors who bear responsibility for failure, transparency would give the public the ability to discover just who to hold accountable, and in doing so, government would at least know who did what.[23]

As the federal government's agenda has expanded over the decades, Hamilton's energetic federal service eventually became the victim of his own vision. Its mission is far broader than its capability; its chains of command are complex and confused; its process for filling the senior offices of government has become a source of embarrassment and delay; its workforce is drawn more by pay, benefits, and security than the chance to make a difference; its future employees would not know how to find a federal job even if they wanted one; its reform agenda has become a destination for fads; and execution of the laws now involves a large and mostly hidden workforce that cannot be held accountable for results.

Hamilton's vision was also undermined by the implementation of the seven attributes, whether in the creation of grand missions, tight chains of command, and so forth down the list, which increased public demand for virtually everything that the new government delivered. As the world became more complex, so did the government's agenda and Hamilton's administrative system. Structures and procedures that made sense in a simpler time began to pull against economy and efficiency, dragging the federal service into needless bureaucracy, increasing the workload without supplying adequate resources to achieve goals, and raising the importance of pay, benefits, and security as motivators for vigorous execution.

Confrontations with Jefferson

Moreover, Jefferson and his Republican Party clearly rejected many if not all of these characteristics, arguing that "drudgery and subsistence" would be "a wise and necessary precaution against the degeneracy of the public servants."[24] Jefferson also argued for a simple and frugal government as a precaution against taking "from the mouth of labor the bread it has earned."[25]

Frugal government. More importantly, Jefferson clearly opposed Hamilton's vision of an energetic executive and the federal service it required. "I own I am not a friend to a very energetic government," Jefferson wrote James Madison from France as the Constitution was still being drafted. "It is always oppressive. It places the governors indeed more at their ease, at the expense of the people."[26] It also nurtured self-aggrandizement, as "hungry cormorants" engaged in "eternal intrigue to turn out one and put in another, in cabals to swap work; and make of them what all executive directories become, mere sinks of corruption and faction."[27]

And it most certainly created needless bureaucracy. As Jefferson argued in his first inaugural address: "When we consider that this government is charged with the external and mutual relations of these States; that the States themselves have principal care of our persons our property and our reputation, constituting the great field of human concerns, we may well doubt whether our organization is too complicated, too expensive; whether offices and officers have not been multiplied unnecessarily and sometimes injuriously to the service they were meant to promote."[28]

It is important to note that Jefferson was not against everything Hamilton proposed. He was known to worry about the intricacies of government, just as he worried about the intricacies of clocks. "In government, as well as every other business of life," he wrote in 1816, "it is by division and subdivision of duties alone that all matters, great and small, can be managed to perfection."[29]

But Jefferson viewed the executive as only one actor in a broader system of governance in which the people, states, and national government worked together toward progress. Writing to Aaron Burr after the 1800 election, Jefferson expressed his regret that Burr had decided not to accept the vice presidency he had won through the popular ballot: "I had endeavored to compose an administration whose talents, integrity, names, and dispositions, should at once inspire unbounded confidence in the public mind, and insure a perfect harmony in the conduct of the public business."[30]

Defining the executive again. Jefferson also took issue with Hamilton's definition of energy in the executive. On unity in the executive, for example, Jefferson believed that the executive had to pursue "a noiseless course, not meddling with the affairs of others, unattractive of notice"; when this occurs, it "is a mark that society is going on in happiness."[31] He also argued for "harmony" in the executive, not tight chains of command. Reflecting on his presidency only two years after leaving office, he recalled that "we never failed, by a contribution of mutual views on the subject, to form an opinion acceptable to the whole. I think there never was one instance to the contrary, in any case of consequence."[32]

On duration in office, Jefferson favored at least some self-imposed limits on reelection. Although he supported "re-eligibility," as Hamilton called it, Jefferson expressed early and forceful opposition to multiple terms: "I dislike, and strongly dislike . . . the abandonment in every instance of the principle of rotation in office and most particularly in the case of the President. Reason and experience tell us that the first magistrate will always be re-elected if he may be re-elected. He is then an officer for life."[33] Once in office, he embraced Washington's two-term precedent, arguing that any president who ran for a third term would be rejected on "this demonstration of ambitious views."[34]

On the adequate provision of support, Jefferson made clear that presidents and their officers should be motivated by duty, not compensation. Indeed, Jefferson frequently complained about the burdens he faced. "I am tired of an office where I can do more good than many others, who would be glad to be employed in it," he wrote during his presidency. "To me, personally, it brings nothing but unceasing drudgery and daily loss of friends."[35]

Finally, on executive powers, Jefferson shared Hamilton's belief in a strong war power, but also promised a restrained and "wholesome" agenda that reflected the will of the people, "who, by the weight of public opinion, influence and strengthen the public measures; it is due to the sound discretion with which they select from among themselves those to whom they confide the legislative duties; it is due to the zeal and wisdom of the characters thus selected, who lay the foundations of public happiness in wholesome laws, the executive of which alone remains for others; and it is due to the able and faithful auxiliaries, whose patriotism has associated with me in the executive functions."[36]

Yet, once in office Jefferson used many of Hamilton's principles of an energetic federal service to reverse the Federalist agenda, which he did quickly and with little resistance. As Stephen Skowronek writes, "the 'system' against which Jefferson set himself . . . had never sunk very deep political footings." He was able to sweep Hamilton's partisans from the army, remove them from senior posts in government, and isolate them from their institutional strongholds.[37]

More significantly, Jefferson took what Skowronek calls "the extraordinary and enormously popular decision to repeal internal taxes immediately. This action simply eliminated the internal revenue service and with it a cadre of placeholders (40 percent of the Treasury Department personnel in the field) representing one of the most visible and noxious offenses of Federalism. Never again would a president be in a position to take such decisive steps in dismantling a regime with so little opposition."[38] The decision not only stopped government growth, it established a key tenet of future wars on waste—the best way to eliminate excessive expenditures was not through direct action, but through starvation.

However, Jefferson was unsuccessful in dismantling Hamilton's concept of an energetic federal service, much as his ideas might have prevented today's erosion. He could not prevent the steady expansion of the federal agenda, for example, the duplication of offices he deplored, the end of the spoils system he helped create, the institutionalization of the civil service, the thickening of the administrative state, the use of compensation and promotion as rewards of service, the steady increase in the number of civil servants, or the creation of a hidden workforce that would eventually outnumber the civil service by four to one. And he could not prevent the steadily increasing size of the federal service as the federal agenda grew.[39]

Nevertheless, Jefferson's views still have merit for addressing the erosion of the energetic federal service. His call for simplification supports the long-overdue flattening of the federal hierarchy, for example, as does his focus on decentralization, broadly interpreted. At the same time, Jefferson's emphasis on civic duty as the primary focus of public service has great merit as the federal government seeks to rebuild enthusiasm among the nation's most talented young Americans.

Confrontations with Reality

Just because Hamilton had a clear vision of the energetic federal service does not mean that Congress and the president followed his outline. As Jerry L. Mashaw writes, the young government violated many of Hamilton's ideals. Although Congress did give the young service what

Mashaw calls an "astonishing" list of missions, thereby creating a substantial government by itself, Hamilton's other criteria were often undermined by simple administrative realities.[40]

Much as he hoped for clarity of command, for example, only a handful of the government's employees resided in Washington within easy reach of the president. And much as he extolled the need for "virtuous execution," most federal employees had little training for their jobs. Writing of the General Land Office, which was responsible for the division and sale of public lands, Matthew Crenson observes that the "department would appoint some respected citizen who lives in the vicinity of a district land office to take a day off from his private labors and look in on the affairs of the register and receiver. Frequently, the examiner was a friend and political ally of both officers, and it was not uncommon for him to know nothing at all about the proper manner in which to conduct the business of a land office."[41] So much for a strong chain of command.

There was also less than a full emphasis on appointing senior officers on the basis of merit, though George Washington talked at length about this necessity. Instead, he appointed what some have called a "regime of notables" and trusted friends—which may have been the only alternative, given the cost of becoming a senior member of the administration.[42] Hard as he may have tried to make "fitness" the sine qua non of merit, Washington soon relied on party affiliation as his guide, thereby bequeathing to Jefferson a government in which vacancies by death were few and by resignation none.

At the same time, Mashaw writes, the "idea of office remained ambiguous." As he notes of all offices, including postal carriers, "Part-timers paid by fees or commissions, and apparently expecting to be policed by criminal penalties, often at the initiative of private parties, are not a professionalized, hierarchically organized civil service."[43]

Congress and the president tried to impose at least rudimentary accountability, however. As Mashaw notes, conflict-of-interest prohibitions were "common" in early statutes. Treasury officials could not engage in trade or commerce; customs officials could not own ships; whiskey-tax collectors could not buy or sell liquor; and agents of the Office of Indian Affairs could not engage in any commerce with Native Americans.[44] So much for Jefferson's idea of a federal service committed entirely to civic duty, and the notion that federal careers would attract the most virtuous in society.

Yet, as Mashaw argues in contradiction to much of the traditional scholarship on the early years of the republic, Hamilton and his

Federalists left a lasting mark on the administrative structure and operations of government:

> Using the tools that came to hand, Federalist Congresses, administrators, and courts struggled to combine techniques of political, managerial, and legal accountability into a system of administrative governances that was simultaneously responsive, effective, and respectful of citizens' rights. They built administrative capacity while binding it to republican politics and existing understandings of the rule of law. They were hardly always successful. But getting the balance right was the preoccupation of the institutional designers who created Federalist administrative law.[45]

And among those designers, Hamilton was the key architect. He offered more than just a philosophy of energy in the executive and the energetic federal service to support it: he established the early precedents for administrative control in building the Treasury Department into what he hoped would be an exemplary organization for the future. More than any other founder, he established the early image of the "good organization." Though he suffered from his own personal obsessions, not least the accretion of minor decisions to the secretary's office and the nearly constant monitoring of day-to-day decisions far down the hierarchy, his definition of an energetic federal service still stands, and forms the backbone of this book.

Plan of the Book

This is not the first time in history that the federal service has faced a crisis. Otherwise, James Garfield might have lived out his term.[46] Yet, the crisis seems different somehow—perhaps because it is exacerbated by the expected retirements of almost half of the federal service over the next decade, perhaps because there is so much pressure to do more with less.

This book will work through Hamilton's definition of an energetic federal service in order, asking whether the federal service still has missions that matter, clarity of command, posts of honor at the top of the hierarchy, a commitment to excellence within the workforce, a strong spirit of federal service among young Americans, steadiness in administration, and accountability for results. The answer, unfortunately, is mostly no. And the federal service is suffering as a result.

The book will examine the erosion of the federal service using the body of research that I have conducted at the Brookings Institution and New York University over the past ten years. The core of each chapter provides a basic review of my past research, updates from recent analysis, and more detailed assessments of what the research reveals about the current erosion. Some of this research is entirely new and some involves a deeper analysis of already-published work.

Chapter 1 asks whether the federal service still has missions that matter for the public benefit. The answer comes largely from my on-going research on government's greatest endeavors and the president's domestic agenda, which explores the continued public demand for extensive and arduous enterprise. The nation has never hesitated to ask government to do more, even as it often applauds tax cuts that deny government the resources to succeed. Much as presidents have attempted to sort or starve government's mission into a more manageable whole, the expansion continues. The result is a government with extraordinary ambition but growing frustration that often undermines its ability to convert its great endeavors into great achievement.

Chapter 2 asks whether the federal hierarchy enhances or obfuscates clarity of command. The answer comes largely from my ongoing effort to track the growth of the federal hierarchy through the proliferation of executive titles while examining the capacity problems such layering presents. The federal government has never had more layers of leaders or more leaders per layer. The towering hierarchy diffuses accountability for what goes wrong or right in government, weakens command and control, and reduces communication to a childhood game of telephone in which messages are distorted at every stop in the chain of command. It also creates extraordinary opportunity for error as information moves up and down the hierarchy.

Chapter 3 asks whether the appointments process assures merit and expertise for the federal government's posts of honor. The answer comes largely from my ongoing analysis of the obstacles embedded in the nomination and confirmation of the federal government's top officials, which addresses the prevailing definition of leadership as more leaders. Burdened by a process that has become more intrusive with each passing administration, presidential appointees have been arriving in office later and leaving earlier. Asked every question imaginable about their private life and subjected to often-random delays, appointees enter office exhausted, while potential appointees wonder if they can endure such an embarrassing and confusing process.

Chapter 4 asks whether the federal service has the vigor and expedition to faithfully execute all of the laws. The answer comes from my 2001 and 2002 surveys of federal, business, and nonprofit employees, which examine the frustrations civil servants face in pursuing their extensive and arduous enterprises. Federal employees may make miracles every day, but often do so in spite of their organizations, which rarely provide enough resources to succeed. In a system unable to attract and hold the best and brightest, the workforce is increasingly composed of employees who come to work in the morning driven by the compensation and who go home unhappy with their leaders, convinced that the personnel system fails at every task it undertakes.

Chapter 5 asks whether the federal government can attract the talent it needs for the future. The answer comes largely from my 2002 and 2003 surveys of college seniors, graduates of the nation's leading schools of public policy and administration, and recent federal recruits while reviewing the capacity crisis that declining student interest creates. The federal government is not only losing the talent war at both the undergraduate and graduate level, but it faces enormous problems holding the recruits it attracts. Even as the federal government has lost its allure as a destination for entering public service, it has become the employer of choice for those who plan to leave early in their career.

Chapter 6 asks how the increasing pace and mix of management reform undermines steadiness in administration. The answer comes largely from my ongoing work on the surge in the amount of reform activity, which suggests the difficulties of renewing government's capacity through a patchwork of often contradictory initiatives. The interval between today's grand reform and tomorrow's has dwindled to a legislative nanosecond, as Congress and the president try one fad after another in search of higher government performance if not public approval.

Chapter 7 asks how a growing and largely hidden workforce of contractors and grantees dilutes safety in the executive. The answer comes largely from my ongoing research on the true size of government, which asks hard questions about the kind of capacity such a workforce creates. The shift of jobs to federal contracts, grants, and mandates has allowed presidents to celebrate the end of big government while encouraging Americans to believe that the federal government can truly do more with less, which has created a vicious cycle of expanding responsibilities and declining resources. With more than 10.5 million contract- and grant-generated employees in 2005 alone, the question is whether the federal government can assure accountability for its off-budget employees.

Finally, Chapter 8 offers recommendations for rebuilding an energetic federal service. To do so, Congress and the president must decide which of the federal government's missions they can sustain, reduce the distance between the top and bottom of its organizations, create an appointments process that makes it easier for talented Americans to say yes to service, provide enough organizational resources to achieve its goals, concentrate on a handful of reforms that might actually work, and create more flexible careers and a clearer purpose as nearly a million of its baby-boom employees retire over the next decade. Government must not just make the invitation to service more vibrant, it must make the service itself more rewarding.

Conclusion

This erosion of the federal service is no longer a quiet crisis easily dismissed. To the contrary, it is now deafening.

The nation has good reason to worry about the continued erosion. Global warming is working its will on the climate, a new generation of terrorists is flexing its muscle in the Middle East, Medicare is straining under rising health costs, Social Security is bending as the baby boomers prepare for retirement, water wars are rising in the western states, energy independence is decades beyond reach, the nation's infrastructure is rusting, many of its public schools are struggling, and many of its greatest achievements of the past sixty years are in jeopardy as an uncertain future bears down on government.

The question is whether the federal government can rise to the tasks ahead. It has never had a more complex agenda, but has never seemed so confused about its priorities. It has never had a greater need for agility, but has never seemed so thick with bureaucracy. It has never had a bigger budget, but has never been so short on the resources to do its job. It has never had a greater need for decisiveness, but has never seemed so dependent on its hidden workforce to execute decisions. It has never had greater cause for commitment, but has never faced so much reform. Although federal agencies such as the National Institutes of Health and Centers for Disease Control continue to perform at high levels, their laboratories are rusting and their workforces are aging ever closer to retirement.

This book is not designed to provide yet another excuse for attacking the federal service, however. It is about reversing the erosion in the capacity to produce a government well executed, whether by creating more flexible careers as the baby boomers leave, building a disciplinary process that actually remedies poor performance, giving federal employees the resources to do their jobs, eliminating layers of needless management, focusing federal agencies and employees on clear priorities, abandoning missions that no longer make sense, or creating an appointments process that makes it easier for America's most talented civic and corporate leaders to say "yes" to a post of honor.

Moreover, with nearly a million baby boomers about to retire from the federal service, the nation has a unique but brief opportunity for radical action to reshape the federal hierarchy, reduce layers of needless management, redistribute resources toward the front lines of government, address the increasing dependency on the hidden workforce of contractors and grantees, and restore student interest in federal careers.

The most powerful advocates for this kind of reform are not outside government, but inside. Federal employees know they do not have enough capacity to do their jobs, and are hungry for change. They also know the time for tinkering is long past. Improving the hiring process will not suffice if new recruits do not have the opportunity to grow; enhancing retention will not help if it produces more layers of management; providing new resources will not matter if they are spread too thin; and setting priorities will not generate clarity if appointees are not in office long enough to make the decisions stick.

There are many reasons to worry about these trends, all of which have worsened since I helped inventory the list as a senior consultant to the first National Commission on the Public Service chaired by former Federal Reserve Board chairman Paul A. Volcker in 1989.

The federal service can hardly become part of the new government imagined for the future if it is not prepared for the present. It cannot focus on problems rather than structures through "one-stop shopping," as Donald F. Kettl recommends, if it does not have the resources to deliver its current agenda; it cannot focus on performance instead of process, as Steven Kelman encourages, if it does not have the talent to measure and discipline results; and it most certainly cannot produce stronger networks for delivering federal services, as Stephen Goldsmith suggests, if it cannot bring strength to its bargaining.[47] Most importantly, it cannot faithfully implement the laws if it does not have the aptitude and tendency to do so.

At least for now, Americans have little interest in rebuilding the federal service, especially in light of seemingly unending stories of fraud, waste, and abuse. They want the federal government to be involved in great endeavors such as protecting voting rights, reducing disease, and providing health care to low-income Americans, but also think government wastes the vast majority of the money it spends.[48] They think the federal government mostly has the right priorities, but also think federal employees take their jobs for the pay, benefits, and security, not the chance to accomplish something worthwhile, make a difference, or help people. They want the federal government to maintain its programs to deal with important problems, but believe it deserves most of the criticism it receives.

In a very real sense, Americans are getting the government they deserve. They demand more, yet create a climate that encourages their leaders to exploit their distrust. Although the current erosion of the federal service is not just the public's fault, it reflects the tension between what Americans want and what they are willing to pay for.

CHAPTER ONE

For the Public Benefit

The first characteristic of an energetic federal service is missions that matter for the public benefit. Why would the federal government worry about creating what Hamilton called the "aptitude and tendency" to produce a good administration if it is mostly directed to unimportant missions? Why worry about an energetic federal service if it is not used for the faithful execution of what Hamilton called "extensive and arduous enterprises for the public benefit"?[1]

Hamilton never defined "extensive and arduous enterprises" specifically, but did write at length in *Federalist No. 72* about the challenges the federal service would face in the administration of government, which he considered "peculiarly within the province of the executive department." His list was understated, but broad: "The actual conduct of foreign negotiations, the preparatory plans of finance, the application and disbursement of the public moneys in conformity to the general appropriations of the legislature, the arrangement of the army and navy, the directions of the operations of war—these, and other matters of a like nature, constitute what seems to be most properly understood by the administration of government."[2]

Not all the challenges involved such general duties, however. "If we mean to be a commercial people, or even to be secure on our Atlantic side," Hamilton wrote of one particularly onerous task in *Federalist No. 24,* "we must endeavor as soon as possible, to have a navy. To this purpose there must be dock-yards and arsenals; and for the defense of these, fortifications, and probably garrisons."[3] Building fortifications was not necessarily a dramatic mission, but it was a mission that mattered nonetheless, as well as an extensive and arduous task.

Despite Hamilton's call for a government dedicated to ambitious enterprises, today's federal service knows that some of its missions might matter more than others, particularly after the 9/11 terrorist attacks. More importantly, perhaps, some missions are more motivating than others. Thus, 9/11 may have created a greater sense of purpose at the federal departments and agencies such as Defense and State involved in the new war on terrorism. But it may have diluted a greater sense of purpose at other departments and agencies such as Agriculture, Commerce, Education, Housing and Urban Development, Interior, and Labor. Never called upon to help fight the war on terrorism, the federal service in these domestic agencies must have wondered whether and how their missions still mattered.[4]

Hamilton would be troubled by this disparity between missions that matter and those that do not, for he believed that large-scale (extensive) and arduous (difficult) missions would generate economic growth and national expansion. "Under a vigorous national government," he wrote in *Federalist No. 11,* "the natural strength of the country, directed to a common interest, would baffle all the combinations of European jealousy to restrain our growth." By creating a vigorous national government, "we might defy the little arts of the little politicians to control or vary the irresistible and unchangeable course of nature." Hence, extensive and arduous enterprise had to include something more than what Hamilton called "passive commerce."[5] It had to include bold action to address the kind of important, difficult problems and equally important, difficult opportunities for growth that confronted a fragile republic in a rapidly changing world.

The federal government's commitment to an extensive and arduous agenda has ebbed and flowed over the decades as Congress and the president have pushed for and against action. But there can be little question that the nation has often called upon the federal service to embrace a long list of seemingly intractable problems. To the extent a nation is known by the problems it attempts to solve and the opportunities it seeks to exploit, the United States has been very ambitious indeed.

The ambition has never let up. Old missions do not fade away, and rarely die. Rather, they mostly continue growing as Congress amends and expands each of the individual programs and laws that underpin its major missions, even as new goals are added to the agenda. Even when the nation actually completes a mission, it is quickly replaced with another great goal. Rebuilding Europe ends and urban renewal begins; the cold war ends and the war on terrorism begins; the interstate highway system is barely finished when the expansions (and repairs) begin.

As this chapter will suggest, Congress and the president have been asking the federal service to do more with less for the past thirty years, often using harsh campaign rhetoric to attack fraud, waste, and abuse, embracing deep tax cuts to "starve the beast" of big government, yet simultaneously adding new endeavors to the federal agenda. Whether by accident or intent, Congress and the president have asked the federal service to do the impossible, jeopardizing its ability to execute all the laws.

Measuring Missions

Despite their persistent opposition to big government, most Americans want more of almost everything the federal service delivers. Ask them whether they want federal government programs cut or maintained, and a majority will answer maintained. Ask them whether the bigger problem with government is the wrong priorities or inefficiency, and a majority will answer inefficiency. Ask them whether government should be involved in issues such as voting rights, health care for the poor, promoting financial security among older Americans, and expanding home ownership, and a majority will answer yes.[6]

But the critical question for this book is not whether Americans want small government and big ambitions, but just how much they ask the federal service to do.[7] Unfortunately, there are relatively few studies of the actual size of the agenda beyond simple counts of the number of laws passed year to year. This work has fallen to a relatively small group of researchers, starting with James L. Sundquist, who tracked issues such as civil rights and environmental policy through the 1950s and 1960s; Sarah Binder, who drew upon *New York Times* editorial coverage to develop a list of issues that were frozen by gridlock from 1947 to 1996; and Frank Baumgartner, Bryan D. Jones, and John Wilkerson, who used *Congressional Quarterly* almanacs to identify the 576 "most important" laws enacted between 1948 and 2004, which are organized into 19 issue topics and 225 sub-topics.[8]

Merely passing a law is no guarantee of actual success, of course. As Sundquist argued, a government's ability to make policy decisions on big issues is only one test of its capacity to govern: "Other dimensions are substantive and administrative—the policies must be appropriate to the problems with which they deal, and they must be made effective through adequate appropriations and competent administration."[9] Simply put, it is one thing to give the federal service missions that matter, and quite another to provide the resources to faithfully execute the laws. Congress can pass great laws as part of even greater missions, but enactment is only the beginning of achieving actual success. Some federal missions have been stunning successes, while others have been equally stunning disappointments.

Yet, even when missions fail, it is hard not to be impressed by what the federal service has been asked to do since World War II. Having emerged victorious from war and economic catastrophe, Congress and the president called upon the federal government and its employees to pursue some of the most important, difficult goals imaginable. Some of the missions were launched by a Supreme Court decision, others by a presidential order, and still others by a federal regulation or budget request. But all involved laws that are deemed major by the *Congressional Quarterly* almanacs. If Congress is serious about creating missions that matter, *Congressional Quarterly* will have the data.

Congress has been very serious, indeed. According to my reading of *Congressional Quarterly* histories that other researchers have used to track legislation, there were 553 major laws enacted between 1944 and 2000 that created a long list of missions that matter: rebuilding Europe after World War II, creating the interstate highway system, expanding voting rights, ending workplace discrimination, reducing disease, winning the cold war, improving air and water quality, advancing science and technology, exploring space, and strengthening financial and health security of older Americans.[10]

All were missions that mattered greatly at the time they were launched, and many are missions that matter greatly today.[11] However, as already noted, some matter more than others, at least measured by the amount of effort embedded in the major laws and the missions they combined to create. Table 1.1 provides short descriptions of the fifty missions that involved the greatest effort between 1944 and 2000. The table also provides a sampling of the major laws that help define each mission, including enactments that codified a

Table 1.1 Government's 50 greatest endeavors, 1943–2000

1. Advance human rights and humanitarian relief—e.g., United Nations charter of 1945, Comprehensive Anti-Apartheid Act of 1986, appropriations for the Kosovo intervention of 1999.

2. Contain communism—e.g., aid to Greece and Turkey 1947, North Atlantic Treaty of 1949, appropriations for the Korean War, Gulf of Tonkin Resolution of 1964.

3. Control immigration—e.g., Immigration and Nationality Act (McCarran-Walter) of 1952, Immigration and Nationality Act amendments of 1965, Immigration Reform and Control Act of 1986, Immigration Act of 1990.

4. Develop and renew impoverished communities—e.g., Appalachian Regional Development Act of 1965, Demonstration Cities Act of 1966.

5. Devolve responsibility to the states—e.g., State and Local Fiscal Assistance Act of 1972 (creation of general revenue sharing), Unfunded Mandate Reform Act of 1995, Personal Responsibility and Work Opportunity Reconciliation Act (welfare reform) of 1996.

6. Enhance consumer protection—e.g., Food, Drug and Cosmetics Act amendments of 1962, Fair Packaging and Labeling Act of 1966, Consumer Product Safety Act of 1972.

7. Enhance access to health care—e.g., Hospital Survey and Construction Act of 1946, Mental Retardation Facilities Construction Act of 1963, Heart Disease, Cancer and Stroke amendments of 1965.

8. Enhance workplace safety—e.g., Federal Coal Mine Health and Safety Act of 1969, Occupational Safety and Health Act of 1970.

9. Ensure safe food and drinking water—e.g., Federal Insecticide, Fungicide and Rodenticide Act of 1947, Wholesome Meat Act of 1967, Safe Drinking Water Act of 1974.

10. Expand foreign markets for U.S. goods—e.g., Bretton-Woods Agreement Act of 1945, General Agreement on Tariffs and Trade of 1947, Organization for Economic Cooperation and Development Treaty of 1961, North American Free Trade Agreement of 1993.

11. Expand home ownership—e.g., Housing Act of 1950, Housing Act of 1959, Tax Reform Act of 1986.

12. Expand job training and placement—e.g., Employment Act of 1946, Small Business Act of 1953, Economic Opportunity Act of 1964, Comprehensive Employment and Training Act of 1973, Job Training Partnership Act of 1982.

13. Expand the right to vote—e.g., Civil Rights Act of 1964, Voting Rights Act of 1965.

Table 1.1 (continued)

14. Improve air quality—e.g., Clean Air Act of 1963, Motor Vehicle Pollution Control Act of 1965, Clean Air Act of 1970.

15. Improve elementary and secondary education—e.g., National Defense Education Act of 1958, Elementary and Secondary Education Act of 1965, Head Start Act of 1967.

16. Improve government performance—e.g., Civil Service Reform Act of 1978, Federal Managers' Financial Integrity Act of 1982, Chief Financial Officers Act of 1990, Government Performance and Results Act of 1993, Federal Acquisitions Streamlining Act of 1994.

17. Improve mass transportation—e.g., Federal Aid to Highways Act of 1956, Urban Mass Transportation Act of 1964, Rail Passenger Service Act of 1970.

18. Improve water quality—e.g., Federal Water Pollution Control Act of 1948, Federal Water Pollution Control Act amendments of 1972, Clean Water Act of 1977, Water Quality Act of 1965, Water Quality Act of 1987.

19. Increase access to postsecondary education—e.g., Higher Education Facilities Act of 1963, Higher Education Act of 1965.

20. Increase arms control and disarmament—e.g., Nuclear Test Ban Treaty of 1963, Nuclear Nonproliferation Treaty of 1969, Strategic Arms Limitation Treaty of 1972, Intermediate Range Nuclear Force Treaty of 1988.

21. Increase international economic development—e.g., Bretton Woods Agreement Act of 1945 (creation of the International Bank for Reconstruction and Development), Act for International Development of 1950, Peace Corps Act of 1961.

22. Increase health care access for low-income Americans—e.g., Medicaid Act of 1965, Children's Health Insurance Program of 1997.

23. Increase market competition—e.g., Airline Deregulation Act of 1978, Gramm-Leach-Bliley Act (financial services overhaul) of 1999.

24. Increase health care access for older Americans—e.g., Medicare Act of 1965, Medicare Catastrophic Coverage Act of 1988.

25. Increase the stability of financial institutions and markets—e.g., Securities Act amendments of 1975, Insider Trading and Securities Fraud Enforcement Act of 1988, Financial Institutions Reform, Recovery and Enforcement Act of 1989.

26. Increase the supply of low-income housing—e.g., Housing Act of 1949, Housing and Community Development Act of 1965.

27. Maintain stability in the Persian Gulf—e.g., Gulf War authorization of 1991.

Table 1.1 (continued)

28. Make government more transparent to the public—e.g., Administrative Procedure Act of 1946, Freedom of Information Act of 1966, Privacy Act of 1974, Government in the Sunshine Act of 1976, Ethics in Government Act of 1978, Inspector General Act of 1978.

29. Promote energy independence—e.g., Atomic Energy Act of 1954, trans-Alaskan pipeline of 1973, Energy Policy and Conservation Act of 1975, Natural Gas Wellhead Decontrol Act of 1989.

30. Promote equal access to public accommodations—e.g., Civil Rights Act of 1964, Open Housing Act of 1968, Americans with Disabilities Act of 1990.

31. Promote financial security in retirement—e.g., multiple Social Security benefit increases, Social Security Act amendments of 1972 (established the Supplemental Security Income program), Employment Retirement Income Security Act of 1974. Social Security Act amendments of 1977 and 1983 (increased taxes and reduced benefits to stabilize the program during funding crisis).

32. Promote scientific and technological research—e.g., National Science Foundation Act of 1950, Department of Defense Reorganization Act of 1958 (created the Defense Advanced Research Projects Agency), Communications Satellite Act of 1962.

33. Promote space exploration—e.g., National Aeronautics and Space Administration Act of 1958, appropriations for the Apollo lunar mission, appropriations for a manned space station.

34. Protect endangered species—e.g., Marine Mammal Protection Act of 1972, Endangered Species Act of 1973.

35. Protect the wilderness—e.g., Wilderness Act of 1964, Wild and Scenic Rivers Act of 1968, Alaska National Interest Lands Conservation Act of 1980.

36. Provide assistance for the working poor—e.g., Earned Income Tax Credit of 1975, Family Support Act of 1988, multiple minimum wage increases, including the Small Business Job Protection Act of 1996.

37. Rebuild Europe after World War II—e.g., Bretton Woods Agreement Act of 1945 (established the International Monetary Fund), Foreign Assistance Act of 1948 (Marshall Plan), North Atlantic Treaty of 1949.

38. Reduce crime—e.g., Omnibus Crime Control and Safe Streets Act of 1968, Violent Crime Control and Law Enforcement Act of 1994, Brady Handgun Violence Prevention Act of 1993.

39. Reduce disease—e.g., Polio Vaccine Act of 1955, Health Professions Educational Assistance Act of 1963, National Cancer Act of 1971.

40. Reduce exposure to hazardous waste—e.g., Resource Conservation and Recovery Act of 1976, Comprehensive Environmental Response, Compensation and Liability Act (Superfund) of 1980.

Table 1.1 (continued)

41. Reduce hunger and improve nutrition—e.g., Food Stamp Act of 1964, Special Supplemental Food Program for Women, Infants and Children (WIC) of 1972.

42. Reduce the federal budget deficit—e.g., Balanced Budget and Emergency Deficit Control Act (Gramm-Rudman-Hollings) of 1985, Omnibus Budget Reconciliation Act of 1990, Omnibus Budget Reconciliation Act of 1993, Balanced Budget Act of 1997.

43. Reduce workplace discrimination—e.g., Equal Pay Act of 1963, Civil Rights Act of 1964, Age Discrimination Act of 1967, Americans with Disabilities Act of 1990.

44. Reform taxes—e.g., Revenue Act of 1964, Economic Recovery Tax Act of 1981, Tax Reform Act of 1986, Economic Growth and Tax Relief Reconciliation Act of 2001.

45. Reform welfare—e.g., Omnibus Budget Reconciliation Act of 1981, Personal Responsibility and Work Opportunity Reconciliation Act of 1996.

46. Stabilize agricultural prices—e.g., Agriculture Act of 1948, Agriculture Trade Development and Assistance Act of 1954, Food Security Act of 1985.

47. Strengthen the national defense—e.g., appropriations for tactical and strategic weapons systems, Department of Defense Reorganization Act of 1958, Goldwater-Nichols Department of Defense Reorganization Act of 1986.

48. Strengthen the nation's airways system—e.g., Federal Airport Act of 1946, Airport and Airways Development Act of 1970.

49. Strengthen the nation's highway system—e.g., Federal Aid Highway Act of 1956, Intermodal Surface Transportation Efficiency Act of 1991.

50. Support veterans' readjustment and training—e.g., Servicemen's Readjustment Act of 1944 (GI Bill), New GI Bill Continuation Act (Montgomery GI Bill) of 1987.

mission such as winning the Korean War simply by appropriating federal dollars or by burying initiatives such as space exploration in continuing resolutions.

The list was created by compressing the 553 laws into discrete missions. There was nothing magical about this sorting. I simply asked how hard the federal government had worked to pursue the endeavor, answering through judgments about the level of interest. It was my judgment alone.

Most of these judgments were easy to make. Some missions focused quite specifically on solving a problem such as racial discrimination, childhood poverty, or the erosion of retirement security. Thus, the Civil Rights Act of 1964 is an easy anchor for efforts to attack segregation in public accommodations, and was followed by other statutes over the decades, while the Omnibus Crime Control and Safe Streets Act of 1968 and its associated amendments easily anchor the federal government's effort to reduce crime.

Other missions involve less coherent collections of laws. Improving mass transportation involves a loosely related group of statutes that range from the creation of the Amtrak rail system to increased federal funding for urban mass transit and creation of the Department of Transportation, while immigration reform involves four mostly contradictory efforts to let more immigrants into the United States or keep more out.

However tight or loose the mission, the list shows the enormous perseverance involved in converting endeavors into achievements, which Charles O. Jones has described as "the ultimate test" of a government of separated powers.[12] Thus, only eleven of the fifty missions described in Table 1.1 were anchored by a single major statute such as the Marshall Plan, the Civil Rights Act, or the Medicare Act, and only eight more involved between two and four laws.

The rest of the missions involved a relatively large number of statutes, passed in sequence over time. For example, Congress passed five separate laws spread out over the decades to help veterans readjust to civilian life, another six to reduce the budget deficit, seven to reduce workplace discrimination, eight each to reduce crime, nine to improve water quality, ten to expand the right to vote, twelve to protect the wilderness, thirteen to increase access to college education, fourteen to find new sources of energy, fifteen to help the working poor, and twenty-one to enhance financial security in retirement.

Jones found similar evidence of perseverance in tracking twenty-eight of Mayhew's major laws over time, labeling most of the laws "part of a continuing legislative story within an issue area."[13] Despite isolated cases in which action involved a single law, such as airline deregulation, twenty-three of his twenty-eight laws "had a substantial legislative heritage, traceable to a basic law and typically exhibiting a short-term history of the immediate bill. Battle lines are already drawn on most important pieces of legislation: committee and subcommittee members and staff are familiar with the issue, other members have participated in previous debates, agency personnel know the administrative and legislative history, and interest group representatives are knowledgeable about who did what and who voted how."[14]

The compression of the 553 major laws into missions helps show the value of bipartisanship in sustaining momentum—the longer an issue is alive and expanding, the more likely it will cross through periods of unified and divided control of Congress and the presidency. Thus, thirteen of the fifty missions included at least one law enacted during divided party control within Congress, and forty-four contained at least one law enacted during divided party control between Congress and the presidency. In addition, only thirteen involved laws that were highly identified with a Democratic or Republican president.

Congress and the president are also able to create and expand the federal government's most extensive and arduous missions. The list of major laws certainly confirms David Mayhew's argument that the federal government is perfectly capable of creating and/or expanding the federal agenda during periods of intense party conflict: "From the Taft-Hartley Act to the Marshall Plan of 1947–1948 through the Clean Air Act and the $490 billion deficit reduction package of 1990, important laws have materialized at a rate largely unrelated to conditions of party control. To see this pattern, one has to peer through a Capitol Hill haze that can feature delay, suspense, party posturing, ugly wrangling, and other presentations."[15] (Readers should note that the pattern may be very different when looking at congressional investigations.)[16]

Growing, but Slowing

The list of government's greatest missions shows more than the ability to legislate during periods of divided government and political intrigue, however. It also reveals the enduring hope that the federal service would deliver on the promises made over six decades of expansion. To use Hamilton's term, it is a list of extensive and arduous enterprise.

The list also shows a willingness to persevere on problems such as hunger, poverty, and disease that have demanded great national commitment. Congress has never stopped asking the federal service to do more, even when it refuses to provide the resources to fulfill each promise. The result is a mission that is simultaneously expanding and starving. Insulated from any public pressure to do more with enough, the expanding federal mission can only reinforce views that government is failing to perform.

Yet, the list also confirms Thomas Jefferson's success in establishing the precedent for limited government. Indeed, much of the recent starvation of the federal agenda reflects a return to Jefferson's philosophy of limited government in the policy debate over the past thirty years. The 1800 election was nothing if not a referendum on Hamilton's extensive and arduous enterprise, and dominated Jefferson's rhetoric throughout his presidency. "I am for a government rigorously frugal and simple," he said at the start of the 1800 campaign, "applying all of the possible savings of the public revenue to the discharge of the national debt."[17]

He repeated the pledge to cut government in his first inaugural address, asking what more might be necessary to make the nation happy and prosperous: "Still one thing more, fellow citizens—a wise and frugal government, which shall restrain men from injuring one another, shall leave them otherwise free to regulate their own pursuits of industry, and improvement, and shall not take from the mouth of labor the bread it has earned."[18]

Even before the campaign, he supported a constitutional amendment to reduce the size of government. He remained opposed to debt throughout his life. "We must make our election between economy and liberty, or profusion and servitude," he wrote in 1816. Without a frugal government, he predicted that citizens would have to subsist on "oatmeal and potatoes," yielding no time to think, no way to call managers to account, and a life of riveting "their chains on the necks of our fellow-sufferers."[19]

At the same time, Jefferson believed in a decentralized agenda that would protect the states from federal encroachment. Believing that the nation's state governments were the best in the world, he argued against the arbitrary assumption of state responsibilities. Toward the very end of his life, he wrote a colleague that he hoped "never to see all offices transferred to Washington, where, further withdrawn from the eyes of the people, they may more secretly, be bought and sold as a market."[20]

The pursuit of limited government has clearly slowed the expansion of the federal agenda. Congress and the president have become far less active in passing new legislation over the past thirty years, which coincides directly with the effort to starve government during the Reagan administration. There are other explanations for the decline in congressional and presidential activity, including the steady erosion of public confidence in government (which has reduced public support of ambitious new missions) and rising polarization in Congress (which has increased the odds against passage of such missions), but starvation emerges as the most powerful brake on legislative activism—especially when that activism has involved new spending for programs such as national health insurance.

The Congressional Agenda

The federal government's long list of obligations has grown with each passing year. However, the rate of expansion has been slowing, and the nature of the growth has been changing. Although the overall effect is still cumulative, resulting in an ever-expanding agenda, Congress and presidents have been adding fewer and fewer major statutes to the list. The result is a form of mission creep that is punctuated by occasional large-scale initiatives such as catastrophic health insurance, welfare reform, education reform, and prescription drug coverage for seniors, but is also characterized by small-scale adjustments in existing programs.

Whatever the form of expansion, there is no question that Congress has become less active in passing major legislation, in large part because tax cuts and budget caps have limited the resources available for new action. It is a pattern described by Sarah A. Binder using issues mentioned on the *New York Times* editorial page to measure the agenda: "In terms of size, the agenda ranges as we might expect. It is smallest in the 1950s, in the quiescent years of the Eisenhower presidency. It jumps sharply under the activist administrations of JFK and LBJ in the 1960s and continues to rise steadily in the 1970s and 1980s. Only in recent years has the number of issues on the agenda declined, most likely reflecting the tightening of budgets and the associated dampening of legislative activism."[21]

It is also a pattern in my list of major laws. Again, congressional action peaked exactly when expected, during the 1960s and early 1970s.

- Between 1944 and 1953, Congress added 68 laws to the inventory, including approval of a variety of federal department and agency reorganizations, appropriations for the Korean War, and passage of the Administrative Procedure, Servicemen's Readjustment (GI Bill), and the Atomic Energy Acts. On average, Congress added just 7 major statutes per year during the decade.

- Between 1954 and 1963, Congress added 103 major laws to the statute books, including creation of the National Aeronautics and

Space Administration, launch of the Peace Corps, a vast expansion in federal funding for higher education, and creation of a federal vaccination program. On average, Congress added 10 major statutes per year during the decade.

- Between 1964 and 1973, Congress added 175 laws to my list, including passage of the Voting Rights, Head Start, Medicare, Food Stamp, and Clean Air and Clean Water Acts, Title IX of the Education Act Amendments, the creation of the departments of Transportation and Housing and Urban Development, and approval of the Gulf of Tonkin Resolution, which laid the foundation for the Vietnam War. In total, the decade accounts for more than 30 percent of the major statutes on my list. On average, Congress passed almost 18 major statutes per year during the decade.

The 1960s and early 1970s marked the high point in creating the federal government's fifty greatest missions. It took Congress and the president two decades to enact the first 169 laws on the list of 553, a single decade to enact another 175, and almost three more decades to enact the final 209. What went up during the 1960s and early 1970s soon came down:

- Between 1974 and 1983, Congress added just 96 laws to the list, including creation of the Department of Energy and the Synfuels Corporation, passage of the Civil Service Reform and the Job Training Partnership Acts, a massive package of budget and tax cuts, a comprehensive set of laws designed to attack government fraud, waste, and abuse, and establishment of the Martin Luther King holiday. On average, Congress passed almost 10 statutes per year during the decade, well below the record-setting pace of 1964–1973.

- Between 1984 and 1993, Congress enacted only 77 major laws, including increases in the minimum wage, elevation of the Veterans Administration to cabinet status, two efforts to balance the federal budget, expanded action against water pollution and toxic waste, creation of Americorps, limits on handgun sales and a ban on assault rifles, and passage of the Americans with Disabilities Act and the Family and Medical Leave Act. On average, Congress enacted 7 statutes per year during the decade.

- And between 1994 and 2000, Congress added 34 laws to the list, including another massive effort to balance the federal budget, and passage of welfare reform, the Children's Health Insurance program, and a package of reforms designed to reinvent government. On average, Congress passed barely 5 statutes per year during the seven-year period.

Despite the obvious slowdown, there was no significant decline in the number of federal missions. Despite several efforts during the period to sort, narrow, devolve, and cap the federal mission, neither Congress nor the president showed an appetite for actually jettisoning missions. Instead, they have continued to expand existing missions and have added massive new programs for fighting the war on terrorism, giving older Americans even greater access to health care, and expanding the federal role in primary and secondary education through one of the largest mandates to state and local government in modern history.

The President's Agenda

Looking back to 1961, the president's domestic agenda shows the same slowdown in activity as that of Congress.[22] Just as the congressional agenda followed a mostly curvilinear path back to a quieter time, so did the activity of the past nine presidents. Each Democratic president sent fewer legislative requests to Congress than the previous Democrat, just as each Republican president sent fewer requests than the previous Republican.

This conclusion is based on my assessment of the 393 major domestic proposals presented to Congress between 1961 and 2004. Presidential requests for congressional action only made the list if they were mentioned in a State of the Union address or omnibus legislative message following a first inauguration, and converted into a major legislative proposal, but covered every year between the beginning of 1961 and the end of 2004. Defined by these criteria, the president's agenda is best viewed as a list of hopes for the future, some of which become law, others of which languish for a lack of support.

According to analysis of the 393 proposals, presidents have been dreaming smaller since the Great Society. The absolute number of proposals on the agenda hit a contemporary high under Lyndon Johnson from 1965 to 1968, and dropped steadily under the next seven presidents: Whereas John F. Kennedy had forty-seven proposals for an average of fifteen per year and Johnson had ninety-seven proposals for an average of nineteen per year, Nixon had sixty-five proposals for an average of eleven per year, Gerald Ford had just sixteen proposals for an average of eight, Jimmy Carter had forty-one proposals for an average of ten, Reagan had thirty for an average of four, George H. W. Bush had twenty-five proposals for an average of six, Bill Clinton had fifty-four proposals for an average of seven, and George W. Bush had eighteen in his first term for an average of five.

The content of the president's domestic agenda has also changed over time, as presidents have turned away from large-scale expansions in the federal mission. They have moved toward modifications of existing programs (old ideas) over changes in existing missions (new ideas), and modest adjustments (small-scale ideas) over significant proposals (large-scale ideas).

Measured by the number of new and old requests, for example, the agenda has narrowed, meaning that it began to concentrate more on expanding existing ideas rather than pursuing pattern-breaking change. Whereas 62 percent of the combined Kennedy, Johnson, Nixon, Ford, Carter, and Reagan agendas consisted of new programs that had not existed before or breaks with past precedents, 68 percent of the Bush, Clinton, and Bush agendas consisted of expansions of old programs already on the statute books.

Measured by the number of large versus small ideas, the agenda has also contracted, meaning that it now focuses on more modest proposals rather than grand expansions. Whereas 49 percent of the combined Kennedy through Reagan agendas contained large-scale requests, 66 of the Bush, Clinton, and Bush agendas that followed consisted of small-scale requests.

When these two measures of scope are combined, the president's agenda is shown to have become a vehicle for mostly small-scale expansions of existing programs, not large-scale pattern-breaking changes in the government's mission. As Table 1.2 shows, the conclusion emerges from two simple facts from the list of proposals on the president's agenda. First, 35 percent of the Kennedy, Johnson, Nixon, Ford, Carter, and Reagan agendas focused on new large-scale requests, compared with just 20 percent of the Bush, Clinton, and Bush agendas. Second, 57 percent of the Bush, Clinton, and Bush agendas focused on small-scale modifications of existing proposals, compared with just 17 percent of the Kennedy, Johnson, Nixon, Ford, Carter, and Reagan agendas. In short, the president's agenda changed from a platform for major new ideas to a list of mostly modest expansions of old ideas, hardly the kind of extensive and arduous enterprises Hamilton favored.

Table 1.2 Large/small programs versus new/old programs on the president's domestic agenda, 1961–2004

President	Large-new		Large-old		Small-new		Small-old	
	Number	Percent	Number	Percent	Number	Percent	Number	Percent
Kennedy/ Johnson	19	36	14	26	9	17	11	21
Johnson	35	39	20	22	15	17	21	23
Nixon	18	28	5	8	28	43	14	22
Ford	4	25	4	25	2	13	6	39
Carter	16	39	6	15	9	22	10	24
Reagan	11	36	2	6	7	23	10	33
Bush	3	12	1	4	5	20	16	64
Clinton I	9	27	7	21	3	9	14	42
Clinton II	4	19	2	10	1	5	14	66
Bush	5	28	1	6	2	11	10	56

N=393.
Note: Percentages may not sum to 100 because of rounding.

George W. Bush's first-term agenda shows the changes. Despite his promise to pursue limited government in a number of policy areas during the 2000 campaign, the second president Bush concentrated most of his first-term domestic agenda on modest expansions of existing federal programs, confirming a "first-do-no-harm" philosophy in keeping government taxes low. Even acknowledging his intense first-term focus on the war on terrorism, and its associated creation of an entirely new set of organizations and statutes, Bush primarily asked the federal government to do more of the same, albeit with less.

It is not clear why the president's agenda has declined, especially given the opportunities created by the congressional slowdown. It could be that presidents simply ran out of new large-scale ideas—that is, that the New Deal and Great Society agendas were mostly exhausted by the 1980s. It could also be that the deep tax and budget cuts discussed below limited presidential maneuvering room by simultaneously forcing the budget deficit onto the list of great missions while limiting the dollars available for major initiatives such as national health insurance.

Finally, it could be that Congress and presidents have lost political support for large/new ideas, whether because the American people have run out of patience for overpromising or because of increased polarization within Congress. Even if Congress and presidents had the ideas, it is not clear they could win passage, although George W. Bush was notably successful with his prescription drug program and No Child Left Behind Act.

The war on terrorism may yet reverse the congressional and presidential slowdowns. Its impact on the federal government was immediate and far-reaching, while creating an entirely new federal mission built around antiterrorism legislation, the wars in Afghanistan and Iraq, and a new homeland security department. Whether this level of activity will continue depends in part on the competition from other missions such as an end to global warming, but the war on terrorism has certainly guaranteed itself a place on the list of the federal government's most important missions far into the future.

Starving Government

Compelling though these explanations for the slowdowns might be, the federal agenda has clearly been starved over the past thirty years. Indeed, the past five presidents have been remarkably consistent in their calls for what Clinton labeled a government that works better and costs less.

These calls have echoed through every presidential campaign since Watergate. They framed Carter's call for a government as good as its people, Reagan's complaint that government was the problem, not the solution, Clinton's attack on government waste, and George W. Bush's promise to give money back to the people. Only George H. W. Bush resisted the temptation to attack government during his run for office, but even he eventually embraced the war on waste. The only problem is that these presidents focused on the bureaucracy, not the mission. Even Reagan grew the federal mission, albeit at a slower pace.

It is not that presidents lack any influence over the mission of government. They can always shorten the list of missions by eliminating unsuccessful endeavors or capping the amount of spending for particularly unsuccessful efforts, narrow the agenda through devolution to the states or deregulation, or starve the mission through deep tax cuts. Yet none of these tools have proven particularly successful in actually reducing the federal government's agenda—not Carter's effort to set the federal budget to zero and force agencies to justify each program through the annual budgeting process, Reagan's 1981 tax cuts, pay-as-you-go budget caps, or further tax cuts. They may have slowed the agenda's growth, but they have never reversed it.

This is not to underestimate the impact of Reagan's 1981 tax cuts on the rate of growth. Not only did the cuts set the stage for future budget caps and further tax cuts in 2001, they clearly affected the future expansion of the federal mission. Having failed to win sweeping cuts in Social Security early in his first year, Reagan turned to tax cuts as the best available tool for constraining government growth. Forged through hard bargaining with a reluctant Congress, the tax cuts created the deficits that slowed the pace of expansion in existing programs, while capping the resources available for new ideas such as Clinton's national health care plan. Table 1.3 shows the effect on the president's agenda pre- and post-1981.

Reagan was the perfect president to pursue the starvation agenda. Referring to the combination of hyperinflation and unemployment under Carter, Reagan launched his presidential campaign in 1979 by arguing that the federal government was the problem, not the solution: "It has outspent, overestimated and overregulated. It has failed to deliver services within the revenues it should be allowed to raise from taxes." He went even further in accepting the Republican nomination in 1980, making tax cuts his top priority. "The American people are carrying the heaviest peacetime tax burden in our nation's history," he argued, "and it will grow even heavier, under present law, next January. We are taxing ourselves into economic exhaustion and stagnation, crushing our ability and incentive to save, invest and produce."[23] But as already noted, Reagan succumbed to demands for an expanded federal mission even as he pursued a frugal administration through hiring freezes and budget cuts.

Table 1.3 The Reagan effect: Presidential requests for legislation, pre- and post-1981 (in percent)

Presidential proposal	Percent proposed pre-1981	Percent proposed post-1981
Large/new	35	25
Small/new	24	14
Large/old	18	10
Small/old	23	50

Note: Pre-Reagan N=266 cases (Kennedy, Johnson, Nixon, Ford, Carter); post-Reagan N=127 cases (Reagan, Bush 41, Clinton, Bush 43).
Percentages may not sum to 100 because of rounding.

Moreover, Reagan never proposed and did not seek a major sorting of government's mission. Despite his rhetoric of smaller, leaner government, Reagan's program was much more about constraining the federal budget, not sorting the federal mission. Having entered office promising to abolish the departments of Education and Energy, deregulate everything from labor to milk prices, and devolve responsibilities to the states, he left office after elevating the Veterans Administration to cabinet status, increasing the federal deficit to the breaking point, expanding federal regulation of toxic waste, and providing catastrophic health insurance to older Americans. The departments of Education and Energy were still standing when he returned to California.

In short, presidents have been talking about streamlining for the past three decades, but actually doing little to reduce the federal agenda. They have promised a sharper mission, but have mostly starved government instead, creating an ever-growing list of missions in or out of favor. And Congress has mostly been a partner in the division of the national agenda into missions that do and do not matter, whether following the president's lead on starving government or pursuing its own wars on fraud, waste, and abuse. As a result, the federal government has emerged with fewer resources but an ever-expanding agenda.

Missions that Still Matter

Perhaps the most important question for the federal service is whether the federal agenda still consists of missions that matter. At least according to my survey of 450 randomly selected leading historians and political scientists, the answer may depend on the relative difficulty, importance, and ultimate success of each endeavor.

In theory, important, difficult, and successful endeavors are more likely to constitute missions that matter than endeavors that are less important, difficult, and successful, especially if important endeavors meet Hamilton's implied definition of "extensive," while difficult endeavors meet his view of "arduous." Although there are substantial ideological disagreements about what constitutes a mission that matters today, there is also substantial agreement that some federal efforts have been more significant than others, meaning that they mostly involve important, difficult issues that only the federal government can solve.

Rating Missions

Determining the relative importance of a given mission involves a sense of time and context, which can be found among many experts, most notably scholars who specialize in post–World War II American history and public policy. If any group of experts should be able to rate the relative importance, difficulty, and success of the federal government's fifty greatest missions, scholars of modern American history and public policy provide an appealing sample.

This assumption is very familiar to those who have attempted to study presidential greatness through polls of historians and other experts. Starting with Arthur Schlesinger's 1948 survey of a hand-picked set of respondents, most of whom were his friends, historians and political scientists have been measuring greatness through the same kinds of methods used in the following section.[24]

Some of these ratings have involved relatively small samples of experts, while others have involved larger samples of C-SPAN viewers or presidential scholars. In addition, some of these ratings have been based on one or two measures of overall greatness, while others have drawn on many more, such as a president's ability to compromise, integrity, intelligence, and luck.[25]

Interestingly, these various studies produce similar results, especially at the top and bottom of the list. George Washington, Thomas Jefferson, Abraham Lincoln, Franklin D. Roosevelt, Theodore Roosevelt, and Harry S Truman are almost always rated at or very near the top, while Ulysses S. Grant, Warren G. Harding, Herbert Hoover, James Buchanan, Richard Nixon, and Andrew Johnson are invariably rated at the bottom. The variation comes in the middle, where presidents such as George H. W. Bush, Jimmy Carter, Clinton, and Reagan move up or down with contemporary history. Although there is certainly some ideology to the ratings, especially with respect to recent presidents, the agreement undermines the notion that presidential greatness is in the eye of the beholder.

The same conclusion seems to fit my 2000 survey of the relative importance, difficulty, and success of the fifty missions. The survey itself involved 450 historians and political scientists randomly selected from lists of modern American history and government scholars provided by the American Historical Association and American Political Science Association. Surveyed by mail in the spring and summer, a year before the 9/11 terrorist attacks, each respondent was asked just three questions

Table 1.4 Ratings of importance, difficulty, and success

Questions: (1) How important was the problem to be solved? (2) How difficult was the problem to be solved? (3) How successful was the federal government in solving the problem?

Percentage rating mission as very important	Percentage rating mission as very difficult	Percentage rating mission as very successful
1. Expand the right to vote: 89%	1. Advance human rights and provide humanitarian relief: 66%	1. Rebuild Europe after WWII: 82%
2. Rebuild Europe after WWII: 80%	2. Increase arms control and disarmament: 65%	2. Expand the right to vote: 61%
3. Increase low-income families' access to health care: 78%	3. Reduce workplace discrimination: 53%	3. Strengthen the nation's highway system: 40%
4. Reduce workplace discrimination: 78%	4. Develop and renew impoverished communities: 52%	4. Contain communism: 36%
5. Promote equal access to public accommodations: 78%	5. Contain communism: 50%	5. Promote equal access to public accommodations: 34%
6. Increase arms control and disarmament: 78%	6. Reduce crime: 48%	6. Reduce the federal budget deficit: 33%
7. Improve elementary and secondary education: 75%	7. Reduce the federal budget deficit: 45%	7. Support veterans' readjustment and training: 29%
8. Ensure safe food and drinking water: 73%	8. Reform welfare: 43%	8. Strengthen the national defense: 26%
9. Improve water quality: 72%	9. Increase international economic development: 41%	9. Increase older Americans' access to health care: 24%
10. Improve air quality: 72%	10. Improve mass transportation: 41%	10. Promote financial security in retirement: 23%
11. Reduce hunger and improve nutrition: 72%	11. Improve air quality: 40%	11. Reduce disease: 23%

12. Increase older Americans' access to health care: 70%
13. Reduce disease: 65%
14. Reduce exposure to hazardous waste: 63%
15. Improve mass transportation: 61%
16. Advance human rights and provide humanitarian relief: 60%
17. Provide assistance for the working poor: 60%
18. Promote financial security in retirement: 60%
19. Ensure an adequate energy supply: 56%
20. Enhance workplace safety: 56%
21. Increase access to postsecondary education: 53%
22. Enhance consumer protection: 51%
23. Increase the supply of low-income housing: 50%
24. Develop and renew impoverished communities: 49%
25. Protect the wilderness: 49%
26. Promote scientific and technological research: 48%

12. Promote equal access to public accommodations: 39%
13. Improve elementary and secondary education: 38%
14. Rebuild Europe after WWII: 38%
15. Control immigration: 36%
16. Increase low-income families' access to health care: 34%
17. Promote space exploration: 34%
18. Reduce exposure to hazardous waste: 34%
19. Expand the right to vote: 34%
20. Ensure an adequate energy supply: 32%
21. Improve water quality: 31%
22. Improve government performance: 29%
23. Reduce disease: 29%
24. Provide assistance for the working poor: 27%
25. Make government more transparent to the public: 27%
26. Increase the supply of low-income housing: 26%

12. Maintain stability in the Persian Gulf: 21%
13. Promote space exploration: 20%
14. Promote scientific and technological research: 20%
15. Expand home ownership: 18%
16. Expand foreign markets for U.S. goods: 15%
17. Increase access to postsecondary education: 15%
18. Ensure safe food and drinking water: 14%
19. Increase market competition: 13%
20. Reduce workplace discrimination: 13%
21. Increase the stability of financial institutions and markets: 11%
22. Reduce hunger and improve nutrition 11%
23. Enhance consumer protection: 11%
24. Stabilize agricultural prices: 11%
25. Enhance workplace safety: 9%
26. Improve water quality: 9%

Table 1.4 (continued)

Percentage rating mission as very important	Percentage rating mission as very difficult	Percentage rating mission as very successful
27. Strengthen the nation's airways system: 47%	27. Protect endangered species: 25%	27. Protect endangered species: 8%
28. Enhance the nation's health care infrastructure: 47%	28. Maintain stability in the Persian Gulf: 25%	28. Improve air quality: 8%
29. Increase international economic development: 46%	29. Enhance workplace safety: 23%	29. Protect the wilderness: 8%
30. Make government more transparent to the public: 46%	30. Expand foreign markets for U.S. goods: 22%	30. Enhance the nation's health care infrastructure: 8%
31. Reduce crime: 45%	31. Increase older Americans' access to health care: 20%	31. Reform taxes: 8%
32. Support veterans' readjustment and training: 40%	32. Enhance consumer protection: 20%	32. Strengthen the nation's airways system: 6%
33. Protect endangered species: 38%	33. Expand job training and placement: 20%	33. Increase international economic development: 5%
34. Reduce the federal budget deficit: 36%	34. Protect the wilderness: 19%	34. Ensure an adequate energy supply: 5%
35. Increase the stability of financial institutions and markets: 36%	35. Enhance the nation's health care infrastructure: 19%	35. Increase arms control and disarmament: 4%
36. Improve government performance: 33%	36. Ensure safe food & drinking water: 19%	36. Devolve responsibility to the states: 4%
37. Expand job training and placement: 33%	37. Reform taxes: 18%	37. Control immigration: 3%
38. Contain communism: 32%	38. Promote financial security in retirement: 16%	38. Increase low-income families' access to health care: 3%
39. Reform welfare: 31%	39. Increase the stability of financial institutions and markets: 16%	39. Provide assistance for the working poor: 3%
40. Strengthen the nation's highway system: 30%	40. Stabilize agricultural prices: 13%	40. Make government more transparent to the public: 3%

41. Strengthen the national defense: 28%
42. Expand foreign markets for U.S. goods: 28%
43. Maintain stability in the Persian Gulf: 24%
44. Stabilize agricultural prices: 18%
45. Expand home ownership: 18%
46. Reform taxes: 17%
47. Promote space exploration: 16%
48. Control immigration: 15%
49. Increase market competition: 13%
50. Devolve responsibility to the states: 8%

41. Reduce hunger and improve nutrition: 13%
42. Strengthen the nation's airways system: 11%
43. Devolve responsibility to the states: 11%
44. Strengthen the national defense: 11%
45. Increase market competition: 11%
46. Increase access to postsecondary education: 9%
47. Promote scientific and technological research: 7%
48. Support veterans' readjustment and training: 6%
49. Strengthen the nation's highway system: 4%
50. Expand home ownership: 4%

41. Reduce exposure to hazardous waste: 3%
42. Reduce crime: 3%
43. Reform welfare: 3%
44. Improve elementary and secondary education: 2%
45. Expand job training and placement: 2%
46. Improve mass transportation: 1%
47. Advance human rights and provide humanitarian relief: 1%
48. Improve government performance: 1%
49. Develop and renew impoverished communities: <1%
50. Increase the supply of low-income housing: 0%

N=450 historians and political scientists.

about each of the fifty endeavors: (1) was the problem that prompted action very, somewhat, not too, or not at all important, (2) was it very, somewhat, not too, or not at all difficult to solve, and (3) was the federal government very, somewhat, not too, or not at all successful in its effort?

Unlike rating presidential greatness, Table 1.4 shows much greater variability among the historians and political scientists on the relative importance, difficulty, and success of the fifty endeavors. Some missions were rated very important and successful, but not particularly difficult, others as unimportant, not particularly difficult, and unsuccessful, and still others as important, difficult, and successful. When the ratings are combined, the most important, difficult, and successful missions might be considered the federal government's greatest achievements, while the more important, easier, and unsuccessful missions might be called its greatest disappointments because success was within reach, and its least important, easiest, and unsuccessful missions its greatest waste of effort.

There are obvious differences in how the historians and political scientists rated the importance of each endeavor, which is a significant measure of a mission that matters. At least during the summer of 2000, these academics saw the right to vote, the need to rebuild postwar Europe, health-care access for low-income Americans, workplace discrimination, equal access to public accommodations, arms control and disarmament, elementary and postsecondary education, safe food and water, and water and air quality as the ten most important problems on the list of federal missions.

Conversely, the historians and political scientists saw devolution as the least important problem, followed by market competition, immigration, space exploration, tax reform, home ownership, agricultural prices, Persian Gulf stability, open markets for U.S. goods, and the national defense. Although there was significant agreement in the importance of each mission in the top and bottom quartiles of the list, there was significant disagreement among the thirty or so missions in the middle.

This variation reflects the influence of both history and ideology. Stability in the Persian Gulf and a strong national defense were less significant issues as the cold war and 1991 Gulf War faded from memory, while space exploration, tax reform, and immigration may have seemed far less important when compared with other problems on the federal agenda. Although rebuilding Europe after World War II was rated as the second most important problem on the list, my sample placed the cold war far down on the list in 34th place, in part perhaps because my respondents saw the seeds of the victory in communism itself rather than in the efforts of the federal government.

The rankings also reflect the bias of mostly white, older, male, and emphatically liberal respondents, which is exactly what one would expect from an academic sample. The ideological bias appears to be particularly important in the top ratings for expanding the right to vote, health care for the poor, increasing arms control, improving air and water quality, and reducing hunger, as well as the relative lack of urgency regarding traditional conservative issues such as devolution and tax reform.

This bias also affects the ratings of difficulty, though perhaps less so given the more objective nature of the question—that is, a mission is either difficult or not. According to the historians and political scientists, human rights was the single most difficult problem on the list of endeavors, followed by nuclear arms control and disarmament, workplace discrimination, low-income communities, the cold war, crime, the budget deficit, welfare reform, international economic development, and mass transportation.

On the other hand, the historians and political scientists rated the highway system, aid to veterans, scientific and technological research, access to post-secondary education, market competition, the national defense, devolution to the states, the nation's airways system, hunger and nutrition, and agricultural price stabilization as the least difficult.

Finally, the historians and political scientists saw significant differences in the federal government's ability to convert the different endeavors into actual success. They viewed rebuilding Europe as the federal government's most successful endeavor, followed by expanding the right to vote, strengthening the highway system, containing communism, promoting equal access to public accommodations, reducing the budget deficit, helping veterans readjust to civilian life, strengthening the national defense, and increasing both health care and financial security for older Americans.

At the same time, the historians and political scientists saw increasing the supply of low-income housing as the federal government's greatest disappointment, followed by renewing poor communities, improving government performance, advancing human rights, improving mass transportation, expanding job training and placement, improving elementary and secondary education, reforming welfare, reducing crime, and reducing exposure to hazardous waste.

A more recent survey might reveal entirely different rankings of success and failure. Making government more transparent to the public might fall even further given the Bush administration's penchant for secrecy, welfare reform might move up given the dramatic decline in case loads under the new timelines established by the Personal Responsibility and Work Opportunity Reconciliation Act of 1996, and improving elementary and secondary education might rise a bit given implementation of the No Child Left Behind Act. Then again, the extraordinary controversy surrounding the cost of implementing the act might drive the endeavor further down.

Nevertheless, the list of achievements and disappointments embedded in these success ratings suggests the importance of consistency and perseverance in achieving impact. The federal government's top achievements reflect an almost single-minded focus on wearing problems down through steady investment, whether in expanding voting rights, reducing disease, cutting the federal budget deficit, or attacking air and water pollution.

Unlike immigration reform, where Congress and the president have never quite agreed on what to do, tax reform, where equity continues to be the enemy of simplicity, or devolution, where the effort has been occasional and often unfocused, government's greatest achievements reflect a clear strategy that governed legislative activity for more than a half century. As such, they suggest that achievement is almost impossible unless Congress and presidents first agree on how they will solve a problem.

Measuring Demand

Despite their own support for smaller government, Americans continue to express significant worries about longer-term issues that have stalled in Congress or that have been set aside for the future. Indeed, according to my July 2006 survey of 1,000 adults, Americans have significant worries about the eight issues addressed in the survey—issues that were selected because they have long-term impacts that are often ignored in the present.[26]

Many of the issues also involve policies that cannot be solved without inflicting significant short-term pain such as higher gasoline taxes and mileage standards (global warming), higher taxes and benefit cuts (Social Security and Medicare), significant costs (terrorism, treat-

ment for new diseases, repairing the nation's roads and bridges), or po-
larizing legislation (immigration reform).

As already noted, at least some of these issues have been widely de-
bated in Congress as an immediate-term issue with no results, in part
because Americans disagree sharply on the policy choices for re-
solving the issue. But as Table 1.5 shows, Americans worried nonetheless.[27]

As the table indicates, there were significant party differences in
worries about the future, with Republicans less concerned about six
of the eight issues. The biggest gaps were on global warming (29 percent), treatments for new diseases (24 percent), Medicare (16 percent), and Social Security (15 percent), all issues closely identified with
Democrats.

The list is particularly important for two reasons. First, it shows the
range of concerns about issues that will shape future legislative action.
Members of Congress are generally remaining silent about their positions on these key long-term issues, in part because elections so often
turn on short-term issues, but in part because members have done so

Table 1.5 Demands for Action, 2006

Question: And how worried are you personally about the future of the country
when it comes to issues involving (insert)—very worried, somewhat worried,
not too worried, or not at all worried?

Issue	Percentage of all respondents who were very or somewhat worried	Percentage of Democratic respondents who were very or somewhat worried	Percentage of Republican respondents who were very or somewhat worried
Social Security	81	89	74
Energy	81	88	77
Medicare	80	85	69
Immigration	80	76	84
Terrorism	78	78	81
Treatments for new diseases	70	81	58
Global warming	52	81	52
Repairing the nation's older roads and bridges	50	50	47

N=491 total; 226 Democrats, 177 Republicans.

little to actually move reform forward. Of course, debates on contentious long-term issues may be best held as far from the next election as possible.

My survey also suggests that Americans are convinced that Congress is not paying enough attention to most of the long-term issues about which they care, a point made emphatically when one examines the percentage of survey participants who said that Congress is paying a great deal of attention to issues about which they are very worried.

These disconnects create a worry/attention gap that speaks to the lack of congressional responsiveness on long-term issues. For example, 81 percent of Americans said they were very or somewhat worried about Social Security, but only 47 percent said Congress is paying a great deal of attention to the issue; 81 percent said they were very worried about energy, but only 48 percent said Congress is paying a great deal of attention to the issue; and 80 percent said they were very worried about Medicare, but only 52 percent said Congress is paying a great deal of attention to the issue. Terrorism was the only issue on which the level of personal worry appeared to match the level of congressional attention.

When coupled with the public's belief that Congress often does not have enough information to act and spends too little time debating long-term issues, the survey reveals a serious dilemma for Congress. On the one hand, the public is worried about these eight long-term issues, thinks Congress is not paying enough attention, and wants Congress to spend more time on each issue. On the other hand, the public thinks Congress does not have the knowledge to do so. If Congress is to act, therefore, it needs to reassure the public that it actually has the knowledge to make thoughtful decisions, which means that it needs to increase its deliberative capacity. It cannot act with strength and reassurance if the public believes it does not have the knowledge to do so.

Nevertheless, Americans are quite clear that they want action now on the long-term issues described above. Their personal worries translate into clear demands for action. Asked whether the nation can wait to deal with these long-term issues or needs to take action now, roughly 90 percent said Congress should act now on immigration reform, terrorism, energy, Medicare, Social Security, and treatments for new diseases, while 75 percent said Congress should act now on global warming, and 65 percent said the same about repairing older roads and bridges. (I surmise that Americans might rate this last issue a bit higher after the I-35 bridge collapse in summer 2007.)

There are only small party differences on these demands except with regard to global warming. Democrats are overwhelming in their demand for action now on the issue, compared to a much smaller majority of Republicans. However, even Republicans have come to believe that global warming demands a response, which remains contrary to the position of the George W. Bush administration.

Regardless of these assorted differences, my 2006 survey suggests that demand for action will remain strong on many of the federal government's greatest endeavors. Whether these missions matter in an objective sense through policy analysis is not the issue. What matters most is the demand itself, which drives the electoral considerations that shape congressional and presidential action. The only problem is that the demand increasingly concentrates on issues that defy resolution in the present tense. Having ignored the opportunity to call for sacrifice after 9/11, action remains well out of reach.

Conclusion

Even the most energetic federal service, no matter how dedicated and talented it might be, is often unable to find the resources to implement missions that no longer matter to the nation.

Some missions simply lose momentum as the nation moves further away from the events that originally inspired action; others lose support as the public tires of the latest pledge to solve intractable problems such as poverty and energy dependency, and still others drift toward irrelevance because social entrepreneurs have taken on responsibilities that government and its networks will not. The missions may still matter, just not to the federal service.

At the same time, many of the missions that no longer matter have been starved into submission under the enormous pressure on the federal government to do more with less. Unwilling to abandon missions because of continued pressure from agencies and constituents, Congress and presidents continue to expand the federal agenda, albeit at a slower pace.

Thus, instead of compiling a list of government's greatest triumphs, I could just as easily have focused on government's greatest frustrations. As Hamilton might have argued, the federal government simply does not have enough resources to cover an ever-expanding mission. Nor is the federal government well configured to pursue every extensive and arduous enterprise that Congress and presidents might ask it to execute, especially when they divide the responsibilities across multiple agencies and different chains of command.

This duplication and overlap is not a major issue in this book, but it was a major issue for the 2003 National Commission on the Public Service, which was chaired by Paul A. Volcker. Characterizing the federal organization chart as "an accumulation of particular organizations that follow no logical pattern," the commission argued that "public servants often find themselves in doubt about the relevance and importance of their agency's mission while spending inordinate amounts of time coordinating or battling with their counterparts in other agencies."[28] Hence, the commission called for a sweeping reorganization of the federal hierarchy into a limited number of mission-related executive departments.

Much as one can acknowledge the allure of mission-centered government, the problem is less the fragmentation and more the expansive agenda. Until Congress and presidents reconcile the agenda with available administrative capacity, no amount of reorganization will provide the needed focus and resources. Reorganization might make the chains of command clearer and inspire a greater sense of unity among employees who have long battled across departmental and agency lines, but will not address the simultaneous growth and starvation of the agenda, which is ultimately at the root of many of the federal government's greatest disappointments. They must either make every mission matter or drop the ones that no longer make sense. In doing so, they might recall Jefferson's belief that the government agenda should pursue "a noiseless course," not missions of national aggrandizement.[29]

Despite the slowdowns in both congressional and presidential activity, there is little reason to believe that Congress and future presidents will stop expanding the federal mission or reverse course by abandoning existing agendas in a pattern-breaking dismantling of the federal mission. Ideas in good currency still exist, as do ample opportunities for expansion. As the recent prescription drug legislation shows, even small-government presidents are not averse to major expansions, especially as they pursue reelection.

Moreover, like the nation's aging highways, the federal government's greatest missions desperately require repairs as the future bears down with great uncertainty. Sooner or later, Congress will have to address the impending Medicare crisis, immigration reform, and global warming, which are on the agenda, but remain mired in uncertainty and political controversy. The rate of increase may have declined, but is unlikely to turn negative any time soon. Through the accretion of new missions, whether because of crises such as the war on terrorism or the continued belief that the measure of a just society lies in its effort to solve intractable problems, the federal mission is likely to expand, and with it the demand for an energetic federal service to faithfully execute the goals.

CHAPTER TWO

Clarity of Command

The second characteristic of an energetic federal service is a clear chain of command. Hamilton and Jefferson both understood that there would be officers and subordinates in the new government, although Jefferson hoped for fewer. In turn, both wanted to make sure these officers and subordinates would be accountable to the president and, therefore, to the public. How else to assure the faithful execution of the laws?[1]

But Hamilton also believed that the federal service had to be given exact orders, which he described as "execution in detail." Nothing was too trivial for his attention. Hamilton even specified that the provisions on his new Coast Guard cutters should include ten muskets, twenty pistols, one broadax, and two lanterns.[2]

Hamilton exercised this "execution in detail" through tight supervision of his chief officers, who exercised tight supervision of their chief officers, and so forth down the chain of command of every organization he served during his abbreviated career. Writing as inspector general of the War Department in 1788, he warned about the dangers of too little supervision: "It is essential to the success of the minister of a great department, that he subdivide the objects of his care, distribute them among competent assistants, and content himself with a general but vigilant superintendence. This course is particularly necessary when an unforeseen emergency has suddenly accumulated a number of new objects to be provided for and executed."[3]

Once issued, orders required a clear chain of command from the top to the very bottom of government. "From the earliest times," Luther

Gulick argued nearly two hundred years later, "it has been recognized that nothing but confusion arises under multiple command. . . . As a result the executive of any enterprise can personally direct only a few persons. He must depend on these to direct others, and upon them in turn to direct still others, until the last man in the organization is reached."[4] Hamilton could hardly have said it better.

As the federal agenda grew, however, so did the federal hierarchy. But the thickening of the hierarchy with more layers of leaders and more leaders per layer is not entirely related to the mission. Indeed, the thickening of government has been accelerating much faster than the agenda has been growing, driven by an indelible belief that more leaders equals more leadership and an unstoppable spread of every new title imaginable. Departments began inventing new titles almost immediately after the founding, and the invention has never stopped.

This thickening of the hierarchy thereby undermines the health of the federal service by denying the clarity of command necessary for faithful execution of the laws. The more the public wants from government, the more Congress and presidents have felt the pressure to provide the leadership to deliver. Convinced in part that the career civil servants are unresponsive, they have added more hierarchy at the top and middle of government to make sure departments and agencies do their jobs.

What they fail to realize is that more leaders does not equal more leadership. Rather, more leaders may actually weaken government's capacity to act by diffusing accountability for what goes right or wrong in the faithful execution of the laws.

As this chapter will argue, Hamilton may have started with the right idea for a clear chain of command, but history has taken his commitment to unity in guiding the federal service well beyond the point of reason. Hamilton's principle made perfect sense in a department of a few hundred employees, but steadily evolved into a complex hierarchy that denies the clarity of command needed for an energetic public service.

A History of Thickening

Thickening does not occur just at the top of government, although much of this chapter focuses on the senior hierarchy. It also occurs down through the middle and lower rungs of the organizational ladder.

This is certainly the case in the federal government, where the federal hierarchy has been changing shape since the 1930s when it resembled a traditional bureaucratic pyramid—the vast majority of federal employees worked at the bottom of government. By the 1970s, the hierarchy was shaped more like an isosceles trapezoid—with growing numbers of federal employees steadily pushing out at the senior and middle levels of government. And by the 1990s, the hierarchy was beginning to look like a pentagon—the majority of federal employees worked at the middle of government rather than at the bottom. If current trends continue, the federal hierarchy may eventually look like an ellipse, with a vast middle of professional and technical employees and their supervisors and a much smaller number of frontline employees who actually deliver services at the bottom.

The evidence is in the federal personnel data files, which show the changing shape:

1. Between 1983 and 2003, the number of lower-level employees fell from 780,000 to 525,000, while the number of middle-level employees increased from 485,000 to 655,000. The two numbers crossed in 1995.

2. During the same period, the number of middle-level supervisors rose from 125,000 to 161,000, then fell to 119,000. The ratio of middle-level supervisors to lower-level employees changed from 1:6 in 1983 to 1:5 in 2003, despite the steep cut in the actual number of middle-level supervisors.

3. In an employment system with fifteen grades, or ranks, the average lower-level grade increased from 8.4 in 1983 to 9.9 in 2003, while the average middle-level grade increased from 12.3 to 12.4, regardless of whether the employees were supervisors or not.[5]

Explaining the Shift

This changing shape obviously involves much more than the executive hierarchy, which is the subject of this chapter, and reflects a number of trends. The federal workforce contains large numbers of baby boomers, who have aged upward through the hierarchy through automatic grade increases after specific periods of time. The average age of the federal worker was just under 44 in 1993 and over 47 in 2003, which has created great pressure for promotion, which in turn has become a way of circumventing pay freezes.

Moreover, many of the jobs that were once located at the bottom of the bureaucratic pyramid have either been erased by new technologies or contracted out to private firms. The number of lower-level clerical staff dropped dramatically with the arrival of the personal computer, for example, while the number of federal cafeteria workers, janitors, and building security guards has dropped to almost zero. The cafeterias still exist, of course, but the food is served by contractors.

Finally, much of the downsizing of the federal service during the 1990s involved attrition, not deliberate decisions. Because turnover rates at the lower levels of government are much higher than those at the middle levels, the number of lower-level employees had to drop. But as just noted, those jobs did not necessarily disappear. Some were filled at a higher level, creating a growing corps of middle-level clerical workers, while others were contracted out. In essence, the bottom of the federal pyramid still exists, just not on the federal payroll.

This thickening has persisted throughout a growing inventory of research on the problems of centralization. As Richard Stillman argues, the 1960s and 1970s witnessed the awakening of a vision of public organizations that was neatly juxtaposed against much of the Hamiltonian model.[6] Romanticism was expressed in calls for decentralization in lieu of hierarchy, popular participation rather than neutral expertise, fragmented structure instead of unity of command, subjectivity and feeling rather than economy and efficiency, even as advocates struggled to develop their distinctly Jeffersonian vision of public management into recommendations for action.

Stillman's 1985 article anticipated a flood of arguments in favor of what David Osborne and Ted Gaebler call "steering not rowing" in government management.[7] And it clearly anticipated Vice President Al Gore's "reinventing government" campaign to "empower employees to get results." According to the vice president, decentralization was a key to giving the federal service the freedom to act. By encouraging "federal employees to become their own managers of their own work," as the first Gore reinventing government report argued, a sharp reduction in managers would offer "employees in dead-end or deadly dull jobs a chance to use all their abilities," which in turn would make "the federal government a better place to work," which in turn again would "make federal workers more productive."[8]

Gore's ideas clearly challenged classic theories of public administration that followed Hamilton's model. But they also challenged the notion that the federal government must meet a higher standard in executing the laws than simply satisfying customers. As Lawrence E. Lynn, Jr., writes, "A reconsideration of the traditional literature leads to the ironic insight that contemporary critics of traditional thought pose a greater threat to democratic values than the authors of the so-called bureaucratic paradigm. Traditional habits of thought exhibited far more respect for law, politics, citizens, and values than customer-oriented managerialism or civil philosophies that, in promoting community and citizen empowerment, barely acknowledge the constitutional role of legislatures, courts, and executive departments."[9]

Lynn and his colleagues would hardly argue for the kind of thickening described in this chapter, but they do understand that clarity of command provides an element of constitutional accountability and essential oversight for the faithful execution of the laws. At the same time, they recognize that thickening can become a risk to faithful execution by slowing the movement of information up and down the hierarchy, while diffusing the clarity of command that also provides constitutional accountability. And they can see the value of the agility and adaptability embedded in the flattening, decentralizing, and networking that have become so prevalent in calls for reform. Thus does thickening have at least some salutary effects, albeit at much lower heights and widths than in the current hierarchy.

Reshaping Government

Members of the federal service certainly recognize that there are too many layers of management between the top and bottom of government. According to my 2001 survey of more than 1,000 randomly selected federal employees, only a tiny fraction said there were too few management layers above them, while 40 percent said there were too many, and the rest said the number was just right.[10]

Not surprisingly, only 11 percent of members of the Senior Executive Service said there were too many layers above them, compared with 28 percent of middle-level managers and 41 percent of lower-level employees. Although these numbers are generally consistent with those for the business employees I interviewed at the same time, they speak to the frustrations many lower-level employees feel every day as they try to send messages up the hierarchy and seek guidance that flows downward.

They also underscore problems in virtually every federal failure of the past twenty-five years, from the complacency that led to the Challenger and Columbia tragedies to the aborted leads that might have alerted the Federal Bureau of Investigation and the rest of government to the 9/11 attacks. In each case, lower-level employees tried to send information upward, only to be rebuffed at the middle or higher levels, giving secretaries and administrators ample cover to profess a lack of knowledge about the problems below.

In theory, the thickening of government is the natural consequence of its ever-expanding missions. Medicare required an entirely new agency (the Health Care Financing Administration, now Centers for Medicare and Medicaid Services), as did space exploration (the National Aeronautics and Space Administration), expansion of the nation's highway system (the Department of Transportation), the attempt to secure energy independence (the Department of Energy), and even helping veterans readjust to civilian life (a new Department of Veterans Affairs built by elevating the old Veterans Administration to cabinet status).

In theory, too, the ever-expanding mission of government has some impact on the growing number of presidential appointees who either require Senate confirmation or serve at the pleasure of the president. Congress and presidents have long believed that presidential leadership is essential to program and agency performance, and readily commit new resources to what is often described as a relatively tiny percentage of the total federal workforce.

In reality, the thickening of government involves far more than the political layers of government. It also appears in the civil service executive corps, which often bulks up in response to the political layering. As Forrest MacDonald writes of Hamilton's management style:

> Hamilton was at pains to ensure that collectors, loan officers and other supervisory personnel were fully instructed in their duties. . . . He was well aware that not every contingency could be provided for, but he tried to lay down policy guidelines to govern subordinates in the exercise of discretionary authority, and when they reported successful innovations in the handling of unanticipated problems, he often used such reports as the basis for supplementary circulars of instruction.[11]

More than two hundred years later, even agencies with relatively few presidential appointees—such as the Bureau of Prisons, the Census Bureau, and the National Aeronautics and Space Administration—bear the imprint of Hamilton's philosophy of control, albeit through civil service employees, not presidential appointees. Like stalactites, the presidential appointees drip downward onto and into the senior layers of government, but, like stalagmites, the career executives build upward. If there is one word that describes the mechanism of modern thickening, it is copying. Once established somewhere in government, titles spread like kudzu as departments and agencies copy each other at will.

Measuring the Hierarchy

The best method for assessing the height and width of the federal hierarchy is to "let your fingers do the walking," as the old Yellow Pages slogan goes. Simply start at the top of the organizational phonebook and ask who reports to whom all the way to the bottom. My analysis assumes that special assistants are not in the chain of command, but I include any variation of secretary, deputy secretary, undersecretary, assistant secretary, or administrator in my list. Although this approach no doubt overstates the height of the hierarchy, it provides a benchmark against which to compare the accretion of layers over time.

The first problem in tracking the reporting chains is that the federal government employs more than 1.8 million civil servants, 850,000 postal workers, and nearly 1.5 million military personnel, meaning that department and agency phone books are nearly impossible to collect.

The second problem is that many federal jobs carry somewhat different titles across government. Bureau chiefs in one agency are sometimes called unit heads in another and section leaders in still another, meaning that it is often difficult to know whether a given employee is a supervisor or nonsupervisor, a team leader or frontline employee.

Fortunately, the *Federal Yellow Book* contains the titles, names, addresses, and phone numbers of all executives located in Washington, D.C., including presidential appointees and civil servants. Published by Leadership Directories, Inc., the *Federal Yellow Book* is considered the most reliable source of information on the 44,000 employees who occupy the executive hierarchy.

Because of resource constraints, the following analysis is limited to the very top of the hierarchy and the fifteen departments of government, counting the executive titles therein at four-year intervals dating back to the winter of 1960. It is also limited to executives in the top five compartments of the executive hierarchy: secretaries at Level I of the presidential appointee pay scale, deputy secretaries at Level II, undersecretaries at Level III, assistant secretaries at Level IV, and administrators at Level V. Thus, the analysis focuses on Senate-confirmed appointees and their associated "title-riders."

Continued Expansion

The executive hierarchy has never had more layers or more occupants per layer than it does today. Despite George W. Bush's promise to bring businesslike thinking to the federal government, his administration has overseen, or at the very least permitted, a significant expansion in both the height and width of the federal hierarchy well beyond best practices anywhere else, most notably in the business sector. According to my most recent analysis, which covers the past twenty years in six-year increments, the thickening of government has been punctuated by occasional efforts to slow it, with respect to either the height or width of the executive hierarchy.

The thickening has produced a long list of titles now open for occupancy, all variations of one of the five titles listed above and subject to Senate confirmation.[12] As Table 2.1 shows, the list now includes almost every variation of these five titles imaginable, but is likely only to grow as executives invent new ways of combining key words such as "principal," "deputy," "associate," "assistant," and "chief." Of the sixty-four titles open for occupancy in 2004, twenty-one existed in at least half the federal departments, which is a number that hints at a hierarchy well beyond the six layers often recommended for business firms.

The number of occupants per title has also multiplied. Presidents have never had more leaders to supervise. Part of the recent growth is due to creation of the new Department of Homeland Security, which grew from just 3 layers and 3 occupants when it first started paying employees in the winter of 2003 (secretary, deputy secretary, and undersecretary) to 21 layers and 146 occupants a year later.

Table 2.1 Titles open for occupancy at the top of government, 2004

Secretary[a]
Chief of staff to the secretary[a]
Deputy chief of staff to the secretary[a]
Deputy secretary[a]
Chief of staff to the deputy secretary
Deputy chief of staff
Deputy deputy secretary
Principal associate deputy secretary
Associate deputy secretary
Deputy associate deputy secretary
Assistant deputy secretary
Undersecretary[a]
Chief of staff to the undersecretary[a]
Principal deputy undersecretary
Deputy undersecretary[a]
Chief of staff to the deputy undersecretary
Principal associate deputy undersecretary
Associate deputy undersecretary
Principal assistant deputy undersecretary
Assistant deputy undersecretary
Associate undersecretary
Assistant undersecretary
Assistant secretary[a]
Chief of staff to the assistant secretary[a]
Deputy chief of staff to the assistant secretary
Principal deputy assistant secretary[a]
Associate principal deputy assistant secretary

Table 2.1 (continued)

Deputy assistant secretary[a]
Chief of staff to the deputy assistant secretary
Principal deputy deputy assistant secretary
Deputy deputy assistant secretary
Associate deputy assistant secretary[a]
Chief of staff to the associate deputy assistant secretary
Deputy associate assistant secretary
Assistant deputy assistant secretary
Principal associate assistant secretary
Associate assistant secretary[a]
Chief of staff to the associate assistant secretary
Deputy associate assistant secretary
Principal assistant assistant secretary
Assistant assistant secretary[a]
Chief of staff to the assistant assistant secretary
Deputy assistant assistant secretary[a]
Administrator[a]
Chief of staff to the administrator[a]
Deputy chief of staff to the administrator
Assistant chief of staff to the administrator
Principal deputy administrator
Deputy administrator[a]
Chief of staff to the deputy administrator
Associate deputy administrator
Deputy associate deputy administrator
Assistant deputy administrator
Deputy assistant deputy administrator
Senior associate administrator
Associate administrator[a]
Chief of staff to the associate administrator
Deputy executive associate administrator
Deputy associate administrator
Assistant administrator[a]
Chief of staff to the assistant administrator
Deputy assistant administrator[a]
Associate assistant administrator
Associate deputy assistant administrator

Note: The list includes all positions defined in statute as Executive Level I–V, and includes positions that are not necessarily called secretary, deputy secretary, undersecretary, assistant secretary, and administrator titles respectively. The assistant secretary list includes a long list of Executive Level IV titles, for example, including inspector general, chief financial officer, general counsel, assistant commandant, and so forth. Hence, some titles such as assistant assistant secretary sound odd, but actually refer to positions such as assistant inspector general, assistant general counsel, and so forth.

a. Title exists in at least seven departments out of fifteen.

But the thickening has occurred in almost every department, including many that are not involved in homeland security or the war on terrorism. Moreover, the increase would have been greater but for the significant thinning of the management ranks at the departments of Defense and Treasury.

As Table 2.2 shows, there are two headlines from my 2004 update on the thickening of the government, which attributes the vast majority of the 1998–2004 growth to George W. Bush. First, the federal hierarchy grew taller; second, it grew wider.

Height. The executive hierarchy clearly grew taller between 1960 and 2004. There were seventeen different executive titles open for occupancy across the departments in 1960, thirty-three in 1992, fifty-one in 1998, and sixty-four in 2004. Although the Bush administration slowed the rate of increase, new layers were still being created at the rate of two per year. Roughly half of the executive layers involve career appointments, while appointees in the other half either require Senate confirmation or serve at the pleasure of the president.

Among the soon-to-be-classic titles are deputy chief of staff to the secretary, principal associate deputy secretary, chief of staff to the deputy secretary, assistant deputy undersecretary, chief of staff and deputy chief of staff to the assistant secretary, principal associate assistant secretary, chief of staff to the assistant assistant secretary, and associate deputy assistant administrator. If the past is prologue, many of these new titles will soon exist across government.

The Defense Department began as the tallest hierarchy in 1960 and remained the tallest in 2004. The department had thirty senior layers in 2004, followed by Transportation at twenty-five, Agriculture, Interior, and Treasury at twenty-four, and Commerce at twenty-two. The State Department had the flattest hierarchy, at just ten layers (in part because it has no administrator-level positions), followed by Housing and Urban Development at fifteen (again in part because it has no administrator-level positions), Veterans Affairs at eighteen, and Education at nineteen.

The Defense Department remained at the top in part because of its long history as an early—often the first—adopter of new layers. For example, in the 1950s it was the first department to create a deputy assistant secretary. This position spread quickly across government, as assistant secretaries soon came to believe they could not do their jobs without more help from below. The title existed in seven departments in the 1960s, but in all twelve by 1968.

Table 2.2 The thickening of government, 1960–2004

Title	Number of departments in which title exists				Number of occupants with each title			
	1960	1992	1998	2004	1960	1992	1998	2004
Secretary	10	14	14	15	10	14	14	15
Chief of staff to the secretary	—	11	13	14	—	11	13	14
Deputy chief of staff to the secretary	—	2	9	13	—	2	10	13
Deputy secretary	3	14	14	15	6	20	23	24
Chief of staff to the deputy secretary	—	2	5	4	—	2	6	4
Deputy chief of staff	—	—	—	1	—	—	—	1
Deputy deputy secretary	—	—	3	3	—	—	5	5
Principal associate deputy secretary	1	—	1	1	2	—	1	1
Associate deputy secretary	—	6	6	6	—	13	12	15
Deputy associate deputy secretary	—	—	1	1	—	—	1	1
Assistant deputy secretary	—	—	3	2	—	—	5	6
Undersecretary	8	9	10	15	15	32	41	53
Chief of staff to the undersecretary	—	—	4	7	—	—	4	13
Principal deputy undersecretary	1	2	2	6	1	8	13	17
Deputy undersecretary	4	11	8	10	9	52	53	79
Chief of staff to the deputy undersecretary	—	—	—	1	—	—	—	1
Principal associate deputy undersecretary	—	1	—	1	—	1	—	1
Associate deputy undersecretary	—	6	—	3	—	11	—	8
Principal assistant deputy undersecretary	—	—	1	1	—	—	5	6
Assistant deputy undersecretary	—	1	1	1	—	11	16	7
Associate undersecretary	—	1	1	3	—	1	1	12
Assistant undersecretary	—	—	1	1	—	—	4	1

Assistant secretary	10	14	14	15	87	225	212	256
Chief of staff to the assistant secretary	—	4	8	10	—	5	21	36
Deputy chief of staff	1	—	—	4	—	—	—	4
Principal deputy assistant secretary	—	8	7	8	1	76	64	74
Associate principal deputy assistant secretary	7	—	1	2	—	—	1	—
Deputy assistant secretary	—	14	14	15	78	518	484	535
Chief of staff to the deputy assistant secretary	—	—	—	2	—	—	—	3
Principal deputy deputy assistant secretary	—	—	1	—	—	—	5	—
Deputy deputy assistant secretary	5	—	1	1	—	—	1	5
Associate deputy assistant secretary	—	4	6	7	20	50	42	24
Chief of staff to the associate deputy assistant secretary	—	—	—	3	—	—	—	6
Deputy associate assistant secretary	—	—	—	1	—	—	—	1
Assistant deputy assistant secretary	—	3	2	3	—	26	16	6
Principal associate assistant secretary	—	—	2	2	—	—	6	3
Associate assistant secretary	1	14	12	12	4	208	148	167
Chief of staff to the associate assistant secretary	—	—	1	1	—	—	2	1
Deputy associate assistant secretary	—	—	11	9	—	121	—	56
Principal assistant assistant secretary	—	—	8	2	—	—	66	4
Assistant assistant secretary	3	14	14	15	16	177	220	269
Chief of staff to the assistant assistant secretary	—	—	1	—	—	—	1	—
Deputy assistant assistant secretary	—	11	13	14	—	57	82	100
Administrator	9	11	9	10	90	128	139	120
Chief of staff to the administrator	—	2	5	7	—	7	12	14
Deputy chief of staff to the administrator	—	—	—	2	—	—	—	2
Assistant chief of staff to the administrator	—	—	1	—	—	—	1	—
Principal deputy administrator	—	3	2	3	—	9	4	4
Deputy administrator	8	10	9	10	52	190	192	187
Chief of staff to the deputy administrator	—	—	2	1	—	15	30	1

Table 2.2 (continued)

Title	Number of departments in which title exists				Number of occupants with each title			
	1960	1992	1998	2004	1960	1992	1998	2004
Associate deputy administrator	—	1	1	2	—	—	1	43
Deputy associate deputy administrator	—	—	3	—	—	48	42	29
Assistant deputy administrator	1	4	1	3	2	—	1	1
Deputy assistant deputy administrator	—	—	1	—	—	—	1	—
Senior associate administrator	—	9	—	1	—	—	—	1
Associate administrator	2	—	9	9	3	105	138	136
Chief of staff to the associate administrator	—	—	1	1	—	—	1	3
Deputy executive associate administrator	—	—	—	1	—	—	—	1
Deputy associate administrator	7	6	4	6	55	28	24	27
Assistant administrator	—	8	8	9	—	159	146	114
Chief of staff to the assistant administrator	—	—	1	—	—	—	1	—
Deputy assistant administrator	—	8	5	7	—	66	54	60
Associate assistant administrator	—	1	—	1	—	12	—	1
Associate deputy assistant administrator	—	—	—	1	—	—	—	1

	Number of titles open for occupancy				Number of positions open for occupancy			
	1960	1992	1998	2004	1960	1992	1998	2004
Total	17	33	51	64	451	2,409	2,385*	2,592*
Absolute increase	—	16	18	13	—	1,958	−24	207
Increase per year	—	0.5	3.0	2.2	—	62	−4	35

* The 1998 and 2004 totals do not include the Social Security Admininstration, which became an independent agency in 1995.

Nevertheless, all but one department added new layers between 1998 and 2004. Veterans Affairs topped the list with six additional titles, followed by Defense, Education, Energy, and Justice with four, and Labor with three. Treasury was the only department to flatten its hierarchy, dropping three executive titles during the period—chief of staff to an assistant secretary, associate deputy assistant secretary, and chief of staff to the assistant assistant secretary.

Like Treasury, Defense also eliminated three executive titles during the period—assistant undersecretary, assistant chief of staff to the administrator, and chief of staff to the associate administrator. However, it also created seven new titles between 1998 and 2004, including its first-ever chief of staff to an undersecretary, chief of staff to an assistant secretary, deputy chief of staff to an assistant secretary, deputy chief of staff to a deputy assistant secretary, and deputy chief of staff to an administrator. The net gain was four.

The fastest-spreading titles in the hierarchy involve chiefs of staffs of one kind or another. Occupied by alter-ego deputies who often stand in for Senate-confirmed appointees, chiefs of staff represent the latest innovation in layering. First created at the Department of Health and Human Services in 1981, the title has been spreading laterally and horizontally ever since. The first deputy chief of staff to a secretary appeared in the hierarchy in 1987, followed by the first chiefs of staff to deputy secretaries, administrators, and assistant secretaries in the early 1990s.

These titles are widely viewed as a sign of executive status in the federal hierarchy. Bluntly put, you are nobody in Washington, D.C., if you do not have a chief of staff. Not only do chiefs of staff act as gatekeepers to their principals, they often exercise the duties of formal officers. And their numbers will continue to multiply in the future as principals look for ways to show their importance in the federal pecking order.

Chiefs of staff are not mere placeholders for their principals, however. Their job descriptions usually include de facto supervisory responsibilities within their units, and they often act as gatekeepers for their principals. Although many of these titles exist in only one or two departments, past experience suggests that they will spread quickly—the first chief of staff to a secretary was created in 1981, spread to ten additional departments by 1992, and now exists in fourteen of fifteen.

Width. The executive hierarchy also grew wider between 1960 and 2004, as presidential appointees and civil servants filled in the new titles. The total number of senior executives, both political and civil service, increased from 451 in 1960 to 2,409 in 1992, and 2,592 in 2004. Although the Clinton administration added more layers to the hierarchy during its eight years in office, the George W. Bush administration added much more girth during its first four years in office. Whereas the number of senior title holders fell by 1 percent between 1992 and 1998, almost entirely because the Social Security Administration became an independent agency and was not counted in the 1998 inventory, the number increased by 9 percent between 1998 and 2004.

Indeed, only five of the federal government's fifteen departments lost width between 1998 and 2004. Treasury trimmed 30 percent of its senior leadership positions during the period, largely due to the Homeland Security reorganization that stripped it of the Customs Service and Secret Service. Defense also trimmed 21 percent of its senior leadership, largely due to a deliberate streamlining designed to improve coordination in the new war on terrorism.

However, except for much smaller declines at Commerce, which trimmed less than 1 percent of its senior leadership, Health and Human Services, which trimmed 4 percent, and Energy, which trimmed 7 percent, the rest of the hierarchy widened. Indeed, when Defense and Treasury executives are removed from the inventory, the federal hierarchy widened 20 percent between 1998 and 2004, rising from 1,785 senior positions to 2,140.

Contrary to conventional wisdom, the war on terrorism was not the primary cause of these increases. Only two of the nine departments that widened had an explicit role in either homeland security or the war on terrorism: Justice, which widened by 13 percent, and State, which widened by 14 percent. The other nine did not have an explicit role in the new endeavor. They widened because of the implementation of new statutes such as the No Child Left Behind Act at Education, the top-heavy focus of highly politicized departments such as Interior, or the steady expansion of existing layers. What began wide mostly grew wider.

Nor does a larger workforce necessarily produce a higher, wider organization, as a quick comparison of Defense and Veterans Affairs suggests. As the two largest departments in government, Defense and Veterans Affairs have very different hierarchies—Defense has the tallest hierarchy in government and the third largest girth, while Veterans Affairs has the third flattest hierarchy and the thinnest width. Weighing in at 200,000 employees, Homeland Security has taken a middle course, coming in much thinner than Defense and its almost 700,000 employees, but thicker than Veterans Affairs and its 250,000 employees.

The Consequence of Thickening

The thickening of government has a host of mostly unsavory consequences for an energetic federal service. It clearly dilutes accountability, but also increases the distance between the top and bottom of government, and shrouds the federal hierarchy in a dense thicket of reporting relationships. It distorts information, weakens the unity of command that presidents seek, and creates enormous frustration in guiding the federal bureaucracy.

These barriers to decision become much more tangible when one looks at particularly visible frontline jobs such as revenue agent, air traffic controller, park ranger, veterans' hospital nurse, and customs inspector, all jobs that matter greatly to the public. According to my last count of the layers between thirteen of the most important service jobs in the federal government, frontline employees face a daunting task sending and receiving information.[13]

On average, these employees reported upward through nine layers of management occupied by formally designated officers (secretaries, deputy secretaries, undersecretaries, and so forth) and sixteen layers occupied by informally designated officers (chiefs of staff, principal assistant secretaries, associate undersecretaries, and so forth) in 1996 when I completed the first round of the count. And on policy and budget questions, which flow downward through a Christmas tree of layers at each level of the hierarchy, the average federal employee received guidance through nearly sixty layers of decision makers. Decisions flow down each branch of the hierarchy, back up, then down the next branch, and so forth through the organization chart.

The nature of each job helps explain the height of its hierarchy. At least in 1996, jobs that involved more hazard (air traffic controller, revenue agent, veterans' hospital nurse, and immigration) or that have been implicated in scandal (public housing specialist) were actually further from the top than those that involve less risk (forest ranger, park ranger, international trade representative). The greater distance clearly insulated top managers from the real world far below, but was generally viewed as essential for tight oversight for those who believe that more leaders equals more leadership. Lower-level staff may know more about how a given policy works or where scarce resources should go, but must pass that information through so many hands that the knowledge never reaches the senior leadership.

This "smudging" is particularly troublesome for the faithful execution of the laws. By the time an idea reaches the bottom of government, it has been translated, reworked, reinterpreted, and formalized to the point of irrelevance and confusion. This interference is almost unavoidable if leaders are to show their worth, but creates a compliance mentality in which frontline employees have little room to innovate. Moreover, long chains of command may create needless checklisting.

Managed to Perfection

The federal hierarchy rises almost inexorably, in part because even the strongest opponent of centralization faces a panoply of laws and habits that encourage thickening. Even Jefferson saw some benefit to the specialization that often produces a denser chain of command. Recall that he wrote in 1816 that "it is by division and subdivision of duties alone that all matters, great and small, can be managed to perfection."[14]

But Jefferson had a greater commitment to simplicity. He wanted the accounts of government to be as simple as a farmer's, and just as easy to understand. Writing to a French journalist in 1803, he said, "We are endeavoring too to reduce the government to the practice of a rigorous economy, to avoid burdening the people, and arming the magistrate with a patronage of money, which might be used to corrupt and undermine the agenda of our government." Convinced that Hamilton and the Federalists had created a bloated bureaucracy, Jefferson promised that the growth solicited "the employment of the pruning-knife."[15]

Jefferson had reason to make the claim. In its first two years alone, Hamilton's Treasury Department had grown from zero to five bureaus and more than eighty employees. "By the standards of the day, this represented a prodigious bureaucracy," Ron Chernow writes in his biography of Hamilton. "For its critics, it was a monster in the making, inciting fears that the department would become the Treasury secretary's personal spy force and military machine."[16]

Equally important, Jefferson believed much more in harmony in the executive than in Hamilton's execution in detail and the chains of command that enforced it. Although he also believed in unity of policy, and remembered the debilitating effects of his own disagreements with Hamilton as a member of Washington's cabinet, he refused to meddle in departmental affairs.

Moreover, where there were disagreements between the chief officers of government, they were to be resolved through mutual agreement, not by isolated conversations with the executive or independent execution. Broad principles, not circulars, would govern administrative conduct. "No man who has conducted himself according to his duties would have anything to fear from me," Jefferson wrote in 1801, "as those who have done ill would have nothing to hope, be their political principles what they might."[17]

By leaving most administrative details to the discretion of his subordinates, Jefferson avoided what he saw as the corruption of centralization and hierarchy: "What an augmentation of the field for jobbing, speculating, plundering, office-building and office-hunting would be produced by an assumption of all the State powers into the hands of the General Government!"[18] The multiplication of offices and officeholders merely created new opportunities for avarice to work its will.

Instead, Jefferson looked to informal communication among his trusted allies to resolve key issues, often calling his cabinet together to reach consensus on an issue that Hamilton would have decided himself. As he wrote his secretary of the treasury, Albert Gallatin, late in the term:

> Something now occurs almost every day on which it is desirable to have the opinions of the Heads of departments, yet to have a formal meeting every day would consume so much of their time as to seriously obstruct their regular business. I have proposed to them, as most convenient for them and wasting less of their time, to call on me at any moment of the day which suits their separate convenience, when, besides any other business they may have to do, I can learn their opinions separately on any matter which has occurred, also communicate the information received daily.[19]

It is little wonder that he would write years later that centralization destroyed liberty itself, especially as it created the demand for more functionaries: "What has destroyed liberty and the rights of man in every government which has ever existed under the sun? The generalizing and concentrating all cares and powers into one body, no matter whether of the autocrats of Russia or France, or of the aristocrats of a Venetian Senate." If the Almighty has decreed that humans shall be free, Jefferson continued, concentrated power in one person and the "higher and higher orders of functionaries" was a path to confusion.[20]

Yet, even as he built his own chain of command to coordinate the day-to-day operations of government, Jefferson understood that new missions such as dividing the Louisiana Purchase would create new hierarchy—in this case, in the form of a General Land Office. It is a pattern that continues to this day. Virtually all of the federal government's fifty greatest missions involved new hierarchy, whether to explore space, reduce disease, improve air and water quality, expand voting rights, or build the interstate highway system.

Virtually all of these new hierarchies were relatively flat when they were created, but quickly expanded to match the rest of the federal organization chart. Thus, the Department of Homeland Security was originally formed around a secretary, deputy secretary, two undersecretaries, and ten assistant secretaries, but soon expanded to five undersecretaries and more than thirty assistant secretaries, not to mention a chief of staff to the secretary.

Even the decision to split an existing department such as the old Department of Health, Education, and Welfare (HEW) can produce a hierarchy greater than the sum of its former parts. According to the *Yellow Books* from the period, the old HEW had a grand total of 64 executive titles, while the new departments of Health and Human Services and Education had a total of 149 as bureaus moved up to the assistant-secretary level, and assistant secretaries moved up to undersecretaries and deputy undersecretaries. The same expansion occurred at the Veterans Administration as it moved up to cabinet status and to the Department of Homeland Security as it underwent two reorganizations in its first three years.

The same phenomenon occurs in the creation of new positions such as the chief financial officers who oversee the budgets of their departments and agencies, and the federal inspectors general who are responsible for monitoring fraud, waste, and abuse. Both were created for perfectly rational reasons, but have added layer upon layer of title riders as they have bulked up to oversee their overlayered subjects. Government's lawyers have followed a similar path, albeit driven by a need to protect their organizations from constant litigation. More is almost always seen as better, even when it comes at a very high cost in lost accountability, increased paperwork, and the failure to communicate effectively during moments of crisis.

The Science of Thickening

The basic argument for government thickening was best articulated in the 1930s with the celebrated *Papers on the Science of Administration* by Luther Gulick, a leading public administration scholar at the time. Arguing that human beings could only handle so many subordinates at any given time, Gulick and his colleagues convinced government that a 1:6 "span of control" between supervisors and subordinates was ideal for effective management. As Gulick's colleague, V. A. Graicunas, wrote at the time, "In the vast majority of cases the 'span of attention' is limited to six digits. The same holds good of other intellectual activities."[21] Thus did the "science" of intellectual capacity create the traditional 1:6 span of control that still governs contemporary thinking about how the federal hierarchy should look.

Gulick and his colleagues were hardly the only advocates of a narrow span of control, however. The concept of tight centralization was a centerpiece of Franklin D. Roosevelt's effort to discipline the federal bureaucracy through the blue-ribbon commission chaired by Louis Brownlow.

The commission did not mince words about the president's problem, opening its final report with a simple sentence, "The President needs help."[22] It then continued with a broad indictment of federal performance. The president was not in charge of the federal hierarchy, the personnel system was straining under often contradictory rules enforced by an independent Civil Service Commission, the financial system was failing, and there was little planning for the future. "We know that bad management may spoil good purposes," the Brownlow Committee argued, "and that without good management democracy itself cannot achieve its highest goals."[23]

The committee made a long list of recommendations for strengthening presidential control, most notably the creation of an Executive Office of the Presidency to oversee hundreds of new agencies. Although it was guided by a fundamental commitment to centralization and to the hierarchy that followed, the committee warned the president that too much control might reduce oversight: "Too close a view of the machinery must not cut off from sight the true purpose of efficient management. Economy is not the only objective, though reorganization is the first step to savings; the elimination of duplication and contradictory policies is not the only objective, though this will follow; a simple and symmetrical organization is not the only objective, though the new organization will be simple and symmetrical."[24]

Simple and symmetrical has come to mean tall and wide, however, an interpretation that has come to violate the tight oversight that the Brownlow Committee recommended. Driven by the search for centralization, Congress and presidents added layer upon layer to the executive hierarchy, always meeting the rough 1:6 span of control as the mark of good administration.

Thickening does not just involve the de facto 1:6 preference, however. It also comes from a number of habits that lead organizations to copy bureaucratic structures. New departments are often a catalyst for new layers, for example, if only because Congress and presidents have the opportunity to add innovations in titling to the organic legislation. Thus, even though the new Department of Veterans Affairs was built entirely from the old Veterans Administration, it added a chief financial officer and two high-level appointees for the renamed Veterans Health and Benefits administrations.

Similarly, the inner cabinet of prestige agencies is often the spark for thickening, accounting for the majority of first, second, and third adoptions of new layers. The so-called inner-cabinet departments of Defense, Health and Human Services, Justice, State, and Treasury do not innovate in the same areas, however. Justice has been more active creating layers at the very top of the department, for example, in part because of the accretion of new responsibilities over the decades, while Defense has been more active at the assistant secretary level, in part because it has tried to centralize control of the armed services at the top.

The Iron Law of Emulation

Much of the subsequent layering reflects what sociologists call "isomorphism," which refers to the tendency of organizations to follow what the late Senator Daniel Patrick Moynihan called the "iron law of emulation."[25] Paul J. DiMaggio and Walter W. Powell put it in somewhat more scholarly terms: "Organizations are still becoming more homogeneous, and bureaucracy remains the common organizational form . . . Today, however, structural change in organizations seems less and less driven by competition or by the need for efficiency. Instead, we contend, bureaucratization and other forms of efficiency change occur as the result of processes that make organizations more similar without necessarily making them more efficient."[26]

This emulation reflects a blend of *coercion,* in which organizations are forced to accept new positions such as chief financial officer and chief human capital officer, *mimicking,* in which organizations copy the latest fads in titles such as chief of staff, *norms,* in which organizations follow what they believe are the structural outlines of the "good organization," and, at least for government, *evasion,* in which agencies use titles and the promotions that go with them to compensate for pay freezes or recruit talented employees at lower salaries than they might otherwise earn.

This isomorphism does not have to create thickening, however. In theory, for example, isomorphism could just as easily lead to flatter organizations, decentralization, and networks instead of continued thickening, which is exactly what Peter Frumkin and Joseph Galaskiewicz found in a relatively large sample of government, private, and nonprofit organizations.[27]

According to their research, there is at least some evidence that coercion and norms can make government organizations behave less like traditional bureaucracies and more like for-profits and nonprofits: "Our results suggest that public sector managers respond to external oversight and professional norms by finding ways to capitalize on the presence of these external pressures to move their organizations away from hierarchy and formalization and toward the mean of all organizations regardless of sector."[28]

In reality, flat organizations, decentralization, and networks are far from becoming the prevailing model of a good organization in the federal government, despite their advance in the private and nonprofit sectors. Thickening continues to be one measure of "good government"— more leaders still equal more leadership.

Moreover, individual public managers may have little leeway to change the substantial incentives toward thickening, which are particularly powerful in organizations that: (1) are dependent on a small number of sources of political or fiscal support, (2) have little incentive to change direction toward an alternative structure, (3) operate under high levels of uncertainty, (4) face significant pressure to measure their professionalism through titles, and (5) operate in a constrained environment with widely accepted norms of bureaucratic behavior.

As if to prove that thickening remains the prevailing wisdom, cabinet-level departments are not the only government organizations that have thickened over the decades. The Office of Management and Budget, Congressional Research Service, Government Accountability Office, and congressional committees and leadership offices have all thickened as well. Although some of this thickening may be part of an effort to control the ever-growing federal hierarchy, it sends the signal that bureaucratization is the safest course given the survival of the fittest.[29]

Although it is not always clear which comes first, the thickening of oversight agencies or the thickening of departments and agencies they oversee, the result is the same: The height and width of the federal hierarchy continue to grow at all levels, often defying the best practices long established in businesses and nonprofit agencies and eagerly embraced by other institutions such as universities and news bureaus. The federal government's hierarchy also reflects the steady aging of the baby boomers, which has put increased pressure on the organization chart to provide the promotions and prestige the generation seeks.

This conclusion stands in direct contrast to that of scholars who argue that agencies vary in their organizational structures due to deliberative choices by Congress and the president. There is no doubt that the two branches do make decisions on whether a given agency should be more or less insulated from the president, with Congress favoring more insulation and presidents favoring less.[30]

Yet, as Terry M. Moe argues, advocates and adversaries of a given policy often favor the same bureaucratic structures regardless. In their effort to protect their victory against future defeat, advocates favor structures that "place formal restrictions on bureaucratic discretion; impose complex procedures for agency decision making, minimize opportunities for oversight, and otherwise insulate the agency from politics." And in their effort to defend their current assets, adversaries favor structures that simultaneously undermine the bureaucracy through fragmented authority and labyrinthine procedures.[31]

In other words, all paths lead to bureaucracy. Indeed, as David E. Lewis argues, this kind of "hardwiring," frustrating though it may be to responsiveness and efficiency, not only increases the lifespan of federal agencies, it protects them from Hamilton's unity of command. It is little wonder, therefore, that presidents might come to believe that more layers of leaders at the top of government might increase their command and control.[32]

Thinning Government

The thickening of government has not gone unnoticed, at least by presidents. But it is thickening at the middle and bottom that has drawn their attention. Hard as they might try to reduce the layering at the middle and bottom, they are often frustrated in the effort, in no small part because of the hardwiring written into law and multiplied by isomorphism.

Nevertheless, every president since Carter has argued that the federal government is too thick, especially at the middle, and several have actually launched initiatives to thin the organization chart. At the urging of the president's Private Sector Survey on Cost Control, which was chaired by J. Peter Grace, the Reagan administration even launched the "Bulge Project" to reduce the thickening of government.[33] Using spans of control as its measure of duplication and waste, the project was designed to eliminate 40,000 middle-level supervisory positions, but had virtually no impact on the actual number in spite of the president's harsh rhetoric about the need to attack fraud, waste, and abuse.

The Clinton administration fared much better in a similar effort led by Vice President Al Gore. Modeled on the Bulge Project, Clinton's reinventing government campaign proposed a rough doubling of the federal government's average span of control. Promising to prune "layer upon layer of managerial overgrowth," the effort involved intense oversight of agency budgets and an explicit effort to move employees either into nonsupervisory positions at the same pay rate or out of government through early retirement incentives such as buyouts.

Led by Vice President Al Gore, the campaign appeared to achieve impressive results. However, many former supervisors carried their supervisory responsibilities into their new nonsupervisory jobs. The Social Security Administration cut nearly 2,800 supervisory positions between 1993 and 1998, for example, but created 1,900 new de facto supervisory titles, including 500 team leaders and nearly 1,400 management support specialists. Although some supervisory titles disappeared from the hierarchy, the amount of layering remained substantial. And a supervisor by any other name can stall the same.

Although the Clinton administration deserves credit for restraining the growth of the senior hierarchy and reducing middle management, it did little to reverse the long-term change in the overall shape of the hierarchy. Implementation of its pledge to reduce overall federal employment by more than 250,000 jobs fell most heavily on the lower levels of government, which dropped by 27 percent during the administration, rather than on the middle levels, which dropped just 7 percent. As a result, the middle levels of government grew relative to the lower levels, accelerating the change in the shape of government from a pyramid to a pentagon.

Part of this shift involved the basic nature of government work as the federal government hired more scientists and engineers, especially in information technology. Part of the shift involved the introduction of new time-saving technologies, which produced greater productivity and less need for lower-level clerical personnel. And part of the shift involved more contracting out of frontline jobs.

Conclusion

Thinning government clearly draws upon Jefferson's philosophy of decentralization and contemporary romanticism for its inspiration. But Jefferson's warnings have not been enough to slow the steady thickening of the federal hierarchy over the past fifty years. As a result, information now passes through layer upon layer before it reaches the *top* of the hierarchy, if it reaches the top at all, while guidance and oversight pass through layer upon layer on the way to the *bottom,* if they ever reach the bottom at all.

It is little wonder that no one can be held accountable, especially in a hierarchy where presidential appointees serve for eighteen to twenty-four months on average, and information is often delivered by word of mouth through a process that has come to resemble the childhood game of gossip.

In such a dense thicket of titles, the officers of government are rarely held accountable for what goes wrong in government, whether because single vacancies anywhere in the chain of command can produce long delays in the movement of information and guidance, or because each stop in the hierarchy creates at least some delay, however brief it might be. For every program director or presidential appointee removed from office after a disaster such as the Space Shuttle Columbia explosion or Hurricane Katrina, many are left in place in the wake of taxpayer abuse, security breakdowns, and intelligence failures. Few are admonished, even fewer are asked to leave, and none of their positions are ever abolished.

At the same time, federal officials rarely get credit for what goes right in government, especially when the federal government succeeds in converting endeavors into achievements. Credit is not only diffused, it is often hidden completely. Much as private foundations and good government groups celebrate government success, the media rarely cover it, and the public rarely believes it. No one is given credit for reducing disease, protecting voting rights, improving air and water quality, and the rest of government's greatest achievements. It is almost as if government's success occurs by magic—no one had anything to do with it.

Thickening also absorbs resources that could be better used in converting missions that matter into achievements that endure. More leaders equals exactly that, more leaders. But more leaders do not necessarily create the conditions for the rest of government to succeed. Often they cost much more in salary and delay than they deliver, and they have been known to create paperwork and regulation to justify their posts. Having been promoted into higher-level positions, they work tirelessly to prove their worth, even if that means the middle- and lower-level ranks must spend needless time and energy satisfying their requests for more information.

Much as Hamilton believed that clarity of command was essential for the energetic execution of the laws, and, therefore, an element of an energetic federal service, his general theory has not passed the test of time. Indeed, there is good evidence that Hamilton's call for extensive and arduous enterprise has added layers to the hierarchy even as it has pushed the federal government toward an inventory filled with missions that matter. In satisfying his aims for an aggressive, centralized government, Hamilton laid the foundation for a hierarchy that now denies the guidance that the federal service so often needs for faithful execution. And this is where a focus on Jefferson's sentiment for simplification and decentralization might stimulate a long-overdue debate about just how much hierarchy is enough.

CHAPTER THREE

Posts of Honor

The third characteristic of an energetic federal service is a fast, simple, and fair appointments process that assures the aptitude and tendency to produce a good administration. A slow, complicated, and abusive appointments process does nothing more than exhaust the talented leadership government desperately needs.

Hamilton believed that the Constitution's checks and balances favored the choice of talented individuals for the federal government's "posts of honor." "It is not easy to conceive a plan better calculated than this to promote a judicious choice of men for filling the offices of government," he wrote in *Federalist No. 76*, "and it will not need proof that on this point must essentially depend the character of its administration."[1] When potential appointees misrepresent themselves to the White House, it is up to the president to stop or withdraw the nomination; when presidents select unqualified nominees, it is up to the Senate to reject the nomination.

Hamilton also believed that the character of an administration would be greatly enhanced if the appointment power resided in a single executive:

> The sole and undivided responsibility of one man will naturally beget a livelier sense of duty and a more exact regard to reputation. He will, on this account, feel himself under stronger obligations, and more interested to investigate with care the qualities requisite to the stations to be filled, and to prefer with impartiality the persons who may have the fairest pretensions to them. He will have *fewer* personal attachments to gratify, than

a body of men who may each be supposed to have an equal number; and will be so much the less liable to be misled by the sentiments of friendship and of affection.[2]

Jefferson also worried about the executive appointment power. As he wrote at the start of his first term in 1801, "There is nothing I am so anxious about as making the best possible appointments, and no case in which the best men are more liable to mislead us, by yielding to the solicitations of applicants."[3]

Unfortunately, the current process does not guarantee character, merit, or reputation, but rather embarrassment, delay, and exhaustion. It is tailored for the best available person, meaning someone willing to endure the process itself. Laden with needless forms, plagued by needless delays, and predisposed to treat every candidate as "innocent until nominated," it has become a confusing test of anything but qualifications for service.[4]

This chapter will explore the appointee process in more detail. It will start with a brief description of the current process, turn to the effects on both past and potential appointees, and conclude with a discussion of how the appointments process has become so cumbersome. Whether readers like the current class of appointees or not, they can all agree that the current process often undermines the merit and reputation of each administration it serves. And it has been doing so with increasing regularity over the past three decades.

A Process Ill Executed

Hamilton and Jefferson both used strong rhetoric in framing the appointee job description. As Hamilton wrote to a colleague about the appointment of a president for Columbia College, "it is essential that he be a gentleman in his manners, as well as a sound and polite scholar; that his moral character be irreproachable; that he possess energy of body and mind, and be of a disposition to maintain discipline without *undue austerity*; and, in the last place, that his politics be of the right sort."[5]

Jefferson agreed. As he wrote in 1800, it was essential to find officers "whose talents, integrity, names, and dispositions, should at once inspire unbounded confidence in the public mind, and insure a perfect harmony in the conduct of the public business."[6]

At the same time, he eventually came to share Hamilton's focus on politics of the right sort.[7] "I have never removed a man merely because he was a federalist," Jefferson wrote late in his second term. But he had removed "those who maintained an active and zealous opposition to the government."[8] Jefferson's frustrations with this opposition came to the surface early in his presidency:

> If the will of the nation, manifested by their various elections, calls for an administration of government according with the opinions of those elected; if, for the fulfillment of that will, displacements are necessary, with whom can they so justly begin as with persons appointed in the last moments of an administration, not for its own aid, but to begin a career at the same time with their successors, by whom they had never been approved and who could scarcely expect from them a cordial cooperation? . . . If a due participation of office is a matter of right, how are vacancies to be obtained? Those by death are few; by resignation, none. Can any other mode than that of removal be proposed?[9]

Yet, the more Republicans he appointed, the less Jefferson seemed to support rotation in office. What had been good for the Federalists just might turn out to be good for Republicans, too, especially if their departures by death were also few, and by resignation none.

This chapter is not designed to explore the benefits of politicization per se, though this issue will arise at several points below. Rather, it is designed to examine the current process for nominating and confirming presidential appointees, whatever their political persuasion.

The New Direction in Presidential Appointments

Whatever the emphasis in filling the federal government's posts of honor, there is no doubt that appointees play a central role in managing the chain of command, interpreting legislation, overseeing regulations, and faithfully executing the laws.[10] Although not all presidential appointees are subject to Senate confirmation, they all derive their authority from the president.

They also matter, to a greater or lesser degree, in implementing the president's agenda. Past research shows that the choice of appointees can affect everything from case processing at regional offices of the National Labor Relations Board to monetary policy at the Federal Reserve.[11]

Moreover, strategically placed agency by agency, they can counterbalance strong interest groups within what one pair of scholars calls a separation-of-powers game, and may be the most important influence for democratic control of the administrative state.[12]

Looking at seven different agencies, including the Food and Drug Administration, Environmental Protection Agency, and Nuclear Regulatory Commission, B. Dan Wood and Richard W. Waterman convincingly argue that presidential appointees not only accelerate and decelerate key decisions and activities, they exert much greater control than changing budgets, legislative action, and administrative reorganizations (though Wood and Waterman find that all these factors have some impact on everything from product seizures at the Food and Drug Administration to rule-making at the Environmental Protection Agency).[13]

Given their importance to governance, one might imagine that the nomination and confirmation process would be tailored for efficiency and effectiveness. But they are actually a vast morass that can be best described as "nasty and brutish without being short."[14] Not only is it flooded by increasing numbers of appointees, it is now governed by a highly centralized review process that provokes the very bureaucratic games it is designed to suppress.[15]

A Flood of Occupants

Current presidents make approximately 3,000 presidential appointments at the start of their administrations: 700–1,000 department and agency executives, independent regulatory commissioners, ambassadors, U.S. Attorneys, and U.S. Marshals, 600–700 members of the Senior Executive Service, and 1,400–1,800 "Schedule C" personnel and confidential assistants. One thousand of these posts require Senate confirmation, while the rest serve entirely at the will of the president.

The number of Senate-confirmed appointees has been growing for decades. Franklin D. Roosevelt started his first term with ten secretaries, three undersecretaries, and thirty-eight assistant secretaries; George W. Bush started his first term with 14 secretaries, 23 deputy secretaries, 41 undersecretaries, 212 assistant secretaries, and 484 deputy assistant secretaries.

According to James Pfiffner, the number of "at will" presidential appointees who serve entirely at the pleasure of the president has also grown.[16]

These are not big numbers compared to the civil service as a whole, however. Indeed, presidential appointees account for just 0.17 percent of the 1.8 million federal servants they oversee.

Yet, measured by the number of layers these appointees occupy, the federal service has never had more political layers or political leaders per layer. Looking down the federal hierarchy all the way to the bottom in 1996, I found presidential appointees in a very large proportion of the layers, leading to thirteen particularly visible federal frontline jobs that existed in Minnesota when I conducted this analysis.[17]

At the St. Paul Veterans Medical Center, for example, a hospital nurse reported upward through seventeen layers to Washington, starting with a nurse supervisor, then upward to a nurse supervisor, associate chief nurse, chief nurse, chief of staff to the St. Paul Medical Center director, and the medical center director, then upward again to the associate regional director, chief of staff to the regional director, regional director, and then upward again to the deputy associate chief medical director for operations, associate chief medical director for operations, deputy undersecretary for health administration and operations, deputy undersecretary for health, undersecretary for health, deputy secretary, deputy chief of staff to the secretary of Veterans Affairs, chief of staff to the secretary, and secretary.

Of these seventeen layers rising from the hospital wards, at least nine were occupied by presidential appointees, three of whom were subject to Senate confirmation and another six of whom were appointed at will by the president. Similar patterns held true for revenue agents, national park and forest rangers, customs inspectors, social security claims representatives, Federal Bureau of Investigation agents, and so on down the list of thirteen frontline jobs studied. Park rangers and international trade specialists reported upward through the largest number of presidential appointees, ten each, and the highest percentages, 77 and 55 percent respectively.

There are a number of reasons to question the need for so many appointees, especially when balanced against the vacancies they create; they come and go after serving eighteen to twenty-four months on average. However, Hugh Heclo's 1987 list of four concerns still stands as the best indictment of continued expansion:

1. Short-term rationale. "Knowing that there will be only a short time to accomplish whatever goals they may have, temporary executives have relatively little reason to worry about the longer-term effects of their actions on government."

2. Discontinuity. "Because political appointees' personal careers are tied to the fate of the administration in power or the bureaucratic machinery, their comings and goings in the executive branch are more likely to be based on calculations of personal benefit rather than the needs of government."

3. Creeping appointeeism. "The in-and-outer system feeds on itself in the sense of encouraging the reproduction of pint-sized political executives throughout government."

4. Biased recruitment: "Accepting a political appointment imposes costs and offers benefits, and the ability to accept this cost/benefit calculus is far from randomly distributed, even within the pool of white, male professionals from which most appointees are drawn."[18]

Selecting from the Center

The flooding of the process has been complicated by the steady centralization of the selection process itself over the past fifty years. Not only does centralization require White House approval of even the most trivial appointment, it also demands more intensive scrutiny to assure maximum political and ideological loyalty to the president. As a result, centralization can make expertise an afterthought in the selection process. Presidents have become convinced that loyalty must come first, a position taken by every president since Nixon, but most significantly by Ronald Reagan and George W. Bush.[19]

This centralizing influence is part of what Terry M. Moe calls the "politicized presidency," which is built in part on the notion that presidents face strong incentives to centralize the appointments process and place loyal lieutenants in control of the levers of government. Writing of this politicized presidency in 1985, Moe rightly concluded that presidents are burdened by expectations that far exceed their capacity for effective action. As such, they have every incentive, perhaps even the obligation, to "right the imbalance by reforming and elaborating the institutional presidency."[20]

One option to "right the imbalance" is to use the appointment power to gain greater control of executive departments and agencies. By appointing some officers on the basis of political and ideological loyalty, presidents could increase bureaucratic responsiveness. "In addition," Moe wrote, "by manipulating civil service rules, proposing minor reorganizations, and pressing for modifying legislation, [the president] can take steps to increase the number and location of administrative positions that can be occupied by appointees."[21]

This is not the book to summarize the ongoing battle between proponents and opponents of the politicized presidency.[22] Rather, it is more important to note the impact of centralization on the merit and reputation of an administration. Extended to its logical extreme, the centralization of the presidential appointments process places a much greater emphasis on political and ideological loyalty as a primary marker of a candidate's qualification for office. Although this marker is not used for every position, it changes the nature of the appointments process in subtle ways, advancing the candidacies of appointees such as Michael D. Brown, the wholly unqualified head of the Federal Emergency Management Agency during and after Hurricane Katrina. Equally important, this centralization produces nominees who provoke intense partisan reactions in the Senate, not to mention among interest groups. This may very well be inevitable, of course, since centralization is one way to ensure that appointees follow the president's strategic direction, especially in agencies dominated by Congress and strong interest groups.

Yet, centralization also has unintended consequences, most notably in efforts to evade it. The tighter the White House has pushed for control, the more its own officers have fought for at least some independence through the use of special assistants that they appoint with minimal White House attention.

It is no coincidence, for example, that the very first chief of staff to a cabinet secretary was created in 1981 by Health and Human Services secretary Richard Schweiker, whose choice for deputy secretary was rejected by the White House in favor of a more loyal alternative. Schweiker responded by appointing his candidate as chief of staff to the secretary, creating an entirely new layer of presidential appointees who owed their loyalty not to the president, but to their department and agency benefactors. Having discovered the ruse, the White House put most chiefs of staff under its oversight.

At least until late in George W. Bush's term, when faced with scandals about politicization in the Justice Department, White House political adviser Karl Rove had weekly conference calls with agency chiefs of staff to coordinate administrative strategies, monitor the distribution of federal largesse to vulnerable congressional districts and friendly campaign contributors, and manage knotty personnel issues such as the firings of seven U.S. Attorneys in 2006.

Centralization created a loyal cadre of presidential appointees who embraced the president's agenda with few questions asked. As if to make the point that the White House was in charge, the Bush administration ordered its second-term cabinet officers to spend at least four hours a week working out of an office suite located in the Old Executive Office Building just across the alley from the White House.[23] It was a perfectly Hamiltonian approach to assuring execution in detail, as well as enforcing loyalty to the president.

Scrutiny Squared

Flooding and centralization both add to the delays in a process already unable to accommodate more than a handful of appointees at a single time. As past presidential recruiters report, there is very little elasticity to cover the increased pressure of the process, certainly not with the war on terrorism occupying the Federal Bureau of Investigation, declining staffing at the Internal Revenue Service and Office of Government Ethics, and static staffing at the White House Personnel Office.[24]

There is a great price to pay just to enter the pipeline, however, and it exists in the sixty pages of questions each appointee must complete and the vetting process that follows. Just to make the entry cost higher, many of the questions repeat each other. Calling the process a "murky fen of executive branch and Senate forms, strategic entanglements, and 'gotcha politics,'" Terry Sullivan argues that Congress and the president have created a "Fabulous Formless Darkness" that could be easily resolved with better computer technology and a bit of institutional co-operation.[25]

The "fabulous formless darkness" emerged in 1953 when the Eisenhower administration instituted the first background checks on presidential appointees as a reaction to increased concerns about the infiltration of government by communist sympathizers. The process is still preoccupied with security threats, but has expanded to include every personal and professional offense possible, including drug and alcohol abuse, payment of nanny taxes, and the employment of illegal immigrants as housekeepers. Although many of the issues involve legitimate questions, it is designed to make the federal government what G. Calvin Mackenzie calls "scandal proof," no matter how small the scandal.[26] As if to make the process even more burdensome, three of the four forms described below have to be filled out, or "populated," by hand or electric typewriter.

The process starts with a White House "Personal Data Statement." As the cover sheet for the other executive branch forms, the data statement currently consists of twenty-three questions, many of which reflect past scandals regarding alcohol abuse, the withholding of federal and state taxes for domestic help (the so-called nanny tax), and controversial writings. The form asks many of the same questions as the national security and financial disclosure forms described below, but in different formats. It also asks for political party affiliation, campaign experience, and finally a pair of questions to elicit what the White House considers the most important information in preventing an embarrassing confirmation battle.

1. Have you ever had any association with any person, group or business venture that could be used, even unfairly, to impugn or attack your character and qualifications for a government position?

2. Do you know anyone or any organization that might take any steps, overtly or covertly, fairly or unfairly, to criticize your appointment, including any news organization?

These last two questions are impossible to answer, especially if the opposition is covert. Who can say where covert opposition will arise? But on the theory that a bad appointment hurts more than a good appointment helps, the questions must be asked, even if the potential nominee rightly concludes that the best answer is always no.

It is important to note that the appointee may already be out of the process before reaching these final questions—depending on the administration, the political affiliation and activity questions can make or break a candidacy. Reagan and George W. Bush put particularly heavy emphasis on these questions as a candidate's primary qualification (albeit not in the case of a Democrat, Norman Mineta, as secretary of the Transportation Department) while the Carter and Clinton administrations clearly paid attention to political affiliation as part of a broad mix of concerns that included gender, race, policy positions, and past management experience.

Once past this first vetting, which merely leads to the announcement of the president's intention to nominate a candidate, potential appointees have two more questionnaires to complete before their formal nomination can be carried to the Senate for confirmation:

The first is the "Questionnaire for National Security Personnel," which is vetted by the Federal Bureau of Investigation. The form dates back to the McCarthy era and has been augmented with new questions covering each passing controversy. The McCarthy era may be over in the country, but it is very much alive in the presidential appointments process.

Virtually nothing is off limits in the eleven-page form. Potential nominees must list every place they have lived over the past fifteen years and the name of a neighbor who knew them at the time; every school they attended since junior high and the name of a former classmate who knew them at the time; every employer they worked for over the past fifteen years and the names of their supervisors; the names and birthdays of spouses and ex-spouses, mother, father, sisters, and brothers (full, step, or half); every prescription drug they have taken; every psychologist, psychiatrist, social worker, or marriage counselor they have seen in therapy; every foreign country they have visited over the past fifteen years, including short trips to Canada or Mexico, and traffic fines over $150. The Federal Bureau of Investigation crosschecks the questionnaire with supervisors, neighbors, and even high-school classmates in the search for possible embarrassments.

The second form is the "Public Financial Disclosure Report" mandated under the 1978 Ethics Act and its subsequent amendments. The form comes with twelve pages of instructions, a main form, and four reporting schedules. The four schedules require nominees to report income, assets, liabilities, and financial transactions such as stock trades in multiple financial bands from "none" to "over $50,000,000." These answers are vetted by the Office of Government Ethics.

Once candidates have been formally nominated, they must fill out one last form that comes from the primary Senate authorizing committee responsible for the department or agency in which an appointee will work. Designed by each committee to fit its own concerns, this form can vary from a few questions about a committee's agenda to pages upon pages of further financial and personal questions.

By the end of this process, an appointee will have answered about 240 separate questions, including 61 on personal and family background, 32 on tax and finance, 35 on legal proceedings, 7 on public and organizational activities, and 1 on domestic help. As Sullivan found, roughly half of these questions request almost the same information, including two-thirds of the questions about tax and finance and more than three-quarters of those about public and organizational activities.[27] Repetitive or not, each question demands a careful response, especially to avoid an investigation that could create embarrassment or even indictment for making a false statement to the federal government.

The Call to Service

It is not surprising that this process would take time, especially since the Federal Bureau of Investigation and the Office of Government Ethics have limited staff for vetting each candidate. However, as the forms and number of appointees have expanded, the process has slowed.

These delays are particularly noticeable, and destructive, at the start of a new administration. John F. Kennedy needed just over two months on average to fill his initial slate of Senate-confirmed positions, compared with three and a half months for Lyndon B. Johnson, four and a half for both Richard M. Nixon and Jimmy Carter, five and a half for

Ronald Reagan, eight for George H. W. Bush, eight and a half for Bill Clinton, and more than nine months for George W. Bush.[28]

The delays come at both ends of Pennsylvania Avenue, where the White House and Senate check and countercheck each appointment to avoid embarrassment. Hence the long list of forms, the endless vetting, and the favoritism toward Washington insiders who have endured the process before. It is little wonder that the majority of appointees, Democrats and Republicans alike, lived inside the Beltway before they accepted their appointments, if only because they have the jobs and histories that permit long delays and provide deep connections to allies and adversaries alike. Who better to survive the process than someone who already has the right commute?

The question facing an energetic federal service is not whether appointees come from inside the Beltway, especially since such appointees often enter their posts with a greater understanding of Washington politics and administration. Nor is it whether the process is too slow, which undermines clarity of command. Rather, the question is whether flooding, centralization, and price of admission reduce the pool of qualified appointees. Simply asked, will talented Americans serve?

One answer comes from presidential appointees who have served in recent administrations (past appointees) and the other from civic and corporate leaders who might accept a future appointment (potential appointees). Together, the answers suggest that the federal service has ample reason to worry that the presidential appointments process may discourage the kind of talent Hamilton and Jefferson both hoped would serve.

Views from the Past

Past appointees clearly believe that the process is broken. According to my 2000 survey of a randomly selected sample of 435 appointees who served between 1985 and 2000, the process provides little information, causes ample frustration, and provokes concerns about the ability to serve.[29] They entered the process with little information concerning what was about to happen to them, received very little help from the White House along their journey, and entered their positions late.

The survey confirms the patterns:

- Only 56 percent of the past appointees said they had enough help from the White House or other official sources about what they were to face when they entered the process itself. As a result, 62 percent sought help from outside sources on the legal aspects of their appointment, while 48 percent sought help on the financial forms. Of these appointees, 90 percent said they spent at least some of their personal funds on that help, including 6 percent who spent more than $10,000.

- Asked which steps in the process took too long, 39 percent said Senate confirmation took longer than necessary, 34 percent said the same about financial disclosure, 30 percent said the same about the Federal Bureau of Investigation's vetting process, and more than a quarter said the same about White House review.

- As Table 3.1 shows, the perceived delays have increased at every stage of the process, especially when compared with a 1985 survey of 536 appointees who served between 1964 and 1984.[30] Whereas 56 percent of the recent appointees said their nomination and confirmation took five months or *more*, 82 percent of the 1964–1984 appointees said their process lasted five months or *less*.

- Asked to describe the process itself, more than 40 percent of past appointees described it as confusing, almost half described it as a necessary evil, and a quarter called it embarrassing. In addition, just 46 percent said the Senate acts reasonably and appropriately in the way it handles presidential nominees, while 30 percent said the White House is so demanding that it makes the process an ordeal.

- Asked about the White House process, only a quarter gave the White House Personnel Office an average letter grade of A for caring about whether they were personally confirmed, while just a fifth gave it an A for competence, responding quickly to their questions, and devoting enough time to their appointment. The Clinton appointees were particularly hard on the White House— 60 percent gave it an A on general competence.

- Nevertheless, 85 percent said they would recommend an appointment to a friend.

There were few differences in these responses across administrations. The process grew longer from Reagan to Clinton; the sense of unfairness and negative views of the Senate and White House also increased. But since most of these appointees moved forward under divided government between the two institutions, it is impossible to attribute the problems to Republicans or Democrats, Congress or the president.

Table 3.1 Speed of the confirmation process, 1964–2000

Question: We are interested in whether you think any aspects of your appointment could have been processed more quickly. What about (insert stage)? Did this take longer than necessary or not?		
Stage	Percentage of 1964–1985 appointees rating the step as longer than necessary	Percentage of 1985–2000 appointees rating the step as longer than necessary
President's personal approval	Not asked	10
White House review	15	27
Clearance with members of Congress	7	18
Federal Bureau of Investigation vetting	24	30
Financial disclosure forms	13	34
Conflict of interest reviews	6	17
Senate confirmation process	24	39

N=585 appointees who served from 1964 to 1985 and 450 who served from 1985 to 2000.

Divided government almost certainly affects the confirmation process, however, as the enormous conflict over appointees late in the Clinton administration confirms. It is just not apparent in my study.

It is much more apparent in Nolan McCarty and Rose Razaghian's research, which looked at more than one hundred years of presidential nominations. As they conclude, "we find confirmations take substantially longer not only in periods of divided government but also in periods in which the Senate is ideologically polarized."[31] To the extent centralization during periods of divided government reflects this polarization by appealing to one side or the other, it has the unintended consequence of longer delays and higher vacancy rates, hardly the elements of tighter White House control.

Once beyond their complaints, past appointees offered a number of simple ideas for improving the process. More than a third urged the White House to provide more information on the process;[32] another third recommended a single common form that eliminated the duplication of questions from the standard disclosure and national security forms; and a quarter urged the White House and Senate to accelerate the process so appointees could get to their jobs faster.

However, relatively few seemed to recognize that the sheer number of appointees might explain the excessive delays, lack of White House support, intense focus on potential embarrassments, and the need for outside help in navigating the legal and financial forms. Asked whether there should be fewer or more appointees in government, roughly a third said fewer, while just a fifth said more. The rest said there were just enough.

Views from the Future

These complaints do not affect the appointees who have actually served in the past, however. They also affect potential appointees in the private and public sectors, whether they are executives at Fortune 500 companies, presidents of the nation's leading universities, chief executives at the nation's largest nonprofits, scholars at large think tanks selected for ideological balance, lobbyists at the nation's largest registered firms, and state and local government officials in the nation's largest jurisdictions. According to a 2000 survey of 580 of these potential appointees, all share a lack of information about how the appointments process works as well as deep concerns about the impact of an appointment on their personal lives.[33]

On the one hand, 66 percent said the ability to make a difference would be much better or somewhat better in a presidential appointment than a position outside government, and 72 percent said it would be an honor to serve. Majorities also said a presidential appointment would help them make valuable contacts and increase their leadership opportunities, the respect of family and friends, the chance to make a difference, and their future earning power. And 83 percent said they would be favorably inclined toward an appointment.

As Table 3.2 shows, the perceived costs and benefits of appointee service sometimes varied greatly depending on a potential appointee's current career. In a "them that's got" phenomenon, Fortune 500 executives, top university presidents, and the chief executives of the nation's largest nonprofits all reported less interest in the future earning power generated by an appointment than think tank scholars, top lobbyists, and state and local government officials. Fortune 500 executives were less likely to worry about losing promotions, and joined with university presidents in minimizing the problems of a return to their previous career. Otherwise, there were few differences across the six groups of potential appointees.

On the other hand, only 15 percent of these potential appointees said they knew a great deal about the appointment process, compared with 47 percent who said they knew little or hardly anything at all; 56 percent

Table 3.2 Cost and benefits of service

Question: For each of the following statements about the impact of serving as a presidential appointee please tell me if you strongly agree, somewhat agree, somewhat disagree, or strongly disagree.

	Total percentage who agree	Percentage of *Fortune 500* executives who agree	Percentage of university presidents who agree	Percentage of nonprofit CEOs who agree	Percentage of think-tank scholars who agree	Percentage of lobbyists who agree	Percentage of state and local government officials who agree
Benefits							
Make valuable contacts	97	95	96	94	99	98	99
Future leadership possibilities	83	73	80	73	84	95	93
Earning power	61	46	41	46	72	80	79
Costs							
Lose valuable contacts	10	14	10	11	8	11	5
Lose promotions and career advancement	23	43	19	19	24	22	13
Prevent return to career	21	32	30	19	15	8	20

N = 100 Fortune 500 executives, 100 top-300 university presidents as listed by *U.S. News & World Report*, 85 nonprofit executives from the list of the largest nonprofits, 95 think-tank scholars selected by size and for ideological balance, 100 lobbyists at the largest Washington, D.C., lobbying firms, and 100 state and local government officials from the largest jurisdictions around the country.

said that living in Washington would be either much less or somewhat less desirable than staying put in their current locale; 45 percent said that relocating their spouse or partner to Washington would be very or somewhat difficult; and three quarters said their employer would not encourage them to take an appointment, even though the vast majority said they would strongly encourage their own employees to serve.

Potential appointees also had a particularly dismal view of the process itself. Only 43 percent called the process "fair," 51 percent called it "embarrassing," 57 percent called it a "necessary evil," and 59 percent called it "confusing." Not surprisingly, therefore, only 48 percent said the White House acts reasonably and appropriately in the process, while 66 percent said that the Senate makes the process an ordeal.

Balancing the positives and negatives, more than 40 percent of the potential appointees said they would be favorably inclined toward an appointment, while just 5 percent said they would be unfavorably inclined.

However, most of these potential appointees did not understand that the federal government does almost nothing to facilitate the transition for an appointee, especially not when compared with Washington, D.C.–area corporations such as America Online, Lockheed Martin, Marriott, or TRW; universities such as American, Georgetown, or George Washington; nonprofits such as the American Red Cross and the Salvation Army; think tanks such as the American Enterprise Institute, the Brookings Institution, and the Heritage Foundation; and local governments throughout the capital area.[34]

Although new presidential appointees receive travel expenses including transportation of household goods and of a mobile home or boat used as a primary residence, as well as a per diem during their travel to Washington, they receive no short-term financial support or assistance in finding temporary housing, help finding a job for their spouse or partner, help finding a house or apartment, or closing costs on a new home, all of which are standard benefits in most of the private and public organizations surveyed on behalf of the Presidential Appointee Initiative.

Compared to the Reagan-Clinton appointees interviewed in 2000, these potential appointees overestimated the unfairness, embarrassment, confusion, and ordeal of the appointments process, perhaps because so many depend on the media and friends for their information about how the process works. They also viewed the White House and Senate more negatively than past appointees.

At the same time, they underestimated the burdens of filling out the financial disclosure forms and curing conflicts of interest through divestiture, if only because so few have direct experience actually working through the forms required of all nominees, including the increasingly intrusive national security clearance process.

Recruiting Appointees

The problem, of course, is that these and other negatives may drive many of the nation's most talented leaders out of the process even before it begins. Although the evidence presented here suggests the value of a simpler, faster appointments process, it also speaks to the need to reduce the sense of unfairness among potential appointees. Presidents can hardly expect their first choices to accept the call to service unless they make a firm commitment to ease the path into office, a point reinforced by further statistical analysis of how past and potential appointees view the decision to serve:[35]

- Among the 435 past appointees, the strongest predictors of the willingness to recommend a post to a friend were whether they thought (1) the appointments process had been fair, (2) their service in government had not been very stressful, and (3) they had earned a higher salary as an appointee than they had in their previous position.

- Among the 580 potential appointees, the strongest predictors of their willingness to serve were the following perceptions: (1) that the appointment would be (a) enjoyable and (b) an honor; (2) that the process would be fair; (3) that the appointment would enhance their future leadership prospects; (4) that the appointment would not sever important contacts they might need in the future; and (5) that the appointment would not disrupt their personal lives.

These findings provide lessons on recruiting appointees. First and most importantly, presidents should emphasize the rewards of service. There is simply no substitute for telling potential appointees that service will be both an honor and an opportunity to serve their country. Nor should presidents be reluctant to emphasize the impact of that service on future leadership opportunities.

Second, presidents must promise to help their appointees navigate the process, and address persistent questions about fairness. Presidents must remember that many potential appointees begin the conversation about service believing that the process is confusing, the White House and Senate will be slow and unfair, and the stress will be great. To the extent presidents commit to creating a fair process, they will increase the odds of a yes significantly.

Third, presidents must convince employers to encourage even their most valued employees to consider presidential service, especially since so many potential appointees worry about maintaining contacts for the future. Presidents might even offer tax incentives for employers whose employees take appointee positions to hold jobs open for future returns and to smooth the transition out of government. In doing so, presidents can only improve the odds that talented appointees will serve.

Finally, presidents should also do everything possible to build an effective White House Office of Presidential Personnel, where Cs and Ds are definitely not good enough for government work. The office must reassure appointees that it actually cares whether they are confirmed, while providing the information needed to survive the process. Although ratings of the office did not significantly influence the willingness of past appointees to recommend an appointment to a friend, it is easy to argue that unresponsiveness from that quarter increases the stress of service, which in turn affects the readiness to recommend.

Is Pay a Problem?

This analysis cannot assess the role of lower federal salaries in discouraging presidential appointees from applying. After all, the surveys of past appointees involve individuals who accepted the call for service, and the surveys of potential appointees involve a hypothetical question about their willingness to serve.

Nevertheless, there is no doubt that pay shapes favorability toward appointment. Potential appointees know they can make more outside government than inside, and clearly recognize the enormous financial costs of moving to Washington. Note, for example, that appointees who made more in their previous jobs were more likely to recommend an appointment to a friend than those who made less.

And there is no doubt that presidential appointee salaries are lagging. According to the Government Accountability Office, presidential appointees lost significant purchasing power between 1970 and 2006. Measured in 2006 dollars, secretaries and administrators who were at the top of the executive pay grade (Executive Level I) made $185,500 in 2006, compared with $250,204 in 1970, a decrease in purchasing power of 27 percent overall, or 0.75 percent per year.[36]

However, this gap does not appear to hold further down the executive hierarchy. Again measuring in 2006 dollars, the Government Accountability Office found that Senior Executive Service purchasing power rose ever so slightly over the thirty-six-year period from $148,058 in 1970 to $152,000 in 2006, or just 0.08 percent per year. To the extent these figures hold for Schedule C appointees, one can understand concerns about keeping pace with private and even nonprofit pay. Indeed, according to a 2003 Congressional Budget Office study, top federal appointees now make less than the chief executive officers of the nation's largest nonprofit organizations, including colleges and universities and hospitals.[37]

Lagging pay may undermine service in other ways, not the least of which is the decision to leave early. Although cabinet officers often stay for long periods, lower-level appointees rarely serve more than eighteen to twenty-four months in the same positions. Some leave government entirely, others take other positions in the hierarchy, and still others join the club of "in-and-outers" who move back and forth between government and much-higher-paying posts in the private sector, notably in lobbying firms along Washington's infamous K-Street corridor.

Quality Strained?

Every administration has its problems with at least some of its presidential appointees, some who are too controversial, others who are unqualified, and still others who are just too zealous. And every administration has its visible failures, from Zoë Baird and Kimba Wood, who were both forced to withdraw as candidates for Attorney General in 1993, to Linda Chavez, who was forced to withdraw as a candidate for Secretary of Labor in 2001.

As the number of appointees has increased, so have the odds of bad appointments. Although there is no systematic method for weighing the relative quality of appointees over time, and ample temptation to generalize from isolated cases, there are at least four ways to measure whether past appointees have been qualified for their posts.

1. Mastering the Job

If the quality of appointments has declined, recent appointees are not acknowledging it. Asked to rate the difficulty of their jobs, the vast majority of past appointees said they had little difficulty mastering specific tasks such as directing career employees and managing a large government organization.

Thus, 67 percent of the 450 past appointees said they had little or no difficulty mastering the substantive details of the policies they dealt with;

59 percent said the same about mastering the decision-making procedures of their department or agency; and 57 percent said the same of dealing successfully with the White House. At the same time, 49 percent also said mastering the federal budget process was either very or somewhat difficult; 49 percent said the same about dealing successfully with Congress; and 42 percent said the same about mastering the informal political networks that affected the work of their department or agency.

These self-assessments do not necessarily match reality, however. According to a study by John B. Gilmour and David E. Lewis, programs headed by presidential appointees during the second Bush administration received lower grades from the Office of Management and Budget than programs headed by senior civil servants.

Looking at the management grades given to 234 separate programs, the two scholars found that presidential appointees appear to be less effective program managers than members of the career Senior Executive Service (SES): "Appointed managers often have less managerial experience, less substantive expertise in the area they are managing, and less on-the-job training than their counterparts in the SES. Appointee-run programs suffer from frequent turnover at the top, and this turnover leads to an accumulation of management problems. Throughout time, these programs become increasingly difficult to manage."[38]

2. Assessing Colleagues

Despite these self-assessments, there is at least some objective and subjective evidence that the quality of appointees is not always high. Asked, for example, about the Senate-confirmed appointees they knew and observed, only 11 percent of the past appointees said their colleagues represented "the best and brightest America has to offer," another 8 percent said their colleagues were not the most talented Americans, but were adequate to perform the tasks they had been assigned, and 79 percent said that some were highly talented, and others did not have the skills and experiences their positions require.

This portrait of competence does not vary across the Reagan, George H. W. Bush, and Clinton appointees surveyed, but likely varies across departments. Some are treated as dumping grounds for politically connected "must" appointees, while others are reserved for the most talented candidates available. The question is not just whether less qualified appointees are the exception or the rule, but how long they can be expected to stay, whether they are in charge of missions that matter, and how much damage they can do before they are removed.[39]

These simple questions involve what Jeff Gill and Richard W. Waterman call the "presidential appointment contradiction."[40] Simply put, if presidential appointees matter, which they do, and are a central tool of presidential control, which they are, how can they serve this representative function if they enter office after long delays and often leave before they learn their jobs?

Again, one sees the unintended consequences of flooding the presidential appointment system and centralizing the process. Presidential appointees simply do not stay long. Turning back to the survey of 450 past appointees, roughly a third of the Reagan and George H. W. Bush appointees served two years or less in their last appointment, compared to 40 percent of the Clinton appointees. Although these percentages do not cover time spent in earlier appointments, one can argue that two years is not enough to master any new job, no matter how long an individual has already been in government.

3. The Ability to Cooperate

There are still other measures of quality that might signal a weakening of quality, including the ability to direct and motivate members of the Senior Executive Service. On the one hand, there may be less political conflict than one might imagine. Comparing samples of appointees and senior executives from three Republican administrations (Nixon, Reagan, and George W. Bush), Joel D. Aberbach and Bert D. Rockman argue that career executives were actually quite responsive to their new Republican leaders, perhaps because the more Democratic and liberal executives either left government or changed posts to create distance.[41]

My survey of past appointees confirms the cooperation—81 percent said the senior career officers in their departments were very or fairly responsive to their directions and suggestions, while 83 percent found them very or fairly competent. In addition, 73 percent said they had little or no difficulty directing career employees. The senior executives either move to other posts, simply believe in faithful execution regardless of ideology, or both.

On the other hand, rank-and-file career civil servants may be far less responsive. Comparing samples of both presidential appointees and civil service employees, Robert Maranto and Karen Marie Hult find significant disagreements between the two groups on management and policy.[42] The differences depended almost entirely on where the executives happened to work—executives at the Defense Department trusted their appointees much more than did their peers at activist agencies such as the Environmental Protection Agency and the Administration for Children and Families. Where career executives stand appears to depend very much on where they sit, which is why the politicized presidency is so tempting.

4. *The Motivation to Serve*

The most damning evidence of the possible decline in appointee quality involves the motivation to serve. Bluntly asked, have presidential appointees become more interested in what they give to government or what they get?

The answer from appointees who served from 1985 to 2000 points more to self-interest. Asked why they accepted the call to service, 38 percent said they wanted to meet and work with stimulating people, enhance their long-term career opportunities, or learn new skills, while 36 percent said they wanted to accomplish important public objectives, deal with challenging and difficult problems, or save taxpayers money. In short, they may have served not because of what they could do for the country, but because of what it could do for them.[43]

This focus on "me" rather than "we" is even sharper when attitudes are compared with those of appointees who served from 1965 to 1985. Asked why they accepted the call to service, just 18 percent of past appointees said they wanted to meet and work with stimulating people, enhance their long-term career opportunities, learn new skills, or participate in important historical events, while 65 percent said they wanted to accomplish important public objectives or deal with challenging and difficult problems. As Table 3.3 shows, today's appointees are more likely to be what Anthony Downs calls climbers or conservors than advocates or statesmen/women. Asked to endure an anxiety-inducing process, subjected to potential embarrassment and humiliation, perhaps they are right to put the focus on what they might receive from government.[44]

Conclusion

Today's sluggish appointments process is the best way to assure the character, merit, and reputation of an administration. Both Hamilton and Jefferson understood that it would be difficult to find individuals fit for office under the best of circumstances, let alone under the kind of unnecessary scrutiny embedded in an increasingly risk-averse system.

It hardly makes sense to streamline the appointments process if nothing is done to flatten the federal hierarchy as a whole, however. Nor

Table 3.3 Motivations to serve, 1964–2000

Question: Now here is a list of some satisfying aspects of an appointee's job. Thinking about all these experiences, which one (is/was) the most satisfying to you (in your current appointment/in your most recent appointment)?

Motivation	Percentage of 1964–1985 appointees rating the motivation as most satisfying	Percentage of 1985–2000 appointees who rated the motivation as most satisfying
Meeting and working with stimulating people	7	19
Accomplishing important public objectives	39	15
Serving a president you admired	11	14
Participating actively in important historical events	8	12
Dealing with challenging and difficult problems	26	10
Helping to save taxpayers' money	1	11
Enhancing your long-term career prospects	2	10
Learning new skills	1	9

N = 585 and 450 appointees respectively.

does it make sense to accelerate the appointments process if the rest of the government cannot assure that its frontline employees are qualified for their jobs. Unless Congress and the president act to restructure the entire hierarchy, a faster, leaner appointments process only hastens the day that appointees realize they have little chance to make a real difference through their work, and thus begin writing their memoirs.

Much as Hamilton and Jefferson would agree on the need for a faster process, Hamilton would be much more likely to favor the flooding of the appointments system, the centralization of selection, and the politicized presidency in general. Like the current administration, he would see great value in appointing like-minded officers, even as he created the structure needed to oversee their every move. Although he did not write deeply about political qualifications for office, he was a tried-and-true Federalist who understood how to use appointments to cement party control.

Jefferson also understood the politicized presidency, however, and worked tirelessly to remove the Federalists from office in an early version of Andrew Jackson's spoils system. But he appeared to do so reluctantly, fighting his own instincts to put merit and reputation above all else. Not trapped in the politicized presidency per se, he longed for a government based on reason and moral judgment, and opposed Hamilton's centralization and execution in detail.

Therefore, it might be time to unwind the politicized presidency by emphasizing Jefferson's commitment to civic duty as the foundation of service. Acknowledging that some presidential appointees play an important role in Hamilton's government well executed, there cannot be so many appointees and so little time in position that the chain of command is always searching for replacements, suffering from inexperience, and mired in the kind of obsessive oversight that even now is eroding the merit and reputation of another administration.

Ultimately, there is simply no way that 3,000 presidential appointees, no matter how qualified or carefully vetted, can substitute for 1.8 million civil servants, no matter how qualified or carefully supervised. But as the next chapter will suggest, the career civil service is currently in crisis. Too many career officers are ready to leave, and too few are well provisioned. They report shortages in virtually every resource needed to succeed, raise serious questions about the qualifications of their presidential and civil service leaders and middle-level managers, and have come to believe that the federal personnel system fails at virtually every task it undertakes. Working with an ever-thickening hierarchy, led by presidential appointees who enter office late and leave early, it is no surprise that they fear that the faithful execution of all the laws might be in jeopardy.

CHAPTER FOUR

Vigor and Expedition

The fourth characteristic of an energetic federal service is the vigor and expedition needed to faithfully execute the laws. Although factors such as pay, benefits, and security are certainly important to any workforce, the federal service must be dedicated first and foremost to the public benefit. It must also be selected for what Hamilton called the "aptitude and tendency" to produce a good administration.[1]

Hamilton argued that the adequate provision of support was the linchpin for both motivation and effectiveness. Although his writings on support for the executive in *Federalist No. 73* deal with the president's salary, which cannot be increased or decreased during the term of office, his other writings suggest that adequate provision also applies to the federal service.[2] Writing of the preservation of the union in *Federalist No. 23*, for example, Hamilton argued that the national defense depended upon "axioms as simple as they are universal; the *means* ought to be proportioned to the *end;* the persons, from whose agency the attainment of any *end* is expected, ought to possess the *means* by which it is [to] be attained."[3]

As the means for executing the laws today, however, the federal service is losing its energy to faithfully execute the laws, especially if vigor and expedition are defined as full exertion on the public's behalf, jobs that allow employees to make a difference, adequate provision of support, rewards and discipline, and the respect of the public served. Indeed, the federal service is at much greater risk than the business and nonprofit workforce. There are few areas where the federal government is competitive in attracting employees primarily motivated by the chance to make a difference.[4]

Hamilton's Federal Service

Many of these challenges can be traced to the very beginning of the federal service and the great difficulty of bringing talented servants into office. As Gordon S. Wood writes of the period, "Public office could no longer be regarded merely as a burden that prominent gentlemen had an obligation to bear. No longer could it be something that gentlemen simply stood by and waited to be called to. And no longer could it be the consequence of a gentleman's previously established social wealth and authority."[5] Public service would be driven by self-interest.[6]

Hamilton extended this "stubbornly unsentimental" view in setting the terms of employment. First, the federal service would be paid. "Public office in this country has few attractions," Hamilton wrote in 1797. "The pecuniary emolument is so inconsiderable as to amount to a sacrifice to any man who can employ his time with advantage in any liberal profession. The opportunity of doing well, from the jealousy of power and the spirit of faction, is too small in any station to warrant a long continuation of private sacrifices."[7]

Second, the federal service would have the possibility of promotion. "In a government like ours, where pecuniary compensations are moderate, the principle of gradual advancement as a reward for good conduct is perhaps more necessary to be attended to than in others where offices are more lucrative."[8]

Finally, the federal service would have tenure in office. As he wrote in *Federalist No. 78*, continuance in office was one of the most important modern improvements in the practice of government. Although he understood the arguments for rotation in office, he argued that tenure avoided the corruption that accompanied a "revocable office."[9] Virtuous exertion would come from pay and promotion in a long-serving workforce, not the simple call of duty that Jefferson hoped would carry talented citizens into office for brief moments of service.

To some extent, Hamilton was merely echoing standard business practices of the period. But just as he designed a basic structure of government that survives to this day, he also designed the basic structure of an energetic federal service.[10] The system evolved over time to include even greater patronage during the 1800s, which eventually prompted a backlash against this spoils system and its replacement by the merit principle that governs the selection of civil servants today. Nevertheless, most elements of Hamilton's vision still guide the federal service, whether in calls for more pay for improved performance or through the thickening of the hierarchy.

Hamilton's terms were hardly easy to implement in the 1790s, however. Most compensation was on a piece rate or commission, promotions were often tied to kickbacks, and tenure was designed more to placate the states and localities, which supplied most federal servants, than to reward virtuous execution.[11] At least for the first few decades, there was no federal service to which to aspire, not with most offices cleaned out by Jefferson's Republicans, and with so many opportunities for manipulating the process to one's advantage.

Jefferson also challenged Hamilton's notion of virtuous execution. He believed that the pursuit of public office reflected a "contemptible ambition." Writing in 1803, he described the evolution of public office as a destination "for every man whose affairs were getting into derangement, or who was too indolent to pursue his profession, and for young men just entering life. In short, it was poisoning of the very source of industry, by presenting an easier resource for a livelihood, and was corrupting the principles of the great mass of those who passed a wishful eye on office."[12]

He also believed that duty, not pay, promotion, and tenure, was the key to the pursuit of perfection in executing the laws: "What duty does a citizen owe to the government that secures the society in which he lives? What can it expect and rightly demand of him in support of itself? A nation that rests on the will of the people must also depend on individuals to support its institutions in whatever ways are appropriate if it is to flourish. Persons qualified for public office should feel some obligation to make that contribution. If not, public service will be left to those of less qualification, and the government may more easily become corrupted."[13]

He certainly opposed pay as a motivation for service, arguing that public offices should be "burthens to those appointed to them," and complained constantly about his own misery in office.[14] He also opposed tenure, writing James Madison in 1793 that "a tour of duty," whatever it might mean, "was due from every individual," but also noted that duty did not require a whole life of service, and "not even of a very large portion of it."[15]

This is not to argue that Jefferson favored a government ill executed. Although his management of his own affairs as a Virginia plantation owner left much to be desired, he understood that government's great missions required effective administration. Wisdom and integrity might reside in honor and duty, but he recognized that government required the vigor and expedition to execute, no matter how much he worried about federal encroachment on the states.

Like Hamilton, Jefferson looked for the aptitude and tendency to produce a good government in an officer's education, family ties, military service, friendship, even marriage. Given a choice between two equally qualified candidates for chief clerk of the State Department in 1792, for example, he chose the candidate who was married on the theory that marriage created a greater need for compensation. Although Republican Party credentials eventually became the most important consideration of all, Jefferson preferred an energetic federal service as much as Hamilton, just not one dedicated to a centralized federal government and managed through tight chains of command.

Service under Stress

The question two hundred years later is whether the federal service meets these expectations for excellence. The answer is troubling at best. Although the federal service has no doubt excelled under harsh conditions before, the threats to a government well executed run the gamut from the long-expected retirements of baby boomers to a cumbersome disciplinary system.

There is no shortage of opinion on the threats:[16]

> Too many of our most talented public servants—those with the skills and dedication that are the hallmarks of an effective career service—are ready to leave. Too few of our brightest young people—those with the imagination and energy that are essential for the future—are willing to join.
>
> THE 1989 NATIONAL COMMISSION ON THE PUBLIC SERVICE, CHAIRED BY PAUL A. VOLCKER[17]

> Talk to a federal manager for 10 minutes: You will likely hear at least one personnel horror story. The system is so complex and rule-bound that most managers cannot even advise an applicant how to get a federal job.
>
> VICE PRESIDENT AL GORE[18]

> There is no time to waste . . . The federal workforce is aging; the baby boomers, with their valuable skills and experience, are drawing nearer to retirement; new employees joining the federal workforce today have

different employment options and different career expectations from the generation that preceded them.

THE CONGRESSIONALLY CHARTERED GENERAL ACCOUNTING OFFICE (NOW THE GOVERNMENT ACCOUNTABILITY OFFICE)[19]

Those who enter the civil service often find themselves trapped in a maze of rules and regulation that thwart their personal development and stifle their creativity. The best are underpaid; the worst, overpaid.

THE 2003 NATIONAL COMMISSION ON THE PUBLIC SERVICE, ALSO CHAIRED BY VOLCKER[20]

Congress and the president have not been oblivious to these problems. To the contrary, they have launched dozens of experiments designed to improve the personnel system over the past thirty years, including efforts to streamline the hiring process, improve training, implement new technologies, and develop alternative pay systems. Unfortunately, the prevailing evidence suggests that the state of the federal service is declining.[21] Indeed, the threats to vigor and expedition are so great that the Government Accountability Office has kept the state of the federal service on its "high-risk" list of the top problems facing the federal government.

This is not to argue there has been complete consensus on the decline of the federal service, however. Researchers have found mixed evidence on the breakdown in the relationship between presidential appointees and career civil servants, for example, and limited evidence of the turnover crisis in government.[22] And there was even an initial body of research trying to explain why the 1989 Volcker Commission was a waste of effort.[23]

But much of the data questioning the threats to excellence is now dated, leading scholars such as Larry M. Lane, James F. Wolf, and Colleen Woodward to write in 2003 about a new wave of research showing continued problems with the federal service: "The quiet crisis of civil service has evolved from a whisper in 1987 to the very public voice of human capital as a high-risk program in the 1st years of the new millennium."[24]

This "deafening crisis" is easy to discern in a host of indicators.[25] Federal employees appear to be more motivated by compensation than mission, ensnared in careers that cannot compete with business and nonprofits, troubled by the lack of resources to do their jobs, dissatisfied with the rewards for a job well done and the lack of consequences for a job done poorly, and unwilling to trust their own organizations.[26] Already at peak load, the federal service is straining to generate enough energy to meet the growing demand for even greater vigor and expedition.

The strain is clear in my 2001 surveys of 1,051 randomly selected federal government employees, 1,005 business employees, and 1,140 nonprofit employees.[27] But before turning to the surveys, readers are warned that perceptions of work problems can be quite different from objective reality. Readers are also warned that these surveys were conducted just after the Bush administration entered office and have not been updated since. Unfortunately, the surveys were prohibitively expensive to conduct and cannot be repeated until the start of the next administration.[28] However, more recent surveys by the Council for Excellence in Government, the Partnership for Public Service, and the U.S. Office of Personnel Management suggest that the federal service remains just as exhausted and dispirited as it was in 2001.

On Overload

If Hamilton had won his duel with Aaron Burr, he might have lived to produce his promised treatise on public administration. Unfortunately, Burr had the better aim. Thus, I have relied on Hamilton's early writing and experiences at the Treasury Department to list his five attributes for vigor and expedition in government:

1. *Full exertion.* Hamilton believed that the federal service would have absolute commitment to what he called "virtuous exertion" for the public benefit. Even though self-interest would play a prominent role in bringing federal servants to work each day, it was to be self-interest put to work pursuing extensive and arduous enterprise to the fullest extent possible.

2. *Work that matters.* Much as Hamilton believed in tight oversight of his employees, he also knew that the work itself had to engage the federal service in the full execution of the laws. Although execution in detail hardly encouraged innovation and risk taking, Hamilton expressed at least some concern about creating jobs that would give employees enough authority to fulfill their missions.

3. *Adequate provision of support.* Hamilton's commitment to adequate provision of support was unquestioned, and can be identified in a host of letters, circulars, and instructions giving his Treasury Department employees the resources needed to do their jobs, whether garrisons for his proposed navy or ledgers and ink for his revenue collectors.

4. *Rewards for a job well done and discipline for a job done poorly.* Alongside his belief in compensation as a reward for service,

Hamilton had little tolerance for poor performance at any level of the hierarchy. He complained bitterly about the failure to execute and had a well-deserved reputation for angry outbursts at any officer who disappointed him. Although firings were few, his temper clearly constituted an intense form of discipline that would eventually cost Hamilton his life.

5. *The respect of the public served.* As Hamilton wrote, safety in the executive depended on the public's trust, albeit within limits. He believed that the "deliberate sense of the community should govern the conduct of those to whom they entrust the management of their affairs . . ." At the same time, he argued that the search for respect did "not require an unqualified complaisance to every sudden breeze of passion or to every transient impulse which the people may receive from the arts of men, who flatter their interests."[29]

Measured against this list, the federal service is beleaguered at best, besieged at worst, especially when compared with business and non-profit employees.[30]

Full Exertion

Hamilton's first attribute of vigor and expedition is full exertion for the public benefit. Unfortunately, Hamilton's own emphasis on pay, promotion, and tenure may have created a federal service that has lost sight of its purpose. Bluntly put, too many federal employees come to work solely for pay, promotion, and tenure, not the chance to make a difference in pursuing extensive and arduous enterprise.

As such, many federal employees may have less of the "public-service motivation" they need for vigor and expedition. As James L. Perry has argued, this public-service motivation is composed of a set of work-related attitudes and behaviors that involve (1) attraction to policy making, (2) commitment to the public interest and civic duty, (3) compassion, and (4) self-sacrifice.[31] Although the measures used in my 2001 survey are blunt, and may overstate the degree of self-interest by forcing employees to choose between sets of motivations such as pay versus the chance to accomplish something worthwhile, there seems to be reason to doubt the public-service motivation of the federal service, especially at the lower levels.

Asked first in my 2001 surveys why they took their jobs, the vast majority of federal employees focused on the compensation. Forced to choose between pairs of reasons, 65 percent said they took their job for pay and benefits, not the chance to make a difference; 59 percent said for

Table 4.1 Motivations for joining the organization, 2001

Question: People decide to accept a job for different reasons. When you first took your job, which of these two things most influenced your decision: Did (insert first phrase) or (insert second phrase) most influence your decision to take the job?

Reason	Percentage of nonprofit employees who selected the first option	Percentage of business employees who selected the first option	Percentage of federal government employees who selected the first option
Job security / helping the public	34	71	65
Salary and benefits / the chance to make a difference	34	72	69
Job security / pride in the organization	39	57	66
Secure paycheck / doing something worthwhile	39	57	66

N = 1,140 nonprofit employees, 1,005 business employees, and 1,051 federal government employees.

job security, not to help the public; 59 percent said for a secure paycheck, not for the chance to do something worthwhile; and 66 percent said for job security, not out of pride in the organization. As Table 4.1 shows, however, nonprofit employees were much more likely to report that they first took their jobs for the chance to make a difference, help people, or do something worthwhile, or out of pride in their organization.

Asked next why they came to work every day and given the chance to give an unscripted, open-ended answer, 31 percent said they came to work for the pay and compensation—for example, the need to pay the bills, access to health insurance, good vacation time, and job security. Another 31 percent said they came to work for personal reasons—for example, the nature of the work itself, their general satisfaction with the job, and intangibles such as the nature of their mission. Another 10 percent said they came to work because of their own work ethic—for example, the need to work itself. The rest of the federal employees either focused on the public good (4 percent) or combinations of compensation, personal interest, and work ethic.

These answers varied greatly in the senior, middle, and lower levels of the federal service, suggesting that public-service motivation may be the product of advancement up the hierarchy or the decision to stay in government long enough to rise to the top. For example, only 25 percent of members of the Senior Executive Service (SES) said they first took their job for the salary and benefits, not the chance to make a difference, compared with 70 percent of middle- and lower-level nonmanagers. Similarly, only 17 percent of the SES respondents said they first took their job for a secure paycheck, rather than to do something worthwhile, compared with 60 percent of middle- and lower-level nonsupervisors.

Federal and business employees were also remarkably similar to their peers in nonprofit organizations in explaining their reasons for coming to work—both groups put the emphasis on pay, benefits, and security. Although federal employees were less likely than business employees to say they came to work for the compensation (31 percent versus 47 percent), nonprofit employees were much more likely than federal employees to come to work because of the nature of the work (41 percent versus 31 percent) and the common good (10 percent versus 4 percent).

For those who argue that the nonprofit sector's pay and benefits are simply too low to be motivating, the surveys show that nonprofit employees understood they could make more in government or business, but chose to come to the nonprofit sector for the chance to make a difference. They were simply willing to make the trade-off between higher salaries and greater meaning.[32]

Work that Matters

Hamilton's second attribute of vigor and expedition is jobs that actually matter to the faithful execution of the laws. Here, the federal government is much closer to Hamilton's ideal. Contrary to the conventional criticisms of the federal service, federal jobs often provide the chance to make a difference.

Instead, almost half of the federal employees I surveyed in 2001 were very satisfied with the chance to accomplish something worthwhile. As Table 4.2 shows, 46 percent strongly agreed that they had a chance to do the things they do best, just 13 percent strongly agreed that their work was a dead end with no future, and only 2 percent strongly agreed that their work was boring. More than half also said their coworkers were willing to help other employees, and 63 percent said their coworkers were concerned about achieving the organization's mission.

Additionally, 29 percent said the word "innovative" described their organization very well, another 52 percent said the same about the word "helpful," 41 percent said the same about "fair," and 45 percent said the same about "trusted." Although only 21 percent said their organizations gave them a great deal of encouragement to take risks and try new ideas, majorities also said they were very satisfied with their jobs overall (49 percent), with job security (66 percent), and with benefits (66 percent).

Perhaps most importantly, 63 percent of federal employees said they could very easily describe how their job contributes to the organizational mission, and 55 percent said they contribute a great deal to accomplish their organization's mission, figures that match business and nonprofit employees' responses almost exactly.

However, federal jobs are not without frustrations. Compared with nonprofit and business employees, federal employees were frequently the least likely to describe their work in the most positive terms. Table 4.2 summarizes comparisons across a number of indicators, indicating that business and nonprofit employees were generally more likely than their federal peers to say they were given the chance to do the things they do best, and to reject descriptions of their jobs as boring or dead ends without a future. They also were also more likely to say their coworkers were very open to new ideas, very willing to help other employees learn new skills, and very concerned about achieving the organization's mission.

The federal government may have challenging jobs and caring workers, but businesses and nonprofits do better in creating jobs that encourage execution. Despite all the calls for government to become more businesslike, Table 4.2 suggests that government would be better advised to become more nonprofitlike. Although nonprofit jobs do not provide the same levels of pay, benefits, and security as those in government or business, nonprofit employees were still more satisfied with their jobs overall (58 percent very satisfied) than either business (44 percent) or federal employees (49 percent).

In addition, nonprofit employees were less likely to report morale problems within their organizations—25 percent of nonprofit employees said morale was either somewhat or very low in 2001, compared with 26 percent of business employees and 41 percent of federal government employees. Like their business peers, nonprofit employees also saw the hiring process as simple and fast, and nonprofits reported relatively little problem recruiting and retaining talented employees.

The federal service is also burdened by a hiring process that is anything but simple and fast. Fifty-seven percent of federal employees described the hiring process as confusing, not simple, 79 percent described it as slow, not fast, and 25 percent described it as unfair, not fair. Asked about recruitment and retention, 32 percent said their organizations were doing not too well or not well at all in recruiting top candidates, compared with

Table 4.2 Comparative views of job quality, 2001

Questions: (1) To what extent are the people you work with (insert)—to a great extent, somewhat, not too much, or not at all? (2) I'm going to read some statements people make about their jobs. Please tell me if you strongly agree, somewhat agree, somewhat disagree, or strongly disagree with them. (3) Does the word (insert) describe your organization very well, somewhat well, not too well, or not well at all?

Measure	Nonprofit employees	Business employees	Federal government employees
Percent who answered that the following characteristics described their coworkers to a great extent:			
Competitive with other employees	11	24	23
Open to new ideas	46	36	33
Willing to help other employees learn new skills	67	51	52
Concerned about achieving your organization's mission	72	56	63
Percent who answered that they "strongly agreed" with the following statements about their job:			
The work I do is boring	7	7	2
I'm given the chance to do the things I do best	68	52	46
My job is a dead end with no future	7	12	13
Percent who answered that the following words described their organization very well:			
The word "innovative"	38	40	29
The word "helpful"	72	50	52
The word "fair"	59	50	41
The word "trusted"	67	56	45

N=1,140 nonprofit employees, 1,005 business employees, and 1,051 federal government employees.

only 19 percent who said very well, while 36 percent said their organizations were doing not too well or not well at all retaining talented employees at their level of the organization.

Business and nonprofit employees were much more positive—nearly three-quarters of each group described the hiring process as fast, roughly half described it as simple, and 90 percent described it as fair. Both groups of employees also said their sectors were more effective at recruitment and retention than the federal government.

Adequate Provision of Support

Hamilton's third attribute of vigor and expedition is the adequate provision of support. After three decades of nearly constant budget cutting, the federal government remains far from meeting Hamilton's test. Employees can hardly be motivated by the chance to make a difference in executing the laws if they do not have the resources to do so. However, federal employees report serious shortages in every resource needed to do their jobs well.

They certainly report shortages of the raw materials needed for execution. According to the 2001 survey, just 38 percent of federal employees said their organization always had the information needed to do its job well, while 35 percent said their organization always had the technology, 23 percent said their organization always had the training, and just 13 percent said their organization always had enough employees.

Federal employees also questioned the competence of other employees at all levels of their organizations. According to the 2001 survey, the vast majority of federal employees rated their senior leaders, middle managers, middle-level employees, and lower-level employees as somewhat competent or worse. Just 37 percent rated their senior leaders as very competent, for example, compared with 32 percent who said the same about their middle-level supervisors, 40 percent who said the same of middle-level employees in general, and just 29 percent who said the same of their lower-level employees.

Most federal employees also said the quality of the workforce had gotten worse or stayed the same. Just 24 percent said the quality of their senior leaders had increased over the past few years, compared with 42 percent who said it had stayed the same, and 34 percent who said the quality had decreased. The pattern continued down the hierarchy, where just 24 percent said the quality of middle-level supervisors had increased, 23 percent said the same about middle-level employees in general, and just 21 percent said the same about lower-level employees.

Finally, federal employees reported shortages in organizational responsiveness. Forty percent said there were too many layers leading to the top of their agencies, while 49 percent said recent efforts to reform or reinvent their agencies had actually made their jobs either somewhat or a lot more difficult to do. Although more than 60 percent said their organizations were basically sound and needed only some reform, almost 20 percent said their organizations needed a major overhaul.

Business and nonprofit employees simply did not complain as much about access to resources, the level of organizational reform, or the competence of their organization's employees. To the contrary, both sets of employees were far more likely than federal employees to report adequate access to the resources they needed, and greater increases in competence at all levels of the organization, while nonprofit employees were more like federal employees in reporting resource shortages in information, technology, and training.

Business and nonprofit employees also reported that there had been both less reform and reinventing within their organizations and much greater success. Of the business and nonprofit employees whose organizations had been reformed or reinvented in the past five years, only 31 percent of business employees and 30 percent of nonprofit employees said the reforms had made their jobs either somewhat more difficult or much more difficult to do. And higher percentages said their organizations did not need much change at all.

Finally, business and nonprofit employees generally saw employees throughout the hierarchy as more competent and getting better.

Rewards and Discipline

Hamilton's fourth attribute of vigor and expedition is the reward for a job well done and the discipline for a job done poorly. The federal service must believe that performance, not time on the job, is the key to pay, promotion, and tenure. Too many simply do not believe it.

Satisfaction. In theory, satisfaction is one of the most important rewards of service. In theory, satisfied employees are more likely to do their jobs well, which in turn increases the odds of successful results.

There are different kinds of satisfaction, however. On the one hand, federal employees were very satisfied with their jobs overall (49 percent very satisfied), their benefits (66 percent), and their job security (66 percent), but not their pay (35 percent). On most measures of extrinsic satisfaction, the federal service outstripped business and nonprofits.

On the other hand, federal employees were far less satisfied with their opportunity to develop new skills (36 percent very satisfied), public respect for the type of work they were doing (36 percent), and their opportunity to accomplish something worthwhile (47 percent). Moreover, on all of these measures of internal, or intrinsic, satisfaction, the federal service trailed business and nonprofits. Two thirds of nonprofit employees were very satisfied with the chance to accomplish something worthwhile, for example, compared with 39 percent of business employees. Again, these results may explain why federal employees express less public-service motivation than their peers—they may simply have fewer opportunities to make a difference in their towering bureaucracies.

Performance. The question is not whether the federal service is satisfied, however, but whether its performance deserves reward. Put simply, is the federal service doing its job well?

There are at least three ways to answer the question. The first is simply to ask federal employees to rate themselves. Here, all but a handful said they do a "very good" or "above average" job. Majorities also said they could very easily describe the mission of their agencies (63 percent), and felt that they contributed a great deal to achieving it (55 percent).

The actual performance appraisal process clearly reinforces the high personal regard. Of the 700,000 employees who were rated in 2001 using a pass-fail grading system, just 0.06 percent failed. Of the 800,000 who were rated using a five-point system, just 0.55 percent of employees were rated as either "minimally successful" or "unacceptable," while 43 percent were rated "outstanding." The rest worked at the Department of Veterans Affairs under an entirely different, but hyperinflated system, or were too new on the job to be rated at all. Whatever the system, however, the federal government now rivals Lake Wobegon as a home for all above average.

The second way to measure performance is to ask federal employees to rate their peers. When asked to make their best guess about what percentage of the people they work with are not performing their jobs well, federal employees put the estimate at 23 percent in 2001, compared with 25 percent among business employees, and 19 percent for nonprofit employees. Simply put, when asked to estimate poor performance, federal employees are just as likely as business and nonprofit employees to use a standard distribution.[33]

However, when asked how well their organizations do at disciplining poor performers, only 9 percent answered "very good," while 67 percent answered "not too good" or "not good at all." When asked what explained the poor performance they saw, 37 percent of federal employees said their organization did not ask enough of its employees, 31 percent said the poor performers were not qualified for their jobs, and 16 percent said the poor performers did not have the training to do their jobs well.

Business and nonprofit employees were just as likely to see poor performers in their midst—business employees estimated that 25 percent of their peers were not doing their jobs well on average, while nonprofit employees put the figure at 19 percent. But both groups of employees had much greater confidence in the ability of their organization's disciplinary process to deal with the problems. Asked how well their organizations did at disciplining poor performers, 22 percent of business employees and 15 percent of nonprofit employees answered "very good."

The third way to test performance is to ask employees to rate their own organizations on three key tasks: (1) spending money wisely, (2) being fair in making decisions, and (3) helping people. Here, there is no dispute about the results. Federal employees were more likely to rate their own organizations poorly than business or nonprofit employees:

- Just 22 percent of federal employees rated their organization as very good in spending money wisely, compared to 36 percent of business employees and 44 percent of nonprofit employees.

- 51 percent of federal and business employees rated their organization as very good in helping people, compared to 51 percent for business employees and 71 percent for nonprofit employees.

- 29 percent rated their organization as being very good in being fair, compared to 36 percent of business employees and 44 percent of nonprofit employees.

Moreover, as Table 4.3 shows, when asked to look at the other sectors on the three tasks discussed above, federal employees rated non-profits and business as almost equal at spending money wisely; non-profits as much further ahead of both business and the federal government in terms of helping people; and the federal government as ever so slightly ahead of nonprofits at being fair. Again, it is little wonder that many federal employees come to work for the pay, benefits, and security—helping people is far from their reach.

The Respect of the Public Served

Hamilton's fifth and final attribute of vigor and expedition is the respect of the people served. The federal service can hardly expect Congress and the president to provide enough resources if the public does

Table 4.3 Federal employees on rating the sectors on doing the best job, 2001

Question: And who does the best job of (insert), the federal government, state and local government, for-profit business, or nonprofit organizations?

Task	Percentage of federal employees who said federal government does the best job at each task	Percentage of federal employees who said state and local government does the best job at each task	Percentage of federal employees who said business does the best job at each task	Percentage of federal employees who said nonprofit organizations do the best job at each task
Spending money wisely	12	7	33	35
Being fair in its decisions	37	8	10	30
Helping people	32	10	6	42

N=1,051 federal employees.
Percentages do not sum to 100 left to right because respondents who answered "don't know" are excluded.

not trust them to spend those resources wisely, nor can the federal service find great pride in its work if the public believes it is hopelessly inefficient. Unfortunately, the public and federal employees have both come to the conclusion that their government cannot be trusted.

According to successive public opinion surveys conducted on behalf of the Center for Public Service, Americans continue to have doubts about the motivation and performance of federal employees. As of July 2001, for example, Americans were convinced that most federal employees are motivated primarily by job security (70 percent), salary and benefits (68 percent), and having a secure paycheck (68 percent).[34]

They also had little confidence in government to do the right thing. Only 2 percent thought the federal government could be trusted to do the right thing "most of the time," only 4 percent had a very favorable opinion of the "federal government in Washington," only 12 percent had a very favorable opinion of federal government workers, and just 30 percent said they would prefer their son or daughter to work in government rather than business. The question may not be whether the public respects the federal government, however, but whether federal employees trust themselves and their organizations.

Unfortunately, federal employees have substantial levels of doubt about their own organizations. Although exactly half of federal employees said they were very proud to tell family and friends where they worked, and 47 percent were very satisfied with the public respect they received for their work, just 25 percent of federal employees said they trusted their organization to always do the right thing, compared to 45 percent who said it would do so most of the time, and 30 percent who thought it would do so only some of the time. By comparison, 37 percent of business employees and 44 percent of nonprofit employees said they always trusted their organizations. The puzzle is why federal employees like their jobs so much, yet trust their organizations so little—a puzzle that further research might resolve.

Haves and Have-Nots

Not all federal employees think alike. Senior-level employees are consistently more positive about their jobs than lower-level employees; supervisors are more positive than nonsupervisors; and employees at high-prestige departments such as Defense, Justice, State, and Treasury are more positive than employees at low-prestige departments such as Agriculture, Housing and Urban Development, and Veterans Affairs.

This variation suggests that the federal service may be dividing into haves and have-nots—that is, into a group of employees who have the motivation, jobs, resources, and so forth to do their jobs well, and a group that does not. In looking for the variation, it is important to remember that the statistical power of a survey is not in huge sample sizes, but in randomness, which is why national election polls can accurately predict outcomes with samples as small as 1,000. The key is to give every member of a population such as eligible voters or federal employees an equal chance of participating in a survey. As the old survey maxim goes, it does not take a gallon of blood to determine blood type, just a single drop drawn carefully.

Views from the Top

There is important variation in the diagnosis of the civil service by levels of government. Regardless of the measure, senior executives were consistently more positive about their motivations, organizations, and performance than middle- and lower-level employees. The view was always more positive at the top.

Thus, senior executives were far more likely than lower-level employees to focus on compensation as a basic motivator for taking their federal job, and much more likely to focus on the chance to accomplish something worthwhile, pride in their organizations, and the opportunity to help people as their basic motivators. They were also the most likely to report a positive work environment, and were more likely to have the resources needed to pursue the public good.

Senior executives were also more likely to see their work as challenging than middle- and lower-level employees. They were far more likely, for example, to say their jobs were interesting, they were given the chance to do the things they do best, their jobs were not dead ends without any future, and they were encouraged to take risks. Senior executives were also more likely to say their colleagues were helpful, to describe their organizations as innovative and trustworthy, and to claim that their organizations were doing a good job on basic tasks such as spending money wisely. They were also more satisfied with the extrinsic aspects of their jobs—pay, security, and benefits.

Not surprisingly given their stations at the top of the hierarchy, senior executives reported more access to every resource described above, perhaps because they had a self-interest in seeing more. After all, they are responsible for marshaling the resources that their employees need. There is little evidence, however, that they heard the complaints from lower-level employees. They were less likely, for example, to say their organizations needed reform, more likely to say that past reforms had been helpful, and less likely to rate their peers as poor performers.

These attitudes reflect both the fact that senior employees have survived the rise to the top and therefore have a vested interest in seeing the positive, and the fact that more positive employees may survive the rise to the top. In other words, particularly unhappy employees may simply exit the federal government early, leaving a pool of relatively happier employees behind. These employees often reach the top of the hierarchy after an excruciating climb, which may help explain their relatively refreshing view from the top.

The 9/11 Effect

My 2002 survey of 673 of the same federal employees interviewed in 2001 clearly shows that federal employees were affected by 9/11. Interviewed just six months after the attacks on New York City and Washington, D.C., federal employees reported declines in every measure of an energetic federal service.

Measuring energy again. The September 11 attacks gave the federal service more than another sober mission. They also changed basic attitudes toward federal service itself, often toward less vigor and expedition.

On Hamilton's first attribute, full exertion in making a difference, the percentage of federal employees who said they came to work for the compensation actually increased by 10 percentage points during the months following 9/11. Although the 2001 economic recession may have heightened concerns about compensation, the increase is troubling nonetheless. At a time when concerns about the mission of government should have gone up, they actually went down.

On Hamilton's second attribute, work that matters, the perceived quality of federal work actually fell after 9/11. While the percentage of employees who felt they were always given the chance to do the things they do best fell by 6 percent, the percentage who described their jobs as a dead end without a future increased by 7 percent. At the same time, the percentage of federal employees who said they were very satisfied with the opportunity to accomplish something worthwhile dropped eight percentage points to 39 percent. Not surprisingly, morale fell seven percentage points during the period.

However, on Hamilton's third attribute, adequate support, federal complaints about access to resources did not worsen appreciably after

9/11, in part because access could not fall much further. Indeed, the 2002 survey suggests that the federal workforce was mostly standing still, often denied the basic resources that produce the high performance the federal government's greatest endeavors require, even as the government failed to strengthen the competence of its workforce, stop the thickening of government, or produce reforms that make jobs easier to do.

On Hamilton's fourth attribute, rewards for a job done well, the vast majority of federal employees still said they were doing a very good job in 2002, estimated that roughly 22 percent of their colleagues were not doing their jobs well, and viewed their organizations as not particularly successful at the four key tasks identified earlier.

However, at least two of the task ratings did drop, albeit incrementally. Whereas 41 percent had rated their organization as very good at delivering programs and services in 2001, only 34 percent agreed in 2002, and whereas 51 percent had rated their organization as very good at helping people in 2001, only 45 percent agreed in 2002. Similarly, the percentage who said they always trusted their organization to do the right thing dropped by four percentage points during the period, confirming employees' continued doubts about their own organizations.

These declines appear to reflect a lack of purpose following the attacks. Asked whether the people they work with have more or less of a sense of purpose since 9/11, 42 percent of federal employees said their colleagues had more of a sense of purpose, while just 1 percent said they had less of a sense of purpose, and 57 percent reported no change at all. Congress and the president rarely talked about the role that federal employees might play in the new war on terrorism, leaving most federal employees wondering whether and how their missions might fit into the new era.

And on Hamilton's fifth attribute, the respect of the public served, trust went on a roller coaster after 9/11, first rising immediately after the attacks, then slowly falling as memories faded. Thus, trust in the federal government to do the right thing just about always jumped from 4 percent in July 2001 to 15 percent in October, but fell back to 8 percent by May 2002. Similarly, favorability toward federal employees jumped from the 12 percent who said they were very favorable in July to 20 percent in October, but fell back to 14 percent in May, while the percentage who would recommend a job in government to their son or daughter rose from 30 percent in July to 39 percent in October, but fell back to 31 percent in May.

Describing 9/11 as a moment of opportunity in which government could convince its citizens that it can be trusted, G. Calvin Mackenzie and Judith Labiner write that Americans had expressed their admiration for what they saw. But as they also write, "the moment passed, apparently without long-term effect."[35] What rose with the expectation that the federal government would quickly win the war on terrorism soon fell with the realization that winning would take years, if at all, starting with the protracted battles in Iraq.

The defense workforce. This heightened sense of purpose was not evenly distributed across the federal agencies, however. Whereas 63 percent of Defense Department employees said they felt a greater sense of purpose after 9/11, only 35 percent of non-Defense employees reported the same reaction. And whereas 30 percent of Defense employees said their jobs had become rewarding after 9/11, only 15 percent of non-Defense employees agreed.[36]

The explanation may be the war on terrorism itself. Defense employees had a very clear sense of their mission after the attacks, while many other federal employees did not, in no small measure because the president and cabinet secretaries did not talk about how traditional domestic organizations such as the departments of Agriculture, Commerce, or Housing and Urban Development could play a role. Asked how their jobs had changed since 9/11, Defense employees also described their jobs as much more challenging. As Table 4.4 shows, they were consistently more likely than non-Defense employees to see their jobs as more difficult, stressful, rewarding, and challenging.

There were other significant changes both within the Defense workforce and between the Defense workforce and the rest of government. As the pre- and post-9/11 surveys show, the Defense workforce became more positive and negative in the early months of the new war on terrorism. On the one hand, Defense employees became more likely to say they were given the chance to do the things they do best, express satisfaction with their job security, give a lower estimate of the number of poor performers in their midst, and note that their organizations had enough employees to do the job.

On the other hand, Defense employees were less likely to report high morale within their organizations, express satisfaction with their opportunity to accomplish something worthwhile, believe they contributed to the mission of their organization, and report adequate access to training. They also reported an increase in the number of layers leading to the top of their organizations.

Table 4.4 Challenging jobs, post-9/11

Question: Has your job become more (insert) since September 11 or has it stayed about the same?

Description	Percentage of all federal employees who said their jobs were more	Percentage of Defense Department employees who said their jobs were more	Percentage of non-Defense employees who said their jobs were more
Difficult	27	31	25
Stressful	37	46	15
Rewarding	19	30	15
Challenging	31	45	26

N = 673 government-wide employees, 174 Defense employees, and 499 non-Defense employees.

Defense employees may have been reacting more viscerally to familiar problems. It is one thing to tolerate layering and a lack of access to training in peacetime, and quite another to accept it during wartime. Defense employees became more sensitive to the bureaucracy because they were highly sensitive to the new mission. At the same time, they saw their jobs as more important. Whereas the percentage of Defense employees who said they were given the chance to do the things they do best went sharply up, the percentage of non-Defense employees who said the same thing went sharply down. And whereas the percentage of Defense employees who said they were personally satisfied with their work stayed the same, the percentage of non-Defense employees who said the same thing went down.

These findings also suggest that non-Defense employees were reacting to confusion regarding their role in the war on terrorism. With little focus on domestic issues, many non-Defense employees may have been expressing their frustration about the lack of engagement. They also may have been expressing their own sense that their work on some of government's greatest endeavors was being ignored by the president, Congress, the press, and the public.

Explaining Poor Performance

As the 2001 survey suggests, there are many potential explanations for employees' rating of performance, including motivation, respect, resources, and so forth. But further analysis suggests that there were five statistically significant predictors of the employees' estimate of poor performance in the federal service:[37]

1. Middle-level employee competence—employees who rated middle-level employees at their organizations as competent perceived less poor performance.

2. The disciplinary process—employees who said the disciplinary process did a very good job perceived less poor performance.

3. The work environment—employees who saw their coworkers as open to new ideas, willing to help others, and committed to the mission of their agencies perceived less poor performance.

4. Resources—employees who said their organization provided enough access to information, technology, and training, and enough employees to do their jobs well, perceived less poor performance.

5. Lower-level employee competence—employees who rated lower-level employees at their organizations as competent were much less likely to perceive poor performance.

In a very real sense, this analysis shows the simple value of investing more in the competence of employees, an effective disciplinary process, and access to resources, all of which are in easy reach provided Congress and the president are willing to act. If Congress and the president want the federal government to improve, they need to do more than just fix the woefully inadequate hiring process, which was an insignificant predictor of estimated performance. They need to fix the system as a whole and give federal employees the resources they need to succeed. As such, poor performance is a drag on more than pursuing missions that matter. It is also a drag on morale.

Explaining Satisfaction

Advocates of a strong civil service have long argued that pay is one of the biggest problems with maintaining an energetic federal service. They argue that federal employees are consistently underpaid compared to private employees, and that this "pay gap" undermines motivation and performance. After all, if federal employees take their jobs for the pay, benefits, and security, and come to work for the compensation, pay becomes a particularly important factor in morale and satisfaction.

Yet, pay turns out to be a relatively weak predictor of overall job satisfaction in the federal government. Further statistical analysis of overall satisfaction suggests that there are eight statistically significant predictors, with pay at the very bottom of the list:[38]

1. Motivation—employees who were satisfied with their opportunity to accomplish something worthwhile were more satisfied overall.

2. Promising jobs—employees who said they were given the chance to do the things they did best were more satisfied overall.

3. Challenging jobs—employees who said their work was not boring were more satisfied overall.

4. Pride—employees who were proud of the organization they worked for were more satisfied overall.

5. Engaging jobs—employees who said their jobs were not dead ends without a future were more satisfied overall.

6. Morale—employees who rated the morale of their coworkers as high were more satisfied overall.

7. Extrinsic benefits—employees who took their jobs for the salary, benefits, and security, not the chance to make a difference, accomplish something worthwhile, and help people were more satisfied.

8. Pay—employees who were more satisfied with their pay were more satisfied overall.

The fact that pay scores so poorly in predicting federal job satisfaction lends partial support to Perry's definition of public-service motivation—at the very least, the results suggest that employees with a greater commitment to making a difference are the most satisfied. At least according to these results, overall satisfaction would rise significantly with an increase in the percentage of those who are very satisfied with the chance to accomplish something worthwhile. Just 47 percent are very satisfied according to this criterion now.

Jefferson might be pleased with the results, too, for they confirm his belief that a sense of duty, not pay, should be the most significant factor in the life of the federal service. At the same time, however, they confirm his disquiet that compensation might become the primary draw for service in the first place. The chance to accomplish something worthwhile may explain satisfaction, but not the decision to take a federal job or come to work each day.

Depleting the Federal Service

As government's own surveys show, the federal service has been drifting for the better part of thirty years. The federal government has become a destination of last resort for making a difference for several decades, and cannot even guarantee that its employees will learn the skills needed to do their jobs.[39] Or, as Patricia Ingraham and David Rosenbloom put it in 1990, the federal service has been in the process of "decomposing" since the 1970s.[40]

It is little wonder, therefore, that there might be declining morale across the workforce as past administrations have tried to create a greater focus on pay for performance and job cuts. As Charles H. Levine wrote in 1986, "It is reasonable to expect that few highly qualified people want to work in a system that is perceived to be failing and which does not promise to be satisfying."[41]

No one knows for sure how federal employees might have answered my surveys before Watergate and the steep fall in public trust in government. Yet, there is good reason to argue that the current disquiet can be traced back to the mid-1970s when members of Congress and presidents campaigned assiduously against the government they led.

The tracks of the recent disinvestment are easy to follow back to Jimmy Carter and his "New Democrat" antigovernment rhetoric. Although Carter often celebrated the federal employees who perform with "spirit and integrity," he campaigned against waste in government and for greater freedom to fire incompetent employees. "There is not enough merit in the merit system," he said in presenting his 1978 civil service reform to Congress, and "too few rewards for excellence and too few penalties for unsatisfactory work."[42]

Carter also drafted a massive civil service reform designed to "let managers manage" and "reward dedication and excellence." At the same time, the reform would help government "single out those who are incompetent or lazy or not dedicated, and discipline them or inspire them or fire them."[43] However, Carter's actual civil-service package may have created the opposite effect by creating a new tangle of regulations governing firings and a longer appeals process. It also produced confusion among federal employees and supervisors as they struggled to manage the new bonus system, and among so-called supergrade civil servants who were given the option to move into the new Senior Executive Service or stay put until retirement. And it produced yet another employment ceiling, as members of Congress sought to cap the growth of government.

Jimmy Carter was hardly the only recent president to focus on poor performance. Ronald Reagan began his presidency by calling government the problem, not the solution, and appointed a personnel director who believed C+ was good enough for government work. Although he wrapped his arms around government in the wake of great national tragedies such as the Challenger accident, he was rarely without a joke about the inefficiencies of government, and never without a plan for capping federal pay and hiring. According to Levine, Reagan also polarized civil-service reform by posing a choice between smaller, efficient government, and a government he described as bloated and wasteful.

In turn, Bill Clinton entered office pledging to create the most ethical, effective government in history, but was embroiled in controversy from beginning to end, culminating in a pardons-for-gifts scandal that took place only days before he left office. Announced only weeks before his national health-care package, his management agenda was designed to show that he could be just as tough on government as Republicans, including cutting more than 250,000 federal employees from the payroll through attrition and voluntary buyouts.

Moreover, even strong advocates of reinventing government recognize that the campaign was oversold as a way of cutting federal spending, rather than as a way of changing the mission of government to fit available resources. Although the job cuts and promised savings of more than $100 billion were important in making the case for reinvention, they also distracted federal employees from the real task of reform, which was empowerment toward better performance. Thus, all that remained from the first round of Clinton's effort was a deep cut in federal employment and growing frustration with the mantra that government should do more with less.

Finally, although George W. Bush began his presidential campaign in 1999 by pledging not to engage in another round of antigovernment rhetoric, he started his administration with yet another civil-service hiring freeze and a commitment to further job cuts through job competitions and aggressive privatization under what his first budget director called the "lawnmower rule." If a job could be found in the Yellow Pages, he said, it should be contracted out.

Moreover, forced by the new war on terrorism and his tax cuts to choose between giving all of government the resources it needed, and concentrating available funding at Defense, Bush took the obvious course. After finally appointing his point person on management reform two years into the administration, Bush launched a mostly tepid management agenda that was poorly linked, if at all, to the budgetary process that might make its scorecards relevant to the federal service.

Only George H. W. Bush seemed to have a genuine affection for the federal service, perhaps because he had spent so much time in the federal service himself. Although he attacked his 1988 Democratic opponent as having the "creed of a technocrat who makes sure the gears mesh, but doesn't for a second understand the magic of the machine," he spoke well of government, greeted Paul Volcker's first National Commission on the Public Service in the Oval Office, and accepted its call for a renewed commitment to the highest traditions of public service.[44] In contrast, his son did not acknowledge the second Volcker Commission in 2003, and dispatched a lower-level aide to receive its report far from the Oval Office.

Throughout this long period of harsh rhetoric and failed implementation, the shape and focus of the federal hierarchy changed. As already noted, the hierarchy thickened with needless layers of management as federal employees aged inexorably upward into higher-paying jobs during repeated pay freezes, while the politicization of government continued with ever-tighter centralization of the appointments process. At the same time, the federal mission continued to expand as federal employees were asked to do more without the resources they needed to succeed.

Conclusion

There are numerous examples of highly motivated federal employees who come to work each day for the chance to make a difference, not the least of whom are the employees celebrated annually by the Partnership for Public Service with a Service to America Medal.

Nevertheless, the federal service as a whole appears to be at the edge of losing the vigor and expedition to execute.[45] Too many federal employees come to work for the pay, benefits, and security, not the chance to make a difference on missions that matter; too many report that their coworkers are closed to new ideas and their organizations are unwilling to encourage risks; too many say they do not have the resources needed to do their jobs well; too many believe their organizations fail at helping people; and too many do not trust their own organizations to do the right thing.

Hamilton bears at least some of the blame for this troubling assessment. After all, he put the focus on pay, benefits, and security as motivators for persuading talented officers to join the early federal service.

He also denied many of those officers the freedom to take risks by demanding execution in detail and binding government in a flood of rules and circulars. And he may have encouraged poor performance by creating a tenure system that makes removal difficult, if not impossible.

Jefferson deserves some of the blame, too. His emphasis on limited government put at least some of the focus on compensation rather than the call of great enterprise, while his unwavering commitment to frugal government has led Congress and presidents toward many of the budget cuts that have starved the federal service of the training and staffing to do their jobs well.

Ironically, the current threats to an energetic executive may demand more of both Hamilton and Jefferson, but in different ways. The federal service could use more of Jefferson in moving the federal government away from pay, benefits, and security as a basic motivation for service, a bit of his commitment to harmony in the executive and decentralization in creating jobs that allow execution, and in dealing aggressively with poor performers. Conversely, it could use much more of Hamilton in providing adequate support, celebrating jobs well done, and defending the need for a federal service to a distrusting public, though without his sometimes pretentious, even condescending rhetoric about saving states from doing too much.

Even Hamilton and Jefferson together cannot rescue the federal service from the continued confusion about where bureaucracy ends and the federal service begins. The federal service distrusts bureaucracy as much as ordinary Americans, except perhaps for some of those who occupy the very highest rungs of the hierarchy. Nevertheless, the federal service is almost always blamed for bureaucracy, and rarely celebrated for its role in delivering on government's greatest promises.

The situation did not change with the George W. Bush management agenda, which promised improvements in everything from civil service recruitment to pay for performance. Although Bush was well advised to put the state of the federal service on the agenda, the effort produced little real improvement and ample anxiety. Bush not only abandoned the total quality initiative launched by his father, but was widely and rightly criticized for a series of anti-union proposals and a dramatic increase in federal outsourcing.

These recommendations might be modestly helpful in addressing employee concerns about recruitment and discipline, but do nothing to address the retention, resource, and respect issues raised in my surveys. Encased in "war on waste" rhetoric, they tend to feed the public's ongoing discomfort with big government, which is exactly what the Bush administration appears to intend.

Moreover, even if the Bush agenda succeeded in creating a faster hiring process, it would not address the lingering concerns about the overall vigor and expedition to execute. Fixing the recruitment process merely replaces one problem with another. Indeed, a faster, simpler recruiting process merely hastens the time that it takes for the most committed recruits to start asking whether they want to stay in government at all.

Instead, reformers must focus on the whole problem of a besieged workforce, working from the very top where employees view their leaders as less than fully competent, to the middle, where employees see a profusion of layers, to the bottom, where they are battered with one management reform after another and cannot make the case that federal jobs should be the destination of choice for America's most talented students. Tinkering at any one level will not suffice, especially if the essential purpose of an energetic federal service is the faithful execution of the laws. There are simply too many barriers to providing the aptitude and tendencies to fulfill that duty today to focus on just one aspect of the erosion of the federal service.

CHAPTER FIVE

A Spirit of Service

The fifth characteristic of an energetic federal service is a spirit of service among talented young Americans. The federal government will need to hire thousands upon thousands of employees each year just to keep pace with the increasing number of civil-service retirements and the ordinary turnover of younger employees. Without an increased stream of energized employees, energy can only decline, and with it, the capacity to faithfully execute the laws.

Hamilton had little time to worry about a federal service for a distant future, however. After all, the Washington administration had to build a federal service from scratch. In retrospect, it seems like an easy task. After all, the new government needed only a few hundred employees, and most jobs were tedious at best. "It was not an age of experts," Leonard White notes. "Most civil servants were engaged in finance, record keeping, and the ordinary type of clerical operations, chiefly plain copying. The professional side of the service was modest indeed, comprising the judges, the district attorneys and an occasional legal counsel elsewhere and a small number of physicians and surgeons in the army, navy, and marine hospitals."[1]

Moreover, the Washington administration knew where to look for talent. As Frederick Mosher writes, the federal service divided rather neatly into four classes, each with its own educational requirements: (1) an administrative class composed of individuals who had completed a university education, (2) an executive class composed of those who had completed the highest level of education short of attending a university, (3) a clerical class composed of those who had completed their first major school examinations, and (4) a messenger class of those with a primary school education.[2] Although Mosher describes this as a "government of gentlemen," the new government relied on allies of allies to fill the four classes.

Nevertheless, the Washington administration soon discovered that there was too little interest in serving at the top of government and too much interest in serving at the bottom. At the top, federal service hardly offered an attractive favored career. Then, as now, the federal service had to compete for its share of talent. "Officeholders as a group competed with old social classes of great prestige, notably the clergy, the merchants and the southern gentlemen planters," White writes in his classic history of the 1790s. "In an era of vast opportunity for private enterprise, bold and active men were attracted to buying and selling, land speculation, shipbuilding and the carrying trade."[3]

Yet, at the bottom, the demand for federal jobs was heavy. White supplies the details: "Here there was a craving for public position, even when the income was painfully small . . . On more than one occasion, Washington had his first news of the death of an officer holder through an application from a would-be successor."[4] With so many potential employees besieged by debts in a weakened economy, the call to service had everything to do with Hamilton's system of pay, promotion, and tenure, not Jefferson's notion of civic duty.

Two hundred years later, the federal government no longer fills most of its posts with allies of allies. Rather, it must rely on the willingness of talented young Americans to accept the call of service on the basis of merit. The problem is that the aging of the federal workforce is about to result in a "retirement tsunami," as the U.S. Office of Personnel Management describes it, while among the nation's young people interest in serving appears to be dwindling.[5] Indeed, roughly half of today's entry-level jobs are filled from within the federal government as employees change jobs in search of higher pay, an easier commute, or the opportunity to advance. The vast majority of middle-level jobs are also filled from within—federal employees pay their dues through time on the job and advance upward.

If the federal government wants to fill these vacancies, it must give young Americans the opportunity to make the difference they so desire. If it also wants to meet the public's expectations for more of virtually everything the government delivers, it must give young Americans a shorter, more vibrant pathway toward the top and the talented leadership they expect.[6] Unfortunately, the path to the top is long and arduous—federal employees do advance automatically with time on the job, but only through a mountainous hierarchy that often leaves them well short of the peak.

The key to this chain of success involves much more than a faster, simpler recruitment process, although such a process would certainly help. The federal government must also imagine a very different career path, one that allows talented recruits to enter at any level. It must also confront the resource shortages, disciplinary problems, declining morale, politicization, and diffusion of accountability that are already driving some of its most talented employees out. And it must restore trust in its own organizations, convince its current employees that there is still hope to make a difference, and encourage risk taking, innovation, and cooperation.

This chapter will examine the lack of interest in federal careers among the nation's most talented prospects, including college seniors, graduates of top public-service professional schools, and the federal government's own top recruits who join the workforce under the President Management Fellowship program. The chapter will then turn to explanations for the lack of interest. In a sentence, today's young Americans are not saying "show us the paycheck," but "show us the work." And the work has not been showing well of late.

Supply and Demand

Although he was preoccupied with both creating and filling new jobs in his Treasury Department, Hamilton was a tireless supporter of a national military academy and wrote at length about the need to train future military officers *and* soldiers in the "science of war."

He also supported creation of a national university, as did Thomas Jefferson. According to Hamilton, such a university would extend science and knowledge as "an object primarily interesting to our national welfare." Defending the idea, Hamilton put the emphasis on the need for science: "But, can it be doubted that the general government would with peculiar propriety occupy itself in affording nutriment to those higher branches of science, which, though not within the reach of general acquisition, are in their consequences and relations productive of general advance? Or can it be doubted that this great object would be materially advanced by a university erected on that broad basis to which the national resources are most adequate, and so liberally endowed as to command the ablest professors in the several branches of liberal knowledge."[7]

Hamilton's interest in education may have been influenced by his exceedingly dismal view of human nature. Speaking to the Constitutional Convention in 1787, he argued that mankind was driven by passion and power: "There may be in every government a few choice spirits, who may act from more worthy motives. One great error is that we suppose mankind more honest than they are. Our prevailing passions are ambitions and interest: it will ever be the duty of a wise government to avail itself of these passions, in order to make them subservient to the public good."[8]

Not surprisingly, Hamilton sought to harness these passions with pay, promotion, and tenure. But he also saw the wisdom in recruiting those "few choice spirits" who came into the federal service through a love of liberty. Hamilton also seemed to believe that the nation needed a steady supply, or reserve, of talent to step into positions of authority should the need arise. Not only would the nation need strength on the Atlantic Ocean to guard its coast, it would need diligence in collecting the revenues that were essential to retire the Revolutionary War debt.

Hamilton's support for active recruiting of a talented service is still relevant today. Assuring a steady supply of talent has never been more critical, and not just because the number of job openings is rising with the baby-boomer retirements. A steady supply is also essential if the federal government is to fill the openings created through natural turnover at the bottom of the hierarchy. All told, the federal government will hire roughly 200,000 new employees a year until the 2020s, only a third of them in response to the retirement tsunami.

The challenge is not to find just anyone for the federal service, however. The capacity to execute the laws depends on having the most able recruits possible. Thus, the federal government must confront two very simple questions as it looks to the future. First, is there an adequate supply of talent upon which to draw? Second, is the federal government expressing its need for that talent in ways that appeal to the most talented?

The Supply Side

Few question the federal government's need for talent in the coming decades. The data is in the average age of the workforce, which drives eligibility for retirement.

As the nonpartisan Partnership for Public Service notes, 40 percent of the Homeland Security Department's managers will be eligible for retirement in 2009, 42 percent of the Senior Executive Service is expected to retire by 2010, and the attrition rate among air traffic controllers is expected to triple by 2012.[9] At the same time, the equally nonpartisan Council for Excellence in Government reports that 60 percent of the federal government's white-collar workforce and 90 percent of the Senior Executive Service will be eligible to retire by 2016.[10]

It is one thing to highlight the demand for replacements, however, and quite another to prove a supply shortage. To the contrary, there is ample demographic evidence that the U.S. economy will survive the baby-boom retirements with just enough room to spare. When the basic trends are compiled, according to demographer Peter Cappelli, the labor shortage disappears. Baby boomers are likely to work longer than expected, and the "echo" generation of the baby boom's children has already begun entering the workforce.[11]

The problem for the federal service lies in attracting the most talented employees into government. Many may be called, but will the right ones be chosen? The answer depends in part on basic changes in what young Americans want from a job.

It is already clear that expectations have changed dramatically since the 1970s, when most young Americans saw government as a destination of choice for long-term careers. As a result of the exceptional growth in government in the 1960s and 1970s, Patricia W. Ingraham writes, workers in the federal service are older than the national workforce as a whole, which generates higher short-term retirement rates, and requires greater agility in dealing with at least three facts that are reshaping the federal government's labor supply.[12]

First, the federal government's labor supply is becoming more diverse. More women are working today than ever, and more people of color are entering the federal workforce. Just as the face of America has changed, so has the face of the labor supply. The federal government is still far from being a "majority minority" employer, but many of its field offices will be located in just such communities by the 2020s, as some already are in cities such as Los Angeles.

Yet even as the percentages of women and people of color remain at or above national averages in the rest of the labor force, the federal government may not be changing fast enough to accommodate an increasingly diverse labor supply. Although women and people of color are moving up the hierarchy in no small part because older white men are retiring, many are still trapped in lower level, lower-paying jobs by "sticky ladders" and "glass ceilings" that prevent upward movement and encourage turnover.[13]

Second, the federal government's labor supply is motivated by a mix of contradictory goals. When asked about their objectives, two-thirds of college freshmen interviewed for a study by the Cooperative Institutional Research Program at the University of California at Los Angeles in 2006 said helping others was a very important objective, while nearly half said the same about influencing social values.[14] At the same time, when asked why they were attending college, the vast majority answered to learn about things that interest them, get a better job, make more money, and increase their earning power. Assuming that these answers shape calculations about career choices, the federal government has to be careful in crafting jobs that meet the intrinsic and extrinsic goals that young Americans seek.

It is a mix that is likely to make the future federal labor supply less distinctive, at least according to Sue A. Frank and Gregory B. Lewis. Whereas federal employees once put interesting work and the opportunity to help people first on their list of goals, Frank and Lewis suggest that pay is becoming more important, even as they report that the work ethic is declining.[15]

Third, the federal government's labor supply is increasingly divided between haves and have-nots, the debt-free and the debt-laden.[16] The growing income inequality is particularly visible among the 2006 college freshmen polled by the Cooperative Institutional Research Program, who come from much wealthier homes on average than the rest of America.

Yet, just as this wealth itself creates a divided workforce between employees who attend college and those who do not, it also creates divisions within each group. Although two-thirds of all freshmen said they had "some" or "major" concerns about financing their education, the greatest concern was exactly where one would predict, among students from lower-income families.[17] "As colleges and universities continue their financial policies of increasing tuition and fees, we are seeing direct effects on students that come from poorer families," said José Luis Santos, assistant professor of education at UCLA and an author of the report. "Poorer students alter their choices of whether or not to go to college at all, or choose a college based on financial costs and packages."[18] The result is division within division within division, and mixed pressure for loan relief as a recruiting tool for recruiting some, but not all future employees.[19]

The Demand Side

Having cut more than 450,000 total jobs from the payroll during the 1990s, the federal government has spent the better part of the past decade learning how to recruit again. But it is still far from effective in making the case for federal careers, especially given its reputation for the bureaucratic meddling that came from Hamilton's tight chains of command and execution in detail. No wonder that young Americans believe government is a great place to work for almost anyone but themselves.[20]

There is a deep inventory of research on how the federal government became a destination of last resort for so many young Americans already committed to public service. Some scholars argue that the federal government has "branded" its careers as the best option for security cravers;[21] others believe that the federal recruiting system has failed to keep pace with the changing labor supply identified above;[22] others believe that federal careers carry the cumulative imprint of "bureaucrat bashing" on the campaign trail;[23] and still others write of the impact of ambiguous goals, poorly designed performance measures, and the overall failure to improve communication.[24]

However, the ultimate culprit may be the federal government itself. Facing a rapidly changing labor supply, the federal government has been slow to develop the kind of organizations that provide the meaningful work and chance to make a difference so many talented young Americans want. As Donald P. Moynihan and Sanjay K. Pandey conclude, the longer employees stay in government, the lower their public-service motivation, in part because of red tape, hierarchy, and failed reforms.[25] Although their research focused on state, not federal, employees, the results are troubling nonetheless.

The longer employees stay, the more likely they are to experience downsizing. As Mary Ann Feldman argues, two decades of downsizing have severed the psychological link between loyalty and employee trust, making "downsizing" itself the "most feared word in the contemporary quest for economic security."[26] According to Feldman, government downsizing has reduced employee trust, morale, and commitment: "In addition, downsizing strategies have diminished the public service ethic based on the altruistic values of civic duty, social justice, and compassion."[27] The findings are particularly ironic given Jefferson's dual commitment to reducing federal employment and promoting civic duty among the employees who remained.

Once past these systemic problems, federal recruiting tactics are also to blame for the failure to convert demand into success. It is a point well made by Cappelli in summarizing the challenge of the future: "Employers may well face new and more difficult challenges in recruiting and hiring than previous generations faced. But the challenges have to do with changes in the employment relationship that increase retention problems, not a shortfall of workers caused by demographic changes. And the solutions are not public policy interventions designed to raise the overall supply of labor in the economy. Instead, they focus back on employers and their own human resource strategies."[28]

These and other threats to public-service motivation have not gone unnoticed in the federal government, which has adopted a number of changes in how it recruits new employees. As Carolyn Ban writes, the federal government has mostly abandoned the highly centralized, one-size-fits-all recruitment process that once forced every employee through a single funnel.[29] And federal organizations now have much greater freedom to post their own jobs, make quick hiring decisions, and put employees on the payroll without exhaustive reviews.

Yet, even acknowledging this progress, the motivation to accept a federal job appears to be most affected by the reputation and reality of actually working for the federal service. It is not enough to enhance the invitation to service; the service itself must be inviting as well.[30] Women and people of color are still not advancing fast enough, meaningful work is still hard to find in sclerotic organizations, and new federal programs for loan forgiveness and recruitment rarely receive adequate funding.

Who Wants a Federal Career?

The key question for the rest of this chapter is not whether young Americans are interested in the federal service—there is plenty of evidence that many give very serious consideration to government careers. Rather, the question is whether the federal government is well configured to handle the changing supply of potential recruits. Simply put, do the *right* young Americans want a federal job?

At least according to my surveys of young Americans, the answer is no. Acknowledging that many people say one thing about their preferences for work, then make entirely different decisions,[31] the following pages focus on the results of three sets of surveys. The first involves college seniors I interviewed in 2002 and 2003; the second involves graduates of the nation's top public-service graduate schools; and the third involves Presidential Management Fellows who entered the federal government through its most prestigious recruitment program.

Because the surveys of college seniors and actual employees are not linked, there is no way to tell whether preferences translate into actual decisions. But assuming that preferences reveal insights about who wants a federal career, the federal service is clearly struggling to make its case to potential and actual recruits. The federal service comes in last in almost every indicator, from the motivation to make a difference to organizational resources.

College Seniors

The following discussion is based on my surveys of 1,015 randomly selected college seniors interviewed in 2002 and 1,002 randomly selected seniors interviewed in 2003. Although these surveys are neither the first made of college seniors nor the most recent, they involved much larger sample sizes than past surveys, longer survey questionnaires, and explicit comparisons of nonprofit, business, and federal careers. And they produced a simple finding: in a sentence, college seniors are not saying "show me the money," but "show me the job." At least according to my 2002 and 2003 surveys, federal jobs have not been showing well lately.[32]

Considerations. The 2002 survey asked three specific questions about the goals and expectations that college seniors bring to the job search:

- Asked first what factors would influence their decision about where to work after graduation, 84 percent said the opportunity to do interesting work was a very important consideration, followed by the opportunity to help people at 70 percent, the opportunity to learn new skills at 66 percent, benefits at 63 percent, the opportunity to do challenging work tied with job security at 62 percent, the opportunity for advancement at 60 percent, the opportunity to repay college loans at 49 percent, public respect at 49 percent, and pay at just 32 percent.

- Asked next how much thought they had given to specific jobs, 31 percent said they had given very serious consideration to a job in business, 20 percent to a job in state or local government, 18 percent to a job in a nonprofit organization, and 13 percent to a job in the federal government.

- Asked last about what they wanted from a job, 78 percent said their most important expectation was to be treated as a professional, 68 percent said they wanted meaningful work, 67 percent said they wanted training and new skills, 60 percent said they wanted challenging work, 47 percent said they wanted to participate in decisions that affect the way work is performed, 43 percent said they wanted to be recognized and rewarded for high performance and productivity, and 21 percent said they wanted to be promoted quickly.

Despite these shared priorities, Tables 5.1 and 5.2 suggest that seniors saw at least some distinctions among taking a nonprofit, business, and federal job. Compared to seniors who were very interested in business and federal jobs, seniors who were very serious about working for a nonprofit put more emphasis on the opportunity to help people as a very important consideration in their decision about where to work. They also placed much less emphasis on pay and the opportunity to be promoted quickly. In contrast, seniors who were very serious about working for a business or the federal government put a greater emphasis on pay and benefits as a very important consideration in their decision about where to work. They also had higher expectations about being recognized for high performance.

Destinations. These findings were confirmed in my 2003 survey, which asked about the relative strengths of nonprofits, businesses that perform work for the federal government under contracts and grants, and the federal government itself.[33]

The survey started with a simple question about the definition of public service—the starting point for imagining potential public service careers. To the extent it is defined as a way to make a living, for example, seniors might favor business and the federal government over nonprofits; to the extent it is defined as helping people, they might favor nonprofits over business and the federal government.

At least according to the 2003 survey, seniors view service through a nonprofit lens. Asked what the words "public service" meant to them, the college seniors gave three broad definitions:

- 36 percent focused outwardly on helping others, using terms such as "doing things for the public," "helping everyone in the community," "helping the less fortunate," "working for the good of society," or "helping people."

- 30 percent focused inwardly on their own obligations, using terms such as "giving back to your community," "doing things that help the community," or "being a contributing member of society."

Table 5.1 Job goals and destinations, college seniors 2002

Question: How important is each of the following in your decision about where to work after you graduate? Is the (insert) a very important consideration, somewhat important, not too important, or not a consideration at all in your decision about where to work?

Very important considerations in considering a job	Percentage who were very serious about working for a nonprofit	Percentage who were very serious about working for a business	Percentage who were very serious about working for the federal government
Opportunity to do interesting work	91	84	86
Opportunity to help people	84	57	69
Opportunity to learn new skills	67	68	61
Benefits	59	69	59
Opportunity to do challenging work	65	64	67
Job security	50	62	63
Opportunity for advancement	46	77	71
Opportunity to repay college loans	50	47	46
Public respect	48	39	44
Pay	27	43	40

N=1,015 college seniors.

Table 5.2 Job expectations and destinations, college seniors 2002

Question: People have different job expectations. To what extent do you expect to (insert)—to a great extent, a moderate extent, not too much, or not at all?

Job expectations expressed to a great extent	Percentage who were very serious about working for a nonprofit	Percentage who were very serious about working for a business	Percentage who were very serious about working for the federal government
Be treated as a professional	69	83	83
Be given meaningful work	72	62	66
Receive training and acquire new skills	64	66	69
Be assigned challenging work	61	59	68
Participate in decisions that affect the way work is performed	46	51	48
Be recognized and rewarded for high performance and productivity	35	52	53
Be promoted quickly	20	33	28

N=1,015 college seniors.

- 15 percent focused inwardly on their reactions to service, using terms such as "doing things for the community and not expecting to get anything back except that warm feeling," and "doing your part."

At least for these seniors, the words "public service" spark thoughts of the kind of one-to-one work that is often found in nonprofit agencies, not in the federal government. Indeed, when asked to rate specific careers, 58 percent of these seniors said working for a nonprofit agency was a form of public service, compared with 28 percent who said the same about working for government, and 23 percent who said the same about working for a business that works for government.

Considerations Again. Given these definitions, it is no surprise that seniors might rate career destinations differently. As Table 5.3 shows, nonprofits were viewed as the best at helping people, making a difference, and gaining the respect of family and friends; government was seen as most attractive for someone who wanted good benefits and the chance to serve the country; and businesses that contract with government were seen as the preference for someone who wanted the best salary. As Table 5.4 shows, my respondents also viewed a job in government as a long-term commitment.

Nor is it a surprise that these seniors preferred nonprofits as a destination for public service. Among the 26 percent who had very seriously considered a public service job, 42 percent said their first preference would be a nonprofit, 19 percent said the same about state and local government, 14 percent said the federal government, and 13 percent said a business that works for government.

The lack of interest in the federal service is not a matter of demographics—men and women, younger students and older, those with large amounts of debt and no debt at all had a much stronger preference for nonprofits. Nor are the ratings explained by political ideology—18 percent of Republicans and 21 percent of Democrats said they wanted to work for the federal government if they took a public-service job, compared with 22 percent of liberals and 16 percent of conservatives. Rather, the preferences appear to reflect a persistent view of government as unable to provide the kind of mission-driven jobs these seniors wanted.

It is no surprise, therefore, that these preferences were closely related to what the seniors wanted in a job. As with the 2002 survey, these 2003 seniors put the opportunity to help people, learn new skills, have challenging work, benefits, and job security at the top of their lists of

Table 5.3 Comparing rewards, college seniors, 2003

Question: Thinking of public service jobs you might hold in government, nonprofits, or businesses that provide products or services to government, do you think (insert) would be better in government, nonprofits, or businesses that provide products and services to government?

Reward	Percentage of college seniors who said reward would be better in a nonprofit	Percentage of college seniors who said reward would be better in a business working for government under a contract or grant	Percentage of college seniors who said reward would be better in the federal government
Chance to help people	66	8	22
Ability to make a difference	66	7	22
Respect of family and friends	42	15	32
Benefits	2	59	37
Pay	1	59	37
Chance to serve your country	22	8	66

N = 1,002 college seniors.

Table 5.4 Time on the job and destinations, college seniors, 2003

Question: If you take a job in public service, how long do you think you'll stay in the job— 1–2 years, 3–5 years, 6–10 years, more than 10 years?

Length of time	Percentage whose first preference was working for a nonprofit	Percentage whose first preference was working for a business that works for government	Percentage whose first preference was working for the federal government
1–2 years	23	17	11
3–5 years	32	35	24
6–10 years	13	14	16
More than 10 years	28	28	44

N = 1,002 college seniors.

very important considerations, and opportunity to repay college loans and pay at the very bottom.

Interestingly, students with high levels of debt were no more interested in salary than students without any debt at all. Rather, they were interested in jobs that provided the opportunity to repay college loans: 67 percent of students with more than $20,000 in debt said repaying college loans was a very important consideration in their decision about where to work after graduation, compared to just 11 percent who had no debt at all. (One can only wonder why seniors with no debt would worry at all—they may have simply associated loan repayment as part of a generally good compensation package.)

As Table 5.5 shows, these seniors clearly understood that nonprofit, business, and federal jobs offered different rewards. Among students who preferred a nonprofit job, the opportunity to do interesting work was rated as the most important consideration in their career decision, followed by the opportunity to help people, learn new skills, benefits, and the opportunity to do challenging work, while pay was rated last.

Confusions. Whatever the destination, these seniors were generally confused about how to find work with government, nonprofits, or contractors. Just 44 percent of the 2003 respondents said they knew a great deal or a fair amount about finding a job in either government or a nonprofit, and even fewer, 30 percent, said they knew a great deal or a fair amount about finding work for a contractor.

What they did know, or at least believe, is that finding a job in government would be the most difficult of all: 78 percent described the

Table 5.5 Jobs and considerations, 2003

Question: How important is each of the following in your decision about where to work after you graduate? Is the (insert) a very important consideration, somewhat important, not too important, or not a consideration at all in your decision about where to work?

Very important considerations in considering a job	Percentage whose first preference was working for a nonprofit	Percentage whose first preference was working for a business that works for government	Percentage whose first preference was working for the federal government
Opportunity to do interesting work	91	84	86
Opportunity to help people	84	57	69
Opportunity to learn new skills	67	68	61
Benefits	59	69	59
Opportunity to do challenging work	65	64	67
Job security	50	62	63
Opportunity for advancement	46	77	71
Opportunity to repay college loans	50	47	46
Public respect	48	39	44
Pay	27	43	40

N=1,002 college seniors.

general government hiring process as slow and 63 percent as confusing, even as they viewed nonprofits and businesses that work for government as relatively fast and simple. Not surprisingly, 62 percent of these seniors said that finding a nonprofit job would be easy, compared with just 34 percent who said the same about finding a job with a business that works for government under a contract or grant, and 28 percent who said the same about finding a federal job.

It is particularly interesting to note that students are much more willing to give businesses that work for government the benefit of the doubt on the hiring process, while reserving their greatest scorn for government. Perhaps they simply assume that businesses that work for government will have at least some of the attributes commonly associated with making profits, meaning speed and simplicity. Or perhaps they simply assume that all government hiring will be bad. Even seniors who said they preferred a job in government were hardly enthusiastic about the hiring process: only 40 percent described it as simple, and only 16 percent described it as fast. However, 83 percent described it as fair.

These findings suggest that all public-service organizations should be very careful about drafting a "one-size-fits-all" message to potential employees. Students do not value all things equally—not surprisingly, for example, two-thirds of students with college loans put a much higher value on repaying those loans than students with no debt at all. Although all students value the nature of the job equally, they are unlikely to react with equal passion toward messages that emphasize pay, security, and benefits. Moreover, I believe public-service organizations should also be careful about building a message that emphasizes the benefits of pay, promotion, and tenure—they should be very careful about what they wish for. If they ask for security-seekers, that is what they will likely get.

The survey also suggests the importance of internships and voluntary service as a way to encourage interest, whatever the destination. More than half of the seniors had at least some past contact with nonprofits through internships, no doubt because of on-campus volunteer programs or high-school service learning, compared to just 8 percent who had had experience with the federal government, 10 percent with contractors, and 11 percent with either state or local government.

- 61 percent of the seniors said the word "valued" described the jobs they saw in the nonprofits very well, compared to 43 percent in government and contractors.

- 48 percent and 50 percent said the word "challenging" described the jobs they saw in nonprofits and contractors very well, compared to 38 percent in government.

- 13 percent said the word "frustrating" described the jobs they saw with contractors, compared to 24 percent each in nonprofits and government.

In other words, students who spent time in the nonprofit sector came away feeling the jobs were more valued, challenging, but frustrating than students in the other sectors. Students who spent time with contractors came away feeling that the jobs were challenging and less frustrating, but not as valued. And students who spent time in government came away feeling that the jobs were only more frustrating.

Predicting interest. Among all seniors, further statistical analysis suggests that there are nine significant predictors of interest in a federal government career:

1. Knowledge about finding a job in the federal government— seniors who said they knew a great deal about finding a job in government were more likely to prefer working for government.

2. Lack of knowledge about nonprofits—the less seniors knew about nonprofit jobs, the more likely they were to prefer the federal service.

3. Government benefits—seniors who said the federal government was better at providing benefits were more likely to prefer federal jobs.

4. Advancement—seniors who said the federal government was better at providing opportunities for advancement were more likely to prefer federal jobs.

5. Helping people—seniors who said the federal government was better at helping people were more likely to prefer federal jobs.

6. Serving the country—seniors who said that serving their country was a very important consideration in a job were more likely to prefer the federal government.

7. Volunteering in government—seniors who spent at least some time working for the federal government as an intern or volunteer were more likely to prefer federal jobs.

8. Lack of knowledge about how to find a job in businesses that work for government—the less seniors knew about finding a job in business, the more they preferred a federal job.

9. Respect of family and friends—the more seniors felt a federal job would earn the respect of family and friends, the more they preferred a federal job.[34]

This advanced analysis provides an outline for rebuilding the federal service to some extent. Although recruiters can hardly promote ignorance of the alternatives as a comparative advantage for the federal service, they can emphasize the chance to help people, serve the country, and earn the respect of family and friends. And they can promote internships and other forms of early contact.

Public-Service Graduates

As already noted, it is one thing to ask seniors about their preferences, and quite another to ask actual federal employees about their experiences. That is why I surveyed graduates of the top professional schools of public service such as Harvard University's John F. Kennedy School of Government, New York University's Robert F. Wagner Graduate School of Public Service, and Syracuse University's Maxwell School of Citizenship and Public Affairs. By asking these graduates where they went and why they stayed or left, one can see the actual impacts of federal service on the kind of talent the federal service should seek.[35] Unfortunately, graduates who took jobs in the federal government were harshly critical of the sector and appeared far less willing to stay.

According to my survey of 1,000 alumni from the classes of 1973–74, 1978–79, 1983, 1988, and 1993, government slowly lost its standing as a preferred starting point after graduation.[36] The percentage of graduates who started their careers in a federal job dropped from 76 percent in the class of 1973–74, which was combined to create a larger sample size, to 49 percent in 1993, while the percentage that started their careers in a nonprofit doubled from 12 percent in 1973–74 to 25 percent in 1993, and the percentage that started in a business doubled from 11 percent to 25 percent.

The federal government also lost the largest percentage of employees drawn from the classes I studied. Fifty-nine percent of the graduates who started in the federal government eventually left government later in their career, compared with just 38 percent of graduates who started in a business and 31 percent who started in a nonprofit organization.

Table 5.6 First and current jobs by class, public service professionals, classes of 1973/74–93

Questions: (1) Thinking about (the first/next) place you worked after your master's program was/is your employer—government, a private company, or a nonprofit group? (2) And what about your current place of work? Is it in government, a private company, or a nonprofit group?

Class of graduates

Job location	Percentage of class of 1973/74		Percentage of class of 1978/79		Percentage of class of 1983		Percentage of class of 1988		Percentage of class of 1993	
	First job vs. current job		First job vs. current job		First job vs. current job		First job vs. current job		First job vs. current job	
Government	76	50	62	46	68	51	55	39	49	41
Business	11	28	21	38	21	30	21	32	23	26
Nonprofit	12	15	15	12	12	15	23	25	25	28

N=200 for 1973/74; N=231 for 1978/79; N=171 for 1983; N=192 for 1988; N=196 for 1993.

Moreover, as Table 5.6 shows, most graduates who left government never came back, compared with at least small percentages of graduates who left nonprofits and business.

Asked about the most important consideration for staying in their current job, graduates across the sectors generally agreed on the opportunity for advancement, chance to make a difference, job security, and public respect, but federal employees were somewhat more likely to say they were most concerned about salary. Although graduates in all sectors were generally satisfied with their work, more recent graduates were less satisfied than their peers, and expressed stronger agreement with the proposition that it is not wise to spend too much time in any one sector.

Whether they stayed put or switched in from another sector, graduates who were in federal jobs at the time of the survey were less trusting of their own organization. Just 20 percent of federal employees said they trusted their organization just about always, compared with 37 percent who were working in a business and 45 percent who were working in a nonprofit. Although these graduates were more trusting toward the federal government in general, somewhat more likely to describe their jobs as public service, and more satisfied with their current work than their nonfederal peers, they were the least likely to say they wanted their son or daughter to pursue a career in public service.

Regardless of their graduating year, these former students saw different strengths in each sector. As with college seniors, these graduates consistently ranked nonprofits as the best at helping people, the federal government as the best at representing the public interest, and nonprofits as the best at spending money wisely. They also had somewhat different views of what matters most in their day-to-day work. Graduates working in the federal government were the most likely to emphasize salary, job security, and the chance to affect national issues as very important considerations. As Table 5.7 shows, 68 percent of the graduates who went federal said affecting national issues was very important to them, compared to 57 percent of graduates in nonprofit jobs, and just 38 percent in business jobs.

According to an informal survey of leading graduate schools, the preference for nonprofit and business jobs has continued since 1998. In 2005, for example, roughly a third of the Kennedy School's masters of public policy students started their careers in a business, another quarter started in a nonprofit, a quarter started in the federal government, and the rest split between state, local, and international government organizations.

Table 5.7 Confidence in sectors by current job, public service professionals, classes of 1973/74 vs. 1988 and 1993

Question: More specifically, who does the best job of (insert)—government, private contractors, or nonprofit organizations?

	Type of current job					
	Government		Business		Nonprofit	
Task	Percentage of 1973/74 and 1978/79 classes combined	Percentage of 1988 and 1993 classes combined	Percentage of 1973/74 and 1978/79 classes combined	Percentage of 1988 and 1993 classes combined	Percentage of 1973/74 and 1978/79 classes combined	Percentage of 1988 and 1993 classes combined
Spending money wisely						
Government	26	18	13	4	4	5
Business	25	35	53	59	48	33
Nonprofit organizations	30	32	24	30	42	52
Representing the public interest						
Government	73	68	52	49	46	36
Business	6	1	7	12	4	3
Nonprofit organizations	10	20	26	30	42	47
Helping people						
Government	43	26	25	16	14	18
Business	4	4	10	11	10	11
Nonprofit organizations	42	46	54	71	58	70

N=378 for the classes of 1973/74 and 1978/79 combined; N=349 for the classes of 1988 and 1993 combined.

Syracuse's Maxwell School showed a similar pattern, as did Indiana's School of Public and Environmental Affairs, the University of Minnesota's Hubert H. Humphrey Institute of Public Affairs, and the University of Texas's Lyndon B. Johnson School of Public Affairs.

Presidential Management Fellows

Concerns about the nature of government jobs were echoed in my survey of a subsample of 107 randomly selected Presidential Management Fellows who were part of my 2001 survey of 1,051 federal employees.[37] Under the Fellows program, created by executive order in 1977, professional-school graduates are recruited to government at a higher level than usual, and given the option to enter government as full-time employees at an even higher level. They are the very best and brightest the federal government can recruit, and demonstrate the availability of a highly motivated federal labor supply.

According to the 2001 survey, these talented young employees have come to believe the federal service lacks the capacity to fully execute the laws. Returning to Hamilton's five attributes of vigor and expedition in the federal service, they see too little motivation to make a difference, a lack of jobs that allow execution, persistent shortages of the resources they need to succeed, few rewards for a job well done and almost no discipline for one done poorly, and little respect from the public they serve.

On Hamilton's first attribute, full exertion to making a difference, the Fellows clearly came to work for what I believe are the right reasons. They were by far the most likely of all federal employees to say that they had taken their job in government for the opportunity to help the public (92 percent), do something worthwhile (90 percent), make a difference (81 percent), and out of pride in the organization (74 percent)—not the pay, benefits, and security. The Fellows were also the least likely to say they came to work each day for the compensation, and the most likely to emphasize the public good.

On Hamilton's second attribute, work that matters, the Fellows were less positive than other federal employees about their jobs. As Table 5.8 shows, they were consistently the least likely to say that other people who worked with them were competitive with other employees, open to new ideas, and concerned about achieving the organization's mission. Although some discount such opinions as an expression of hubris by a privileged group of employees, these low ratings must have some effect on retention. To the extent Fellows are known by the company they think they keep, they are quite critical, indeed.

Table 5.8 Measures of job quality, Presidential Management Fellows, 2001

Question: To what extent are the people you work with (insert)—to a great extent, somewhat, not too much or not at all?

Measure	Percentage of General Schedule nonsupervisors who answered to a great extent	Percentage of General Schedule supervisors who answered to a great extent	Percentage of Senior Executive Service members who answered to a great extent	Percentage of Presidential Management Fellows who answered to a great extent
Competitive with other employees	22	32	36	13
Open to new ideas	32	41	55	29
Willing to help other employees learn new skills	51	55	68	52
Concerned about achieving your organization's mission	51	66	68	42

N = 554 General Schedule nonsupervisors, 213 General Schedule supervisors, 177 members of the Senior Executive Service, and 107 Presidential Management Fellows.

The Fellows were by far the most likely to describe the hiring process as slow (94 percent) and confusing (85 percent); they were often the harshest critics of their coworkers, and they saw enormous difficulties attracting and retaining talented employees at their levels of the organization. More than a third said their organization did a poor job attracting top candidates, and almost half said their organization did a poor job retaining them.

They were also the most critical about access to challenging work. Only 34 percent said they were always given the chance to do the things they did best, only 29 percent said their colleagues were very open to new ideas, and just 10 percent said their organization gave a great deal of encouragement to take risks. Although they were generally satisfied with the opportunity to advance and develop new skills, they were the least satisfied with public respect for the work they were doing, and among the least satisfied with the opportunity to accomplish something worthwhile.

On Hamilton's third attribute, adequate resources, the Fellows were intensely dissatisfied. Only 18 percent said their organization always provided the information needed to do its job well, only 16 percent said the same about access to technology, 10 percent said the same about training, and just 7 percent said there were enough employees to do the job. All these percentages were far lower than the corresponding responses of the other employees interviewed. The Fellows were also the most troubled by the degree of competence of employees at all levels of their hierarchies, and less likely to believe their organization had been reinvented or reformed over the past five years.

On Hamilton's fourth attribute, rewards and discipline, the Fellows were not more likely to see a higher percentage of poor performance in their midst, but were the most critical of the disciplinary process. Eighty percent said their organization did a poor job disciplining poor performers, compared to just 56 percent of senior executives; 56 percent of the Fellows said the poor performance was because their organization simply did not ask enough of its employees. And the Fellows were consistently the most critical of their organization's performance in spending money wisely, being fair in its decisions, and helping people.

And on Hamilton's fifth attribute, respect for the public served, the Fellows were less likely than other federal employees to believe that their own organizations deserved respect. As Table 5.9 suggests, they not only were the least trusting that their own organizations would do

Table 5.9 Federal employee ratings of organizational performance, 2001

Question: And how good a job does your organization do (insert)—a very good, somewhat good, not too good, or not at all good job?

Task	Percentage of General Schedule nonsupervisors who answered the federal government was very good at:	Percentage of General Schedule supervisors who answered the federal government was very good at:	Percentage of Senior Executive Service members who answered the federal government was very good at:	Percentage of Presidential Management Fellows who answered the federal government was very good at:
Spending money wisely	35	50	24	14
Being fair in decisions	42	27	60	20
Helping people	57	50	52	40

N = 554 General Schedule nonsupervisors, 213 General Schedule supervisors, 177 members of the Senior Executive Service, and 107 Presidential Management Fellows.

the right thing, they were also the least trusting about their organization's ability to spend money wisely, be fair in decisions, and help people. Although they were the proudest to tell their friends and neighbors where they worked, they were the least likely of all federal employees to say that the words "innovative," "helpful," "trusted," and "fair" described their own organization very well. Whereas 54 percent of senior executives said the word "helpful" described their organization very well, for example, just 36 percent of the Fellows agreed.

These are not the only measures of dissatisfaction among the Fellows, however. According to my tracking survey of another 95 randomly selected Fellows drawn from a separate survey of the members of the class of 2001, there is plenty of cause for concern about the development of the federal government's future leaders.[38] Although some indicators improved over time, almost every indicator of job satisfaction—quality of work, access to resources, respect for their peers, and trust in their own organizations—fell over the two years of their fellowships, which should have been a positive, not negative introduction to the federal government.

Satisfaction with salary did go up over these first two years in government, for example, but satisfaction with the opportunity to do challenging work fell. The freedom to work independently on projects did go up, too, but the sense that the job met expectations fell. Moreover, the longer the Fellows stayed, the less trusting they became. Whereas 38 percent said they trusted their organizations just about always in the fall of their first year, only 19 percent agreed two years later. And whereas 23 percent rated the morale of their agency as very high when they arrived, just 11 percent felt the same two years later.

Not surprisingly, more than half said they would limit their time in government. Asked why they intended to leave, 55 percent cited personal reasons, while 52 percent said there were too few opportunities to develop new skills, 42 percent said there were too few opportunities to do challenging work, and 40 percent said there were too few opportunities to accomplish something worthwhile. Asked which reason was most important to their future, the number one answer was too few opportunities to accomplish something worthwhile.

To the extent these Fellows were selected to lead the future federal workforce, the federal government is in deep trouble. Too many of these Fellows were already unsure of their future, and already angry toward their organizations. The federal government is having no trouble getting the very best and brightest to apply and accept these prestigious fellowships, but is facing serious challenges holding onto them over time.

Relative Distrust

It is tempting to blame young Americans for the declining interest in federal careers. After all, they are the ones who have come to view the hiring process as slow and confusing, federal jobs as less than challenging, and public service as more like volunteering than traditional work. They are also the ones who have fashioned the new public service, switching jobs and sectors almost at will in search of challenging work, if not also in search of novelty and higher salaries.

The question, therefore, is how so many college seniors came to hold such negative opinions about federal careers. The answer may be their parents, who teach their children about government and, in turn, the campaigners and leaders who consistently attack government as a source of fraud, waste, and abuse. Because they exert so much influence over their children's career decisions, their view of the federal government matters greatly to the final choice.

Unfortunately, it is difficult to know what parents think of government beyond general measures of trust. These surveys show a simple trend, albeit one interrupted in the early 1980s: General trust in government remains low, and attitudes toward government jobs are not just skeptical, but harshly critical. The vast majority of Americans believe that federal employees take their jobs for the pay, benefits, and security. Young Americans share the view.

Yet, young Americans do not believe everything their parents say. According to a May 2002 survey of 986 adults conducted on my behalf young Americans held different attitudes than older Americans about government trust generally.[39]

On trust in government generally, for example, 18–24-year-olds were more likely than other age groups to say that the federal government does an excellent or good job running its programs and services. Fifty-six percent of 18–24-year-olds gave the federal government an excellent or good rating, compared to just 35 percent of Americans over age 65. These young Americans were also more favorable toward government workers. Although just 19 percent said they were very favorable, another 65 percent said they were at least somewhat favorable, compared with just 12 percent and 54 percent respectively among Americans over age 65.

Young Americans also gave federal employees a greater benefit of the doubt than other age groups. Asked to imagine that they had a son or daughter with job offers from the federal government or a private business, they were somewhat more likely to recommend a job in government. Whereas 35 percent of 18–24-year-olds recommended the federal government, only 31 percent of Americans over age 65 did so.

Young Americans were also more likely to say that federal employees took their jobs in government for the chance to help people, make a difference, and do something worthwhile. Thus, 32 percent said federal employees took their jobs for the chance to help the public, compared to just 10 percent of Americans over age 65; 38 percent said federal employees took their jobs for the chance to make a difference, compared to just 20 percent of Americans over age 65; and 30 percent said federal employees took their jobs because they want to do something worthwhile, compared to 19 percent of Americans over age 65.

At the same time, young Americans were just as likely as older Americans to agree that the federal government controls too much of their lives, that most elected officials are not trustworthy, and that the federal government is too powerful, all of which may reflect their coming of age during Bill Clinton's impeachment trial. Although they were more likely than their elders to say that government is really run for the benefit of all the people, the endorsement was not stunning. Moreover, they were just as likely as other age groups to say that criticism of the federal government is justified and equally likely to say that the bigger problem in government is that it runs its programs inefficiently, not that it has the wrong priorities.

These findings hardly create a ringing endorsement for federal employment. Younger Americans may be more forgiving of the federal government, but are hardly overwhelmingly positive. To the extent these attitudes affect career decisions, the federal government faces an obvious challenge in convincing potential recruits that it can be trusted.

Americans have not always been so mistrustful of their government, however. To the contrary, there have been two moments in recent history when trust has rebounded, albeit only to fall back. The first rise began in the early 1980s as the percentage of Americans who believed that the federal government in Washington could be trusted all or most of the time inched up from 25 percent to 44 percent.[40]

The reason for the rise is not entirely clear. As Arthur Miller and Stephen A. Borrelli later suggested, the jump in trust was particularly ironic because the Reagan administration was so antigovernment. In a sense, the president restored confidence in government through the harshness of his rhetoric. The more he talked about fraud, waste, and abuse, the more the public seemed to believe he was doing something about it.

In addition, Reagan was a particularly effective president on everything from tax cuts to foreign policy.[41] Jack Citrin and Donald Philip Green echoed the findings: "Somewhat paradoxically, the long legacy of failure that preceded his election provided Reagan with an advantage in promoting approval of his performance . . . Moreover, chronic failure can lower expectations about what constitutes success."[42]

The second rise in trust began in the weeks and months following 9/11, as confidence in virtually every civic institution jumped. According to surveys conducted by Princeton Survey Research on my behalf in July and October 2001 and May 2002, the percentage of Americans who trusted the federal government to do what is right always or most of the time went up by 28 points to 57 percent after 9/11, but fell by 17 points to 40 percent in the six months after, and another 8 percentage points to 32 percent by late 2006.[43]

Most importantly for recruiting, 9/11 did not change the percentage of Americans that said federal employees were motivated primarily by job security, salary and benefits, and having a secure paycheck. Asked in July 2001 what influences government employees most, 70 percent of Americans said the job security, not helping the public, 68 percent said the salary and benefits, not the chance to make a difference, and 68 percent said having a secure paycheck, not doing something worthwhile.

There is some hope here that trust can rebound, but the post-9/11 rebound in trust is so unusual, even unique, that the federal government cannot pretend that a turnaround is near, especially not with the eventual collapse of trust in the years following the tragedy. The answer is not to bet on increased trust, but to build the kind of careers that will attract talented young Americans even under the most distressing conditions. Public confidence is nice to have, but federal employees must learn to live without it.

Conclusion

Public distrust is only one of many factors that might influence the decision to consider, let alone accept, a federal job. Indeed, one can easily argue that it is merely another symptom of a general disquiet with the federal government as a destination for talented young Americans. The federal government is simply not prepared for the new labor supply—it is struggling to remove the ceilings that limit advancement for women and people of color, provide meaningful work, and reduce the financial divide through loan forgiveness and other bonus programs.

Others might argue that the media are to blame for the lack of enthusiasm. After all, the media appear to give more coverage to government's disappointments than its achievements, a point well made by the Center for Excellence in Government in its ongoing tracking studies of television content.[44]

However, my ongoing research on media coverage of highly visible events such as the Space Shuttle Challenger explosion and the 9/11 attacks suggests that the media covers government's successes as the product of heroism, and government's failures as the product of cavalier misbehavior and ordinary incompetence. Even successes such as the return to space following the Challenger accident often become another opportunity for reviving coverage of past failures. Thus, the return to space featured a recurring story line: not about how the National Aeronautics and Space Administration had succeeded, but about how it had not failed again.

Others might argue that at least part of the declining interest in federal careers is due to presidential rhetoric that echoes Jefferson's incessant attacks on federal fraud, waste, and abuse. Although constant attacks on government no doubt fuel general public distrust, it is quite possible that Bill Clinton's endorsement of the redemptive value of Americorps and George W. Bush's promotion of faith-based action encouraged at least some potential federal employees to consider the nonprofit sector as a destination of choice, while the constant drumbeat of support for contracting out and privatization elevated interest in and recruiting by the private contractors, who often provide the same kind of meaningful work often found in federal, state, and local government.

However, one need not look far beyond the halls of government for a significant cause of the disaffection. The more young Americans look at federal government careers, whether as potential recruits or new Presidential Management Fellows, the more they rightly ask whether the federal government is the kind of employer that honors their basic interest in making a difference.

Once again, Jefferson's view of the federal service as a noble calling deserves highlighting. Jefferson may have done more than his share to launch a spoils system and fuel the war on wasteful government, but he always believed in the call of duty. Although he understood that government could not be a destination for the destitute, he clearly felt that pay, benefits, and security were poor substitutes for public-service motivation. He also viewed the growing bureaucracy as a detriment to effectiveness, and almost certainly would have appreciated its impact on the willingness to serve.

In a very real sense, the federal government's reputation as a cavalier employer is well signaled in its recruitment process, its lack of consistent advertising of meaningful work, and the attitudes of federal employees themselves regarding the quality of their jobs and access to resources. The federal government may have earned its reputation as a destination of last resort the old-fashioned way, through disinvestment in the basic capacity of its organizations to provide the kind of work that talented young Americans want most. Until it confronts its own negligence, as well as its outright resistance to building meaningful careers, it is hard to imagine how it can reverse the reluctance to serve, let alone the reluctance to stay. And absent both, it cannot meet Hamilton's test of an energetic federal service.

CHAPTER SIX

Steadiness in Administration

The sixth characteristic of an energetic federal service is steadiness in administration. The federal service cannot faithfully execute the laws if it is constantly interrupted by the latest fad in management reform. Presidents may come and go, but the emphasis on improved performance *and* the approach to achieving it should remain constant.

Hamilton clearly believed in this steadiness, although almost all of his writing on steadiness in administration dealt with the executive's ability to pursue extensive and arduous enterprise to the point of completion. As he wrote in *Federalist No. 72*, executives had to be allowed to stay in office as long as necessary, even if that meant two, three, four, or more terms of office—hence, the accusations that he favored a monarchy: "To reverse and undo what has been done by a predecessor, is very often considered by a successor as the best proof he can give of his own capacity and desert . . . These considerations, and the influence of personal confidences and attachments, would be likely to induce every new President to promote a change of men to fill the subordinate stations; and these causes together could not fail to occasion a disgraceful and ruinous mutability in the administration of the government."[1]

Hamilton's defense of "re-eligibility of the executive" seemed to reach beyond the missions of government, however. As he also wrote in *Federalist No. 72,* steadiness was intimately related to the inclination to "secure to the government the wise advantage of permanency in a wise system of administration."[2]

Here Hamilton was addressing the issue of tenure in office, but he could just as easily have focused on the nature of constant administrative reform in unsettling the faithful execution of the laws. After all, how better to keep the federal service from doing its job than by changing the bureaucratic rules so frequently that the administrative state could never settle in? The threat is not too little reform, but too much.

The rest of this chapter will examine the contemporary history of government reform. It will ask where reform comes from, how it changes government, whether it actually works, and why it might reduce the ability to execute the laws. Even the most energetic federal service has limits. To the extent it spends time filling out the paperwork for the latest management fad, it loses energy for implementing all the laws.

An Inventory of Reform

Today's inventory of administrative reforms proves the point. The federal service has never faced so much pressure to alter its basic options, the major problem being that the resulting reforms have instructed government to move across a set of often contradictory philosophies that focus on Hamilton's vision of scientific management for running government and a watchful eye for overseeing it, and Jefferson's liberation management for running government, and the war on waste for cutting it.

These four philosophies, or tides, of government reform are embedded in contemporary efforts to improve performance. Some of these efforts are rooted in the notion that government should follow the "scientific" rules that govern its operation and organization. Others are rooted in the repeated wars on fraud, waste, and abuse that seek to cut costs, reduce vulnerabilities, and deter malfeasance. Still others seek a stronger watchful eye on government through greater transparency and public access to information. And others still seek to liberate government from what advocates describe as the needless rules that tie it in Lilliputian ropes that limit discretion.[3] If government is not getting better, it is not for a lack of trying.[4]

Indeed, at least part of the chaos reflects Jefferson's support for what he called adaptability in administration. Jefferson saw steadiness as the antithesis of adaptability. "Laws and institutions must go hand in hand with the progress of the human," he wrote a colleague. "As that becomes more developed, more enlightened, as new discoveries are made, new truths disclosed, and manners and opinions change with the change of circumstances, institutions must advance also, and keep pace with the times."[5] Whereas steadiness promised perseverance to grand goals, adaptability argued that each generation was a distinctive nation—it could bind itself, but not future generations.

Thinking back to the founding, Jefferson wrote that he knew of "no safe depositary of the ultimate powers of the society but the people themselves."[6] The people had to think for themselves. "Fix reason firmly in her seat, and call to her tribunal every fact, every opinion," he wrote. "Question with boldness even the existence of a God; because, if there be one, he must more approve of the homage of reason, than that of blindfolded fear."[7] Although mistakes were inevitable, they could be tempered by analysis, study, and the application of scientific methods.

Steadiness in administration not only prevented the exercise of reason, it created inertia and resistance. As Jefferson wrote Madison in 1820 of legislation to prohibit the removal of government officers, "The late mischievous law vacating every four years nearly all the executive officers of the government . . . saps the constitutional and salutary functions of the President, and introduces a principle of intrigue and corruption which will soon leaven the masses, not only of Senators, but of citizens. It is more baneful than the attempt which failed in the beginning of the government to make all officers irremovable but with consent of the Senate."[8]

At first glance, Jefferson appears to have been the victor in this debate. But, as this chapter will show, the acceleration of reform over the past few decades has been driven mostly by a nearly uniform rejection of stability, which was once deemed the greatest benefit of bureaucracy.

In recent years, however, stability has been recast as a barrier to performance. "The term *bureaucracy* has become equated with stodgy, hidebound, and inefficient operations," Laurence J. O'Toole, Jr., and Kenneth J. Meier write. "Much of the emphasis among recent proponents of good government has been on finding ways to encourage an escape from or a 'banishing' of bureaucracy—and a move toward alternative forms and processes."[9] At least in the present, stability has become a sign of weakness, not strength, and of complacency, not boldness.

Defining the Tides

Each of the tides makes perfect sense on its own, but has potentially destructive consequences for actual government performance—scientific rules tend to multiply with the thickening of government; wars on waste do generate savings and deter malfeasance to at least some extent; sunshine does create democratic accountability; and liberation gives managers greater authority to manage.

Moreover, when the reforms multiply in random order, they also create the sediment of bureaucratic confusion and distraction that weakens the federal government's ability to operate. They also weaken the implementation of reforms that might actually improve performance.

Philosophical Differences

The four reform philosophies convey very different views of the federal service, and very different implementation approaches. At least two reflect a generally trusting view of the federal service and the capability to execute, scientific management, and liberation management. The other two bear a more distrusting view toward the federal service and its propensity to overspend or hide mistakes.

In turn, two of the four reform philosophies reflect centralization of implementation, scientific management, and war on waste. And the other two use decentralization either inside or outside government to achieve impact, liberation management, and watchful eye. Table 6.1 shows the resulting blend of reform philosophies.

Each of these philosophies has produced major changes of direction in government. For example, the 1946 Classification Act reflected a very traditional vision of a highly specialized, centralized approach to recruiting federal employees; the 1978 Inspector General Act created a highly specialized, centralized approach to the war on waste; the 1994 Government Performance and Results Act tapped the decentralized, employee-empowerment model associated with liberation management; while the 1946 Administrative Procedure Act created a

Table 6.1 Comparing reform philosophies

	Trusting toward the federal service	Distrustful of the federal service
Centralized administration of reform	Scientific management	War on waste
Decentralized administration of reform	Liberation management	Watchful eye

watchful eye through public notice and comment on all government regulations.

As Stephen Skowronek shows, these reform philosophies date back to the late 1800s and the Progressive Era.[10] And they are featured repeatedly in Peri E. Arnold's list of major reform impulses during the 1900s.[11] They can even be found in the Constitution itself, which gives the president control over the officers of government (a bit of scientific management), requires annual audits of accounts (war on waste), mandates both congressional and presidential oversight of the state of the union (watchful eye), and hints of lessened regulation through an elaborate system of checks and balances (liberation management).

Many of these philosophies also reflect multiple attempts to address the same problems. Congress and the president have created dozens of departments and agencies to reconcile competing missions, as well as countless rules for governing the behavior of their employees. They have also tried to measure the results of government, starting with Johnson's Planning Programming Budgeting System, Ford's Management by Objectives, Carter's Zero-Base Budgeting, and Clinton's Government Performance and Results Act. They have attacked fraud, waste, and abuse through the Inspector General Act, which has been amended multiple times to expand both the number of inspectors general and their auditing and investigation authority. And they have tried to make government more transparent through the Administrative Procedure and Freedom of Information acts, not to mention the Government in the Sunshine Act.[12]

Finally, many of these reforms have been legislative "freight trains" that carried secondary and tertiary reforms into law with them. For example, the Clinton administration's "reinventing government" campaign carried elements of all four reform philosophies, including provisions to: (1) cut hundreds of existing programs to save money (war on waste), (2) empower federal employees by eliminating federal reporting requirements (liberation management), (3) reduce the federal payroll by 250,000 positions (war on waste), (4) give citizens more information on government performance (watchful eye), (5) create customer service standards for every agency (scientific management plus watchful eye), (6) measure program performance (scientific management), (7) reduce department and agency "control personnel" such as procurement, personnel, evaluation, and inspector general staffs (liberation management), (8) eliminate duplication and overlap by merging programs and organizations (scientific management plus war on waste), and (9) streamline the federal purchasing process.[13] As Lawrence E. Lynn, Jr., argues, reinventing government turned out to be more of a theme than a consistent reform ideal.[14]

The Pace of Reform

The question is not whether Congress and presidents have adopted eclectic, even contradictory, approaches to reform, but whether there are discernible patterns in reform over time and how these patterns might explain its success or failure. Although there are many ways to track the history of reform, whether through administrative regulations, blue-ribbon commissions, executive orders, budget circulars, job descriptions, organization charts, congressional committee hearings, articles in the *Public Administration Review,* and so forth, this chapter is based on a careful reading of major administrative reform statutes enacted between 1945 and 2002.

Not only are statutes easier to identify and track, they tend to be much more durable over time, in part by spawning offspring through amendments and expansions in future sessions of Congress. Without naively suggesting that they remain relevant or even enforceable in perpetuity, statutes do endure for a moment or two across the boundaries of administrations.

By my count, Congress enacted 177 major reform statutes between 1945 and 2002, of which 43 percent involved scientific management, 24 percent involved watchful eye, 18 percent involved the war on waste, and 15 percent involved liberation management.

However, unlike the expansion of the federal mission, which has slowed appreciably over time, management reform has accelerated. Congress passed 12 percent of the 177 statutes between 1945 and 1954, just 10 percent between 1955 and 1964, 20 percent between 1965 and 1974, 17 percent between 1975 and 1984, 22 percent between 1985 and 1994, and a final 19 percent between 1994 and 2002. Put another way, it took Congress twenty-eight years to enact the first third of the 177 statutes, but just sixteen years to produce the second third, and fourteen years to produce the final third.

Buried beneath these totals by decade, one can easily find spikes in activity, including a large number of statutes enacted in the wake of the two Commissions on the Organization of the Executive Branch of Government chaired by former president Herbert Hoover during the late 1940s and early 1950s, the Johnson administration's Great Society, Nixon's resignation, the end of the Reagan administration, and the

Clinton administration's "reinventing government" campaign. Together, these spikes account for just 10 percent of the years covered by my analysis, but more than a third of the 177 statutes.

Even as the pace of reform increased, the mix of reforms changed. Scientific management was the dominant philosophy of administrative reform from the 1930s to the 1960s, as the Hoover Commissions and Great Society spanned a long list of new organizations and rules; watchful eye reforms opened government to the sunshine after Nixon's departure; a war on waste accompanied Reagan's antigovernment rhetoric; and liberation management was the mark of the Clinton administration.[15]

Viewed over almost sixty years, 42 percent of all scientific management laws were passed between 1945 and 1964, compared with 10 percent of the watchful eye laws, 6 percent of the war on waste laws, and just 4 percent of the liberation management laws. Conversely, just 26 percent of all scientific management laws were passed between 1984 and 2002, compared with 47 percent of the watchful eye laws, 56 percent of the liberation management laws, and 57 percent of the war on waste laws.

Most of the early scientific management laws involved department and agency building. Congress and presidents built the basic structure of the modern administrative state during the first two decades of the post–World War II period, creating one department and agency after another to administer the New Deal and Great Society. Once created, the process reforms followed, whether in the form of new administrative systems, attacks on bureaucratic waste, or efforts to give managers and employees greater space to do their work. The pattern suggests a *Field of Dreams* effect—that is, if Congress and the president build it, process reforms will come.

Scientific management did not disappear entirely from the reform agenda, of course. Indeed, it supplied 33, or 28 percent, of the 1975–2002 reform statutes. But it clearly had to share the reform agenda with process reforms, including the long list of war on waste statutes enacted during the Reagan administration, the watchful eye reforms that increased dramatically after the Watergate scandal and President Nixon's resignation, and the liberation management reforms primarily introduced under the aegis of "reinventing government."

Yet, even as its percentage share fell over time, scientific management marched on, and came back forcefully with reorganizations at the Internal Revenue Service, Food and Drug Administration, and Amtrak, and the creation of the Transportation Security Administration and the Homeland Security Department. It also shaped a new generation of key officers in government, including chief financial officers, chief information officers, and chief human capital officers, as well as new rules governing the procurement process, financial management controls, and the precise measurement of government results.

Patterns across the Tides

Beyond the acceleration of reform over time and basic changes in the mix of reform philosophies, there are at least five other patterns in the mix and match of reform:

1. The percentage of reforms jumped dramatically after Watergate as Congress and the president became increasingly interested in *how* government worked. Of the 177 statutes, 35 percent were passed before Nixon's resignation from office, and 65 percent after. This Watergate effect was amplified by the Reagan administration's tax cuts. Without the resources to launch new spending programs, Congress and the president became increasingly interested in management reform as an alternative for which they could claim the credit; if they could not earn electoral support by establishing new programs, at least they could earn it for fixing government.

2. The percentage of reforms that originated with the president also dropped sharply after Watergate. Only 38 percent of the 177 management reforms can be closely identified as a presidential idea, and, of those, the vast majority came from presidents who served before Watergate. In sense, Congress moved from wholesale to retail on management reform, a change supported by more legislative staff at the key Senate and House government reform committees, and by the dwindling capacity for presidential participation.[16]

3. The percentage of statutes that addressed a specific process of government such as personnel, financial management, or information management increased from 41 percent in 1945–1954 to 67 percent in 1975–1984, 73 percent in 1985–1994, and 88 percent in 1995–2002.

4. The percentage of reforms that represented a more trusting view of the federal service, such as procurement streamlining, fell over time, from 68 percent trusting before Watergate to 71 per-

cent distrusting after. This change tracks public distrust in government closely—by decade, the percentage of trusting statutes fell dramatically after the 1945–64 period, which is roughly when public trust in government also began to tumble. As public mistrust rose, so did the level of distrust embedded in congressional action. Recall that the "reinventing government" movement, which was packaged into a single law in 1994, may have been trusting in content, but not in rhetoric—it was very much born in the antigovernment zeitgeist that the Clinton administration hoped to dispel in advance of national health care reform.[17]

5. The enforcement of reform has focused more on rule-based compliance, not the creation of new capabilities for execution. As the list of 177 statutes shows, compliance accountability rose from just 32 percent of statutes in 1945–1954 to 57 percent in 1974–1985 with statutes such as the Ethics in Government Act, 53 percent in 1985–1994 with expansion of existing statutes such as the Freedom of Information Act, and 64 percent in 1995–2002 with passage of a raft of statutes covering lobbying reform, paperwork reduction, and electronic freedom of information.

Distinguishing the Tides

Further analysis of the 177 reform laws shows significant variation in the timing, origins, and impacts of the four tides. As Table 6.2 shows, scientific management was at its peak before Watergate, is neither a Democratic nor a Republican congressional idea, survives in both divided and unified government (at least the two parties can agree on creating new structure and process), and is the most likely to involve a structural change in government, a trusting view of government, and capacity-based accountability.

In turn, war on waste and watchful eye reform tend to originate during divided government and come from Congress, in part because they both generate information that can be used to embarrass an administration from the other party. War on waste and watchful eye rarely appear when Republicans control Congress, however, no doubt again because Republicans were the exception during the period covered by my analysis. Finally, war on waste and watchful eye reform focuses on distrust and compliance.

Lastly, liberation management is definitely a post-Watergate fashion, does best in Democratic congresses (perhaps because Republicans are

Table 6.2 Patterns in reform, 1945–2002

	Percentage of scientific management	Percentage of war on waste	Percentage of watchful eye	Percentage of liberation management
Enacted before Nixon resignation	71	5	13	12
Enacted under Republican control of Congress	47	28	18	16
Enacted during Republican control of the presidency	37	21	28	14
Enacted during unified government	50	11	17	14
Originated as presidential idea	59	13	2	16
Involved structural change in government	53	21	14	27
Involved trusting view of the federal service	74	6	2	59
Involved compliance accountability	20	72	91	15
Carries a secondary reform philosophy	44	41	19	37

N=177 major management reform laws.

less interested in unraveling the rules that constrict government), is rarely a presidential idea (in part because reinventing government was driven more by executive order and invective than legislation), is much more trusting than war on waste or watchful eye, and focuses on capacity.

The greatest divide across the four reform philosophies is the degree to which each one was accompanied in statutes by provisions from a secondary or tertiary philosophy. The explanation is simple perhaps: Watchful eye is inherently defensible in Congress on its own, especially during periods of divided government, while the other three philosophies must carry extra reforms to justify passage.

Ironically perhaps, the war on waste is most frequently coupled with liberation management en route to final passage. Unable to reduce management rules without facing a public backlash driven by distrust in government, advocates of liberation management may have little choice but to tie their reforms to the hostile rhetoric itself. The risk of this strategy lies in its impact on future reform. Having sold liberation management with heated arguments against big government and overblown estimates of savings, they may reap even tighter rules in the future in the rebound against disappointment.

The Return of Structural Reform

Even the recent return of structural reform can be traced to Congress, not the president. Pressed to show they were doing more than just tinkering with existing structures, Congress created three new organizations in the two years following the 9/11 terrorist attacks: the Transportation Security Administration, the Department of Homeland Security, and a new Office of the National Intelligence Director.

All three organizations reflect an emerging consensus among study groups, think tanks, and blue-ribbon commissions that the structure of government was ill suited for the war on terrorism. Such reorganizations are fraught with risk, however, in part because past reforms create their own sediment of administrative inertia, and in part because an increasingly active Congress often imposes its own preferences on the organization chart. The Homeland Security Department has struggled to integrate the varied missions that its twenty-two agencies brought into the newly merged agency, while the Transportation Security Administration has operated under persistent hiring caps imposed by House Republicans who wanted contractors, not federal employees, to staff the airport security checkpoints.

The war on terrorism also brought new process reforms, notably at the Defense and Homeland Security departments, both of which have struggled to implement the new personnel systems that many in Congress hoped would accelerate the hiring and disciplinary processes and that employee unions opposed as an abridgement of employee bargaining rights. Although the pay-for-performance sections of the new laws are going into effect, it will take years, if not decades, to tell whether agencies have the managerial talent to make the new system work. Designed to replace the antiquated General Schedule, which assures all employees of automatic advance and pay increases, the new systems impose a "pay banding" approach that creates three to five bands in which employees move up, and possibly down, based on managerial assessments.

It is too early to predict whether reorganization, and the process reforms that often tag along, will become fashionable in other policy areas. What is clear is that today's reorganizations are markedly different from those of the 1950s and 1960s, which created a host of new agencies such as the departments of Health, Education, and Welfare, Housing and Urban Development, Transportation, and the National Aeronautics and Space Administration, National Science Foundation, and Environmental Protection Agency.

First, the new organizations were stamped with much more detail as they moved through multiple congressional committees en route to passage. The Aviation and Transportation Security Act (which established the Transportation Security Administration) was loaded with specifications on everything from the choice of logos and uniforms to the installation of baggage screening equipment, while the Homeland Security Act carried a long list of instructions on how the new department was to operate. Both statutes also contained precise language naming officers, duties, and chains of command.

Second, the new organizations carried all the accoutrements of the war on waste and watchful eye, including offices of inspector general, long lists of required studies and reports, and repeated language about spending priorities. The Transportation Security Administration was to spend as little as possible on the new federal screener workforce, while the Department of Homeland Security was to be revenue- and personnel-neutral by using expected economies of scale to reduce budget demand. As a result, the president has relatively little actual authority to design the new agencies.

Thus, even if reorganization is back, it is back in a very different form. Because the Bush administration initially resisted all three agencies,

Congress was very much the designer, which produced a mix of reform philosophies that has required a much greater focus on congressional politics than did the reorganizations that came in the late 1940s and early 1950s. As Congress became more involved, war on waste and watchful eye reform came into vogue, as many members looked for ways to enhance their antigovernment reputations back home.

Predicting Reform

Conventional wisdom suggests that the tides of reform are nearly impossible to predict. As Herbert Kaufman argued in 1969, the "emphasis on one remedy over a prolonged period merely accumulated the other discontents until new remedies gain enough support to be put into effect . . . So the constant shift in emphasis goes on."[18] More than thirty years later, Lois R. Wise made a similar argument, suggesting that reforms are driven by competing pressures that cannot be controlled or predicted: "If we think of administrative reform engines in bundles of normative and rational drivers of change, we can liken the shift back and forth between reform cycles to the movement of a seesaw. One side is likely to dominate the other at a given point in time, but the balance is bound to shift. Both sets of reform drivers remain present, despite the fact that one is more influential than the other. The dominance of rational determinants of change foretells the return to influence of alternative drivers of change such as social equity, democratization, and humanization."[19]

Acknowledging the great variability in reform over time and the complete lack of predictable sequencing among philosophies from one to another, there is at least some predictability buried in the 177 management reforms. Indeed, further statistical analysis of each tide suggests that at least three of the four can be predicted with at least some accuracy by a relatively small number of factors.

Scientific management is the easiest reform to predict—it is the product of presidential proposals that were enacted mostly before Watergate and is associated with the involvement of blue-ribbon commissions such as the 9/11 Commission.[20] Watchful eye is also relatively easy to predict—it is almost entirely the product of congressional action that occurred under Democrats in Congress, and also frequently results from the involvement of blue-ribbon commissions.[21] War on waste is more difficult to predict—it tends to be the product of action in the post-Nixon period, which is the only significant predictor of its rise.[22] Finally, liberation management is impossible to predict given the current state of our information.

This advanced statistical analysis suggests that scientific management, while still present in the panoply of management reform today, is fading, only to be replaced by the more skeptical view of government represented by watchful eye. Having mostly run out of new organizations and rules for running them, Congress is turning increasingly to watchful eye to make sure that the organizations work and the rules are being implemented, which both feeds and feeds off the public distrust for government.

These results tend to confirm Arnold's description of "reinventing government" as a presidential effort to reassert control of administration. As he argued in 1995, "executive reorganization is more than a house cleaning, dutifully undertaken by presidents; presidents are not altruists. Rather . . . throughout this century, presidents have initiated comprehensive reorganization planning to cope with fundamental political issues entailed in the relationship of authority to administration in the American separation of powers regime."[23]

But reorganization is merely one of the four tides of reform, and has been fading for thirty years as the president's reorganizational authority and ability have also faded. Of all these findings, Hamilton might be most discouraged by the dramatic decline in the president's role in shaping management reform. After all, he viewed the executive as the controlling force over administrative behavior, and would likely balk at the heavy congressional involvement in opening government to further oversight and what he would surely describe as second-guessing.

It could be, for example, that presidents have simply given up on legislative solutions to administrative tasks, turning more to executive orders and memoranda, blue-ribbon commissions, task forces, management agendas, and even reinvention labs to accomplish their ends.[24] What such vehicles lack in durability, they may more than make up for in pliability.

Yet, there is also ample evidence that presidents may be participating less because they no longer have the capacity to set the reform agenda through the Office of Management and Budget (OMB). This decline has been well documented by scholars such as Ronald C. Moe, who summarizes the state of the "M" in OMB as follows: "The contemporary presidency has been steadily losing its capacity to lead the executive branch on a day-to-day basis, in large measure because of the absence of a supportive institutional presence to project and protect the President's interests in government operations. It is not enough for management purposes to rely on the budget process with its short-term deadlines and spending biases. Nor can ad-hoc groups tied to some unit without the Executive Office . . . substitute for permanent management leadership, properly defined and understood."[25]

This is not to suggest that presidents are incapable of crafting a reform agenda or unable to participate in the reform process; the Bush administration did so in expanding the homeland security merger to include more agencies. Nor does it mean that presidents are no longer capable of authoring reform legislation, as the Clinton administration did in developing durable and successful streamlining of the federal procurement process.[26] However, it does suggest that presidents cannot go very deep in building such agendas, nor can they mount particularly effective counterarguments to the rising flow of reform from Congress.

Does Reform Work?

There are plenty of opinions about whether reform actually works. Has the Freedom of Information Act actually produced greater access, or just more sophisticated secrets? Has the Government Performance and Results Act actually generated greater performance, or just more internal paperwork? Has the Homeland Security Department produced more homeland security, or just more layers of government? And have all the procedural reforms produced greater accountability and transparency, or just more secrets?

How Federal Employees Rate Reform

Federal employees may have the greatest insight regarding the sediment of past reforms. Asked in 2001 whether their organization had been reformed, reorganized, or reinvented in the past five years, for example, 75 percent of federal employees said yes, compared with 56 percent of business employees and 60 percent of nonprofit employees.

In turn, 50 percent of the federal employees said the reforms had made their jobs either somewhat or much more difficult, compared with 31 percent of the nonprofit employees and 30 percent of the private-sector employees.

As with other measures of the workforce at risk, senior executives were much more positive regarding the impact of reform. Sixty percent of the senior executives said the reforms had made their jobs a lot or somewhat easier to do, compared with 43 percent of middle- and lower-level managers, and 41 percent of middle- and lower-level nonmanagers.

It is not clear who has the better view. Senior executives have the higher perch from which to view organization-wide impacts, but middle- and lower-level employees have the front-row seats.

There are two obvious problems with asking employees whether reform works. First, as Steven Kelman cautions, not all federal reforms are designed to make jobs easier.[27] Moreover, as Terry M. Moe argues, some reforms are designed to make government fail. According to Moe, government organizations reflect an amalgam of choices that lead almost inexorably to disaster: "Just as policy can get watered down through compromise, so can structure—and it almost always is . . . In the economic system, organizations are generally designed by participants who want them to succeed. In the political system, public bureaucracies are designed in no small measure by participants who explicitly want them to fail."[28]

Second, all employees have an obvious self-interest in downplaying the need for major reform, particularly since it might involve more work for them, not to mention the potential loss of their freedom and jobs. Given the heavy dose of compliance in the recent past, one might expect federal employees in particular to worry about any invitation they might give to further reform.

One way to address these biases is to ignore employee impressions of reform altogether, and focus instead on perceptions of their organization's overall performance in four basic tasks: (1) helping people, (2) spending money wisely, (3) being fair in decisions, and (4) running its programs and services. After all, improved performance is the theoretical goal of reform.

Fortunately, perceptions of federal performance in these four areas are highly correlated and sum to a very useful measure of just how well government was doing its job at the time of the 2001 survey, which was completed the summer before 9/11. According to further statistical analysis, there are five significant predictors of organizational performance. Interestingly, the amount of actual reform in each department or agency was not one of them.[29]

1. Employees who viewed their senior-, middle-, and lower-level colleagues as competent were more likely to give their organization high grades on performance.

2. Employees who rated their coworkers as committed to achieving the organization's mission were more likely to give their organization high grades.

3. Employees who said they were very satisfied with their opportunity to develop new skills and advancement, accomplish something worthwhile, and do something worthwhile were more likely to give their organization high grades.

4. Employees who said their organization provided access to enough information, technology, training, and employees were more likely to give their organization high grades.

5. Employees who said their organization had too many layers leading to the top were less likely to give their organization high grades.

These findings provide a simple message to Congress and the president: reform only registers if it actually strengthens organizational capacity. This message should be reassuring to those who worry about the steady erosion of capacity, as well as those who have invested enormous energy in improving the federal government's antiquated personnel system.

The results also confirm worries about layering in government, which emerges as one of the most significant predictors of organizational performance—in this case, poor performance. The further they are from the top, the more employees lose track of the mission of the organization, an understanding of how their job contributes to that mission, and access to the basic resources to do their jobs. And it appears to be a sense of drift and isolation that these employees attribute to their colleagues.

Successes and Failures

None of this is to suggest that past reforms have been an abysmal failure. To the contrary, this statistical analysis did not ask federal employees whether statutes such as the Freedom of Information Act, Inspector General Act, Homeland Security Act, or other iconic reform statutes worked. That assessment must be left to other observers.[30]

However, my 2001 survey of federal employees did ask senior employees which reform efforts had made the greatest impact in their work. Assuming that knowledge would be the greatest at the top of the hierarchy, this section of the survey was restricted only to senior employees with at least five years of experience.[31]

These employees were first asked whether Congress and the president generally acted in ways that improve or worsen the management of their agencies. The answers were hardly positive: Overall, 60 percent of these senior employees said that Congress acts in ways that worsen management, while 41 percent said the same of the president.

These employees were then asked about the amount of reform over the previous five years. Again, the answers were hardly positive. Overall, 60 percent of these senior employees said there had either been too little (29 percent) or too much (31 percent) reform, while just 38 percent said the amount had been just right.

Finally, the employees were asked to think about the past ten years and rate a set of specific initiatives to improve government performance. As Table 6.3 shows, the answers were mixed at best.

Once again, there were sharp disagreements between supervisors and nonsupervisors. Supervisors were more forgiving toward both Congress and the president, much more likely to say that there had been just the right amount of reform in their organizations, and more likely to say that most past management initiatives had been very or somewhat successful.

The question is who to believe—the senior supervisors who implement the ideas or the senior nonsupervisors who supposedly benefit from the efforts. I would bet on the nonsupervisors—if they do not feel the effects, the reform could not have penetrated deeply. In addition, they are not necessarily a disagreeable group. After all, they agreed with the senior supervisors on information technology.

What Federal Employees Want from Reform

Federal employees have their own views about what might improve the performance of their agencies. Among federal employees who said their organizations needed reform in 2001, the priorities were clear: Half focused on improving access to resources, another quarter emphasized the need for better recruitment, retention, and discipline, and the rest concentrated on motivation, performance, and respect.[32] "It is the most inefficient organization on the earth," one federal employee remarked in hitting all of the themes. "It is a colossal waste of taxpayer money, and the more streamlined it can be the better. The civil service system does not hold people accountable. It's all very political and the cream rarely rises to the top."

Employees who focused on resources were most concerned about structure, whether in the form of layering, politicization of the hierarchy, lack of access to technology and training, and need for more innovation. "You have to go through too many people to do your job," one federal employee remarked. "There are too many upper layers in the bureaucracy," said another.

The concerns about the consequences of past reforms were even more pointed. "They need to leave us alone," said one employee. "We

Table 6.3 Ratings of federal government reform, 2001

Question: Thinking about the past ten years, how would you rate the following initiatives? Was the effort to (insert) very successful, somewhat successful, not too successful, or not successful at all?

Reform initiative	Percentage of senior-level employees who rated initiative as very or somewhat successful	Percentage of senior-level nonsupervisors who rated initiative as very or somewhat successful	Percentage of senior-level supervisors who rated initiative as very or somewhat successful
Improve information technology	34/54	27/59	46/45
Reduce fraud, waste, and abuse	14/53	10/51	21/56
Streamline procurement	16/38	12/34	22/45
Improve financial management	11/38	7/34	17/49
Reduce internal rules	7/36	7/32	8/44
Measure government results	4/35	2/32	6/41

N=310 federal employees at General Schedule Grades 13–15 or in the Senior Executive Service *and* who had been in government ten years or longer.

have to realize that the new ways are not always the best ways," said another. "They've reformed our processes to the point that nothing works," said still another. "We ought to either reverse the reforms or reform the reforms so that they actually work."

Employees also worried about the simple impact of age on organizational responsiveness. "I'm fifty-three," one respondent said, "and most of the people I work with are about the same age. Change is difficult for all of us." "We have people who have been here thirty years or so," said another of the huge baby-boom generation of federal employees. "If people don't want to innovate, they are just fine the way they are."

Overall, the reforms proposed by these employees were hardly self-interested. Although a trivial percentage did recommend higher pay, the vast majority wanted the federal government to make good on its promises by providing the basic tools to succeed.

At the same time, most of the respondents did recognize the need for improvement, and wanted Congress and the president to be more serious about engaging in a broader dialogue about reform. After all, federal employees know where the problems are in their agencies, and which employees are not performing well. Although the Clinton administration engaged thousands of federal employees in just such a dialogue, it is not clear that the reinventors listened, at least not to the complaints about having enough employees to do the job and improving the disciplinary process.

Riptides

Reforms fail for many reasons, not the least of which is the burnout that comes from the constant push for reform itself. According to Haksoo Lee, N. Joseph Cayer, and G. Zhiyong Lan, continuous reform efforts produce high levels of employee dissatisfaction.[33]

Looking back over seven of the federal government's own employee surveys, the authors note that most recent reform efforts involved conflict between Congress and the president or budget cuts and downsizing. Not only did most reform efforts end in limited success or in failure, the resulting burnout reduced future support for organizational change. After sorting through all of their data, the authors offer a simple conclusion: "Reforms should not be undertaken based on political opportunism or short-term benefit."[34] Unfortunately, that is precisely why many, if not most, reforms are launched.

But the acceleration of management reform undermines performance in other ways, too.

First, the acceleration distracts federal employees from doing their work. Congress and presidents invariably make the latest reform the top priority, even as they excoriate government for not implementing the previous change. As a result, the federal government has no sense of what comes first, and whether a given reform deserves maximum attention. Given no sense of priorities, many departments and agencies simply wait for the latest reform to pass, which is exactly what has happened with most reforms over the past thirty years. Total Quality Management comes and goes within months, financial management reform stalls quickly, and employee training is always limited.

Second, the rising tide absorbs scarce resources. Many federal agencies made performance management a top priority during the 1990s, for example, despite limited evidence that they had the systems in place to make real progress on setting strategic plans, developing specific measures of success, and using those measures to improve performance. Similarly, despite the desperate need for improved financial management, many federal agencies still do not have the information systems needed to track and link expenditures to performance management, let alone to produce the financial statements that were mandated in the early 1990s under the Chief Financial Officers Act.

Third, the reforms sometimes undermine each other. For example, war on waste often creates more pressure for watchful eye and its tighter rules which clearly conflict with liberation management. Yet, it is often used to sell liberation management to a reluctant Congress, as demonstrated by the Clinton administration's decision to tie its liberation agenda to deep job cuts and more than $100 billion in savings. Such ties often undermine the investments needed to pursue long-overdue reforms in basic systems that would produce needed efficiencies. Although some reforms can produce results quickly, most produce quick criticism when they do not yield the promised savings within a short period.

Fourth, there is so little time between today's reform and tomorrow's that the federal government rarely has time to learn, often repeating the same mistake over and over as proponents seek just one more chance to see their ideas through to fruition. "Rarely do proponents ask why previous efforts achieved only modest success and what this implies for their proposals," George Downs and Patrick Larkey argue. "Those who seek to reform government must realize both that some otherwise commendable schemes enjoy only a miniscule chance of successful implementation and that simple-minded solutions to complex problems are capable of doing as much harm as good."[35]

Fifth, and perhaps most important, the reforms are isolated from each other. Although some reforms such as procurement streamlining do work well in isolation, many others add up to a whole that is less than the parts. As a result, the past three decades of reform have mostly failed to address the systemic problems that have corroded the federal government's ability to execute the laws, not to mention the ability to meet an ever-expanding mission with limited resources. Though most reforms cannot be described as tinkering, many work on isolated corners of need with little lasting impact.

The Market for Reform

There is little doubt that both the pace of reform and the focus on war on waste and watchful eye rose in tandem with increasing public distrust toward government. The vast majority of the pre-Watergate management statutes conveyed a trusting view of government, meaning that legislative text and/or history reflected confidence in the ability of government and its employees to achieve their mission. In contrast, the vast majority of post-Watergate statutes conveyed a distrusting view of government, meaning that the rhetoric and history were either based on specific breakdowns such as taxpayer abuse at the Internal Revenue Service or the security breach at the Los Alamos nuclear weapons lab, or carried sharp language criticizing government waste and abuse more generally.

The rising tide of public distrust also generated increased congressional engagement in reform as members began to see the electoral advantages of running against government. Under pressure to attack the government they hoped to lead, candidates began promising wholesale changes in government operations. Thus, 82 percent of the 110 management statutes that originated in Congress came after Watergate, while 61 percent of the 67 management statutes that originated in the White House came before. Congress, not presidents, became the source of management reform, almost always with a distrusting edge.

Watergate clearly loosened congressional inhibitions about reform. Whereas Congress once gave the benefit of the doubt to the president in reforming government, Watergate gave Congress new reasons to act, not the least of which was the desire to reassert congressional authority after a long period of presidential control. This congressional ascendancy clearly increased the intensity of antigovernment rhetoric and reform. Coupled with its increased activity, war on waste and watchful eye came to dominate the reform agenda. Before Watergate, Congress added just nine war on waste and watchful eye reforms to the statute books; after Watergate, Congress added another fifty-five.

Watergate also weakened presidential interest in reform legislation. Although presidents occasionally ask Congress to create new organizations and reduce internal rules, they have mostly lost the capacity to develop their own reform agendas. Thus, none of the recent homeland security reorganizations originated in the White House, nor did most of the major reforms in basic management systems such as financial management. Whereas presidents accounted for thirty-four of the forty-five scientific management reforms before Watergate, Congress accounted for twenty-one of the thirty-three after. Even liberating government from overregulation has become a congressional specialization. Whereas presidents accounted for five of the seven liberation management statutes before Watergate, Congress was the source of fourteen of the twenty after Watergate.

This may be the best presidents can do given the slow but steady weakening of their own capacity to develop reform legislation. Although Nixon put the word "management" ahead of "budget" when he created the Office of Management and Budget in 1970, the "M" in OMB has dwindled to a handful of staff with little institutional memory of how past reforms were enforced, let alone the knowledge to create new initiatives. Over the past thirty years, OMB's management division has been reorganized and downsized to the point of near irrelevance, forcing presidents to rely on blue-ribbon commissions such as Reagan's Grace Commission and ad hoc task forces such as Carter's reorganization project and Clinton's "reinventing government" campaign. Although presidents still celebrate their reform campaigns as the longest and strongest in history, being long and strong has been redefined to mean temporary and mostly hortatory.

This is not to suggest that presidents are incapable of crafting occasional reforms such as Clinton's "reinventing government" plan. But such reforms often come from ad hoc task forces and blue-ribbon commissions that lack the power to assure both passage and implementation.

Congress and presidents might not be so interested in reform if the public were more confident in government. But the public is anything but confident. The vast majority believes the federal government wastes a great deal or fair amount of money, and think that government is run for the benefit of the few. Even though their personal contact with government may be positive, they think the worst of government as a whole. Just as they love their member of Congress, but hate Congress, they love their bureaucrat, but hate the bureaucracy.

The public is also overwhelmingly supportive of greater efficiency. According to my May 2002 survey of 986 randomly selected Americans, for example, a majority of the public believes (1) that federal programs should be maintained to deal with important problems, but (2) that the bigger problem with the federal government is not its priorities but its inefficiency.[36] It is easy to see how these two opinions create a core constituency in favor of reform. When combined, only 13 percent of the public simultaneously believe that federal programs should be sharply curtailed and that the bigger problem with government is its wrong priorities. These "devolvers" are the only constituents for changes or outright cuts in federal priorities. In contrast, 43 percent of the public believes that federal programs should be maintained to deal with important problems, and that the bigger problem with government is inefficiency. These "reinventors" are the core constituents of the kind of reforms envisioned in the war on waste and watchful eye reforms of the past three decades.

These opinions echo the results of a late 1998 survey conducted by the Pew Research Center for the People and the Press under a grant I shepherded as a senior program officer at the Pew Charitable Trusts.[37] Focused on the Environmental Protection Agency, Federal Aviation Administration, Food and Drug Administration, and Internal Revenue Service, the survey found that each agency's constituents were generally satisfied with its overall performance, but frustrated and even angry regarding slowness and complexity. The complaints were uniform across seventeen different constituent groups across the five high-impact agencies.

For example, taxpayers, business tax officers, and professional tax preparers were generally favorable toward the Internal Revenue Service, but not its rules and procedures; frequent fliers, pilots, air traffic controllers, and business regulatory officers were generally favorable toward the Federal Aviation Administration, but not its administrative systems; and medical professionals, health safety advocates, and the chronically ill were all generally favorable toward the Food and Drug Administration, but not toward its day-to-day operations. In short, these constituents believed in the core missions of each agency, but had serious reservations about the bureaucracy. Although few constituents complained that agency employees were rude or disrespectful, and most said it was easy to contact the agencies and even praised them for making an effort to help explain the rules, most constituents had little good to say about the rules themselves.

Moreover, poor performance hurt agencies much more than good performance helped. Most constituents approached their agency with high expectations, but agencies that met those expectations simply did not reap a dramatic increase in confidence, in part because they do not control the major factors that influence overall favorability. It is residual support for the agency's mission that matters most to perceptions of performance, not actual experience.

Ultimately, constituents will always be unhappy with government if they do not support the basic mission. Given the general public view that government should maintain its programs, but address inefficiency, it is no surprise that Congress and presidents would pick the most attractive targets for reform, which reside in persistent public antipathy toward waste.

Conclusion

The federal government is awash in reform. Hardly a day goes by without some new proposal to make government work, be it scientific management, war on waste, watchful eye, or liberation management. But perhaps the federal government could do with a bit less of both Hamilton and Jefferson on this issue—instead of moving quickly back and forth across the tides, perhaps it is time to stick with a set of reforms for a bit longer than a single Congress.

This does not mean the federal government should stop trying to improve performance. Again, as Patricia W. Ingraham writes, "Performance is a siren for modern government and justly so. Performance promises may be difficult to keep, but they are the right promise . . . Performance is, at its heart, about governance and accountability. For public organizations, and the role they play in governance, that link is essential."[38]

The question is how to honor these promises without flooding government with so much reform that it cannot possibly succeed. The answer perhaps is to take the best of Hamilton and Jefferson, and leave the war on waste behind. Use Hamilton's scientific management sparingly to improve performance measurement so that pay and other resources can be tied to actual impacts; Jefferson's watchful eye sparingly to make sure that government is exposed to the scrutiny needed for honest evaluation; and a mix of Hamilton and Jefferson to liberate the federal government from Hamilton's execution in detail and tight chains of command, and temper Jefferson's attacks on fraud, waste, and abuse.

The challenge is to use the best of Hamilton and Jefferson in a comprehensive effort to improve performance. The federal government has never suffered from a lack of tinkering. Hardly a month goes by without another small adjustment in a major reform, often involving little more than a restatement of the original rationale for action, but rare is the hearing or investigation that asks why a past reform failed. Page through the Hurricane Katrina and 9/11 reports and one will find little mention of the comprehensive problems that led to the failure. Every event is unique.

Rarer still is the moment when Congress and the president attempt comprehensive reform, and that moment almost always involves a dip into the war on waste as a way to make reforms such as the 1978 Civil Service Reform Act and "reinventing" government package more attractive to a doubtful public. By attacking government as part of saving it, Congress and the president foredoom their efforts by carving into the employee support they need to succeed. And by usually exempting their own institutions from reform, most notably by walling off presidential appointees from any cuts in personnel, they undermine both their credibility, while exposing their proposals to divide-and-conquer attacks. As such, tinkering comes in many forms—it can involve a tiny effort to adjust a single structure or process of government, or a large-scale effort that neglects major causes of poor performance. Neither form of tinkering will suffice.

CHAPTER SEVEN

Safety in the Executive

The seventh characteristic of an energetic federal service is safety in the executive, which flows in large part from the ability to oversee those who actually deliver the goods and services for government. The public cannot assign responsibility for what goes wrong or right if they cannot see the federal government's vast, uncounted workforce, nor can it expect accountability if its leaders hide the true size of government from view.

Hamilton made this case for accountability in *Federalist No. 70* by defining the need for a single executive. A single executive would not only provide his hoped-for energy in the executive, it was essential for a *due* dependence on the people and a *due* responsibility to the public good. "Whenever two or more persons are engaged in any common enterprise or pursuit," he argued, "there is always danger of difference of opinion. If it be a public trust or office, in which they are clothed with equal dignity and authority, there is peculiar danger of personal emulation and even animosity."[1]

Concerned though he was with a single executive, Hamilton's vision of accountability can be easily extended to an energetic federal service. As he wrote three paragraphs later in *Federalist No. 70*, one of the greatest dangers of a plural executive was its tendency "to conceal faults and destroy responsibility. Responsibility is of two kinds—to censure and to punishment." And censure and punishment were made infinitely more difficult if more than one principal was in charge:

> It often becomes impossible, amidst mutual accusations, to determine on whom the blame or the punishment of a pernicious measure, or series

of pernicious measures, ought really to fall. It is shifted from one to another with so much dexterity, and under such plausible appearances, that the public opinion is left in suspense about the real author. The circumstances which may have led to any national miscarriage or misfortune are sometimes so complicated that, where there are a number of actors who may have had different degrees and kinds of agency, though we may clearly see upon the whole that there has been mismanagement, yet it may be impracticable to pronounce to whose account the evil which may have been incurred is truly chargeable.[2]

Extending Hamilton's argument to the federal service, today's vast collection of mostly hidden contractors, grantees, and other partners of government vitiates the transparency that provides accountability. Under pressure to deliver more with less, the federal government has steadily expanded its outsourcing to provide goods and services once provided by federal employees. Although outsourcing has been part of the federal repertoire since the Revolutionary War, when businesses supplied the Continental Army, the hidden federal workforce has become indispensable in honoring the federal government's commitment to extensive and arduous enterprise.

As part of the erosion of an energetic federal service, the hidden workforce has also become the de facto destination for fulfilling responsibilities once held by federal employees. Unable or unwilling to convince the public that the ever-expanding mission requires a greater supply of federal employees, Congress and presidents have turned to the hidden workforce as a way to fulfill their often disingenuous promises to deliver more with less.

This is not to suggest that contracts, grants, and other forms of outsourcing are inherently flawed. There are many good reasons to use these tools to procure goods and services, not the least of which is the lack of the federal government's own capacity to produce certain goods and services in bulk. The federal government also uses contractors and grantees to provide talent it cannot recruit, specialized services it cannot produce, competition it cannot generate among its own organizations, and equipment that it cannot and should not build itself.

Moreover, the federal government no longer needs to provide basic goods and services such as soil testing, weather forecasting, satellite technology, basic scientific research, or even dentures, which the Department of Veterans Affairs produced until the 1950s. Although it still conducts a great deal of medical research through the National Institutes of Health, its grants to private and public universities have produced some of the most important breakthroughs in creating new vaccines, reducing disease, and speeding new technologies to the market, such as the Internet.

As such, contractors and grantees are often vital in converting missions that matter into lasting achievements. The federal government managed the budget for the Marshall Plan, for example, but private contractors did most of the work. The federal government controlled the path of the interstate highway system, but private contractors and grantees did most of the construction. And the federal government set the rules for implementing the Clean Water Act, but state and local government employees did much of the monitoring and enforcement, while grantees built the water treatment plants.

Yet, there is also one service the federal government must provide through its contracts and grants. It must achieve and maintain basic accountability for what goes right and wrong, whoever produces the goods and services. It does matter who loads and launches the space shuttle if the federal hierarchy is so thick with needless management that it cannot monitor quality control before and during flight, who makes the body armor if the federal procurement workforce is so thinly stretched that it cannot make sure the armor works, or who builds the new schools and hospitals in Iraq if the contracts are so complex that they cannot be audited.

The federal government does not use contracts and grants just to procure needed goods and services, however. It also uses contracts, grants, and mandates to state and local governments to hide its true size, thereby creating the illusion that it is smaller than it actually is. It also uses this outsourcing to give its departments and agencies much greater flexibility in hiring labor, thereby creating the illusion that the civil service system is somehow working effectively. Not only does the federal government's largely hidden workforce of contractors and grantees encourage the public to believe that it truly can get more for less, it diffuses accountability. Just who was in charge of the launchpad camera that failed to provide a precise image of the damage to the shuttle Columbia's left wing?

The rest of this chapter will examine the true size of the federal workforce, which has increased by almost 2 million employees since the end of the cold war. The chapter will first explore new figures on just how many people actually work for the federal government as civil servants, military personnel, postal workers, contractors, and grantees, and will then turn to a discussion of reasons for the recent growth in the hidden workforce. Although some of the growth reflects the perfectly reasonable growth of demand for goods and services that simply cannot be found inside government, the chapter will suggest that the hidden workforce has simultaneously increased the federal government's dependence on contractors and grantees, thereby possibly increasing costs, while decreasing accountability for faithfully executing the laws.

How Large Is Government?

Notwithstanding the perfectly legitimate reasons for contracts and grants, and acknowledging the temptations of unfunded mandates to state and local governments, much of the recent growth in the hidden federal workforce has been driven by employment caps and freezes designed to make government look smaller than it actually is.[3] In turn, this effort to hide the true size of government makes accountability much more difficult—it is, indeed, nearly impossible to censure and punish national misfortune or mismanagement in cases such as the Space Shuttle Challenger and Columbia disasters if one is dealing with a contractor that provides its goods and services through a bundle of more than 2,000 subcontracts.

No one knows just how much the civil service would grow absent the constraints on how many people it could employ. Would the civil service reach 2.3 million employees, as it did at the height of the Vietnam War? Would it reach 3.4 million, as it did at the end of World War II? Whatever the guess, intuition suggests that the civil service would certainly be much larger than the 1.8 million employees on the federal payroll in 2005. At least some of the contract- and grant-generated jobs now carried "off budget" would be "on budget" inside government.

The caps can actually be traced back to the downsizing that took place after World War II, and to repeated efforts to restrain the growth of the federal workforce. Even as the federal government's greatest endeavors expanded, Congress and presidents tried, and mostly succeeded, in keeping the federal workforce under a 2.25 million threshold that was only breached in 1968. Although the president's budget office claims that departments and agencies are free to hire as many civil servants as their budgets will allow, woe be to the president who presides over an increase.

The Whitten Influence

No one was more important to the politics of federal headcounts than Jamie L. Whitten, a Democratic member of the House of Representatives from Mississippi. Frustrated with what he saw as a rapidly expanding federal workforce during the Korean War, Whitten drafted a nearly perfect employment freeze.

Under Whitten's 1951 amendment to a Korean War spending package, Congress placed a ceiling on total federal employment while prohibiting the creation of any new permanent positions. As he explained his amendment in 1954, "I had no ax to grind, and have none now, except to do what I can for orderly government. Sometimes I think politically it would be much wiser to get a staff and keep count of Federal employees and release it to the press complaining about the total number now and then. Had I followed that course, I might have gotten an award."[4]

His amendment was simple enough. It merely ordered the Civil Service Commission to use its authority to make temporary appointments in order to prevent any growth in the total number of permanent posts. But effected in executive orders and repeated reauthorizations, the amendment affected both temporary and permanent positions. Federal employment has remained virtually flat at plus or minus 2 million employees since the mid-1950s, driving departments such as Defense and Energy, and agencies such as the National Aeronautics and Space Administration and Environmental Protection Agency to build large de facto federal workforces through contracts and grants.

These organizations were not the only ones to contribute to the growth of the hidden workforce, however. The hidden workforce, which is sometimes called the shadow workforce, has expanded in almost all federal departments and agencies regardless of mission, in part because the federal government is prohibited under an Eisenhower-administration order from performing any work that is commercially available and not inherently governmental. Under the order, which is enforced to this day under Budget Circular A-76, the federal government is required to subject all commercially available/not-inherently-government jobs to competition with businesses that want to do the work.

Although federal departments and agencies have evaded the order by defining jobs as a no/yes combination of commercially available and/or inherently governmental, and although neither term has been precisely defined in recent revisions of Budget Circular A-76, federal employment has remained fixed. Again, the federal civil service is unlikely to pull many of the current contractor, grantee, and other jobs back into government, nor should it. B-2 bombers should be built outside government, for example, if only because government lacks the expertise to build them, and high-end research on everything from stem cells to the modeling of the impact of catastrophic events can be done within government at the National Institutes of Health or outside government in colleges, universities, research firms, and nonprofit laboratories.

Estimating the True Size of Government

It is difficult to know precisely how many contractors, grantees, and state and local government employees actually work for the federal government, however. Contractors and grantees do not keep an exact count of their employees, in part because doing so would allow the federal government and scholars like me to estimate actual labor costs and profit. At the same time, state and local governments make no effort whatsoever to quantify the number of hours their employees spend administering federal mandates.[5]

Given these obstacles to developing a hard headcount of the hidden workforce, I estimate the number of contractors and grantees by using the input/output model of the U.S. economy that is constantly updated by the U.S. Bureau of Economic Analysis. Based on actual transactions, the Bureau is able to convert contract spending into an estimated headcount. Building a missile would involve much more material than labor, for example, while providing building security or management consulting would involve much more labor than material.[6]

The information needed to produce the estimate of the true size of government is contained in two federal databases: the Federal Procurement Data System, which tracks contract transactions, and the Federal Assistance Awards Data System, which tracks grants. According to Eagle Eye Publishers, the Virginia-based research firm that developed the estimating methodology on my behalf, these databases contain enough information to create reasonable estimates of the total number of full-time-equivalent employees who work in the federal government's hidden workforce. But they are still estimates, and should be taken as such.

Indeed, absent a hard headcount by contractors and grantees themselves, my estimates are more a basis for measuring the change in the true size of government than an absolutely precise count of actual employees. Unfortunately, such estimates are only available back to the mid-1980s when the Federal Procurement Data System was first established.

Moreover, it is impossible to estimate the number of state and local mandate employees, though I did try to do so in 1997 by asking state and local employees to estimate the time they spent working under federal mandates, whether funded or unfunded. The resulting numbers, while provocative at 4.4 million, are simply too speculative to use in the following discussion. Nevertheless, readers are free to add 4.4 million to the 1996, 1999, 2002, and 2005 totals discussed below if they want a glimpse of the truly phenomenal number of de facto federal employees who work under contracts, grants, and mandates. Much as they complain about the impacts of unfunded mandates on budget and personnel, states and localities simply do not know themselves how much those mandates actually cost.

Readers should note that the following figures reflect a good deal of rounding, in part because rounding makes the text easier to read, and partly because it reduces the perceived precision of the estimates. Although the civil service, postal worker, and military personnel figures come from federal sources, including historical tables of the U.S. budget, the contract and grant estimates are just that, estimates, and should be treated as such. The trends matter far more than the estimates, and the trends suggest that the true size of government is growing rapidly.

Caveats. It is important to note that the following analysis focuses solely on the true size of government, not on who should be doing the work of government per se. As such, I do not engage the vast privatization literature,[7] examine state and local outsourcing,[8] or consider the norms that should guide outsourcing.[9] I am merely asking how many employees it takes to deliver on the promises that the federal government makes, whether that number is growing, and how it affects safety in the executive.

Given the difficulty in measuring the true size of government, readers should note three caveats in reading the following history. First, the estimates capture the indirect jobs created by a particular transaction—that is, jobs that are created under primary contracts and grants, which include everything from subcontracts for additional goods and services in launching the space shuttle to small purchases at the Office Depot.

Second, the numbers rely on the Bureau of Economic Analysis's estimates of how much labor is required for each federal transaction.

Although the Bureau updates these estimates every year, they are still only estimates of the number of jobs created by specific transactions, and should be treated as such.

Third, the final estimate of the true size of government mixes apples and oranges to some degree—the measures of the number of federal civil servants, military personnel, and postal workers do not include the indirect jobs they create in their communities through the purchase of other goods and services. These indirect jobs are considered to constitute an exceedingly small percentage of the total created by federal and hidden workers alike.

Given these caveats, readers are wise to view my estimates as a way to illustrate the changing size of government. Because the same methodology was used for every year discussed below, one can easily see the fall and rise of the true size, particularly its growth over the past fifteen years.

The 1990 baseline. Eagle Eye's 1990 estimates provide a mark against which to measure the changes in the true size of government. Expenditures in 1990 reflect the last decisions of the year before the end of the cold war, and show the true size of government after the end of one of the largest defense buildups since World War II. As Table 7.1 shows, this buildup helped create a true size of government of more than 12.6 million employees: roughly 2.2 million civil servants, 820,000 postal workers, 2.1 million uniformed military personnel, 5.1 million contractors, and 2.4 million grantees.[10] As of 1990, there were roughly three and a half contractors and grantees for every federal civil servant.

A true size of 12.6 million employees is no small number, but is significantly smaller than the number estimated for 1984, when the true size of government reached just under 14 million, albeit at a time when the Federal Procurement Data System was still so new that its tracking was often unreliable.

Nevertheless, the number of contract-generated employees had fallen by 400,000 by 1990, with much of the decline in Defense and Energy Department contracts. Although the total number of military personnel remained virtually unchanged over the six years, the end of the cold war had already produced the start of a peace dividend that would increase by 1993.

1993. By 1993, the true size of the federal government showed the effect of the post–cold war peace dividend. Although there were small

Table 7.1 The true size of government, 1990–2005

Measure	1990	1993	1996	1999	2002	2005	Change 1999–2002	Change 2002–2005
1. Civil servants	2,238,000	2,157,000	1,934,000	1,820,000	1,818,000	1,872,000	–2,000	54,000
2. Contract jobs	5,058,000	4,884,000	4,704,000	4,441,000	5,168,000	7,634,000	727,000	2,466,000
3. Grant jobs	2,416,000	2,400,000	2,440,000	2,527,000	2,860,000	2,892,000[a]	333,000	32,000
4. Military personnel	2,106,000	1,744,000	1,507,000	1,386,000	1,456,000	1,436,000	70,000	–20,000
5. Postal service jobs	817,000	820,000	852,000	872,000	810,000	767,000	–62,000	–43,000
The true size of government	12,635,000	12,005,000	11,437,000	11,046,000	12,112,000	14,601,000	1,066,000	2,489,000

a. Grant data are from 2004, the last year for which complete data were available at the time of this analysis.

cuts in the number of contract-generated and civil service jobs between 1990 and 1993, the number of military personnel fell by almost 500,000, while the Defense Department's civilian workforce fell by 100,000. All told, the true size of government was 12 million jobs: roughly 2.2 million civil servants, 820,000 postal workers, 1.7 million military personnel, 4.9 million contractors, and 2.2 million grantees. At the time, there were barely three contractors and grantees for every federal civil servant.

In a very real sense, the declining number of military personnel had become a leading indicator of future cuts in the contract-generated workforce. Fewer soldiers needed fewer weapons, which meant lower contract spending. Reducing the size of the armed services can be done almost immediately at the recruiting stations, while contracts usually run their course. Moreover, a significant drawdown in military personnel requires at least some increased outsourcing just to study the impacts and handle the eventual base closings it produces. Military downsizing also puts pressure on Congress and the president to help state and local governments convert military bases to civilian use; such conversion became a growth industry in contracts and grants during the early 1990s.

However, the grant-generated workforce did not decline during the same period, as federal grants continued to hold steady. Unlike total procurement spending, which fell by $60 billion, grant spending increased ever so slightly as the federal government continued to pursue endeavors such as reducing disease and strengthening the highway system through its grants. Although grant-generated employment is particularly difficult to estimate given the lack of hard transactions to track, grant employment appears to have increased during the period by roughly 200,000 jobs.

1996. The true size of government continued to decline between 1993 and 1996. By the end of the second year of the Clinton administration, the total federal workforce stood at just 11.4 million: roughly 1.9 million civil servants, 850,000 postal workers, 1.5 million military personnel, 4.7 million contractors, and 2.4 million grantees. The peace dividend was clearly continuing with the huge downsizing that had begun at the Department of Defense, which dropped almost 300,000 civil servants and 500,000 contract jobs.

These declines were well telegraphed by decisions made under George H. W. Bush, and allowed the Clinton administration to claim that it was about to shave more than a quarter million federal employees from the payroll, which led to Clinton's famous statement that the end of the era of big government had begun. Even before the promise was made, the administration had already met its target, which allowed it to make even greater claims as the downsizing continued through the mid-1990s and beyond. However, as the 1999 estimates show, portions of the Defense Department savings were reinvested in domestic growth.

1999. By 1999, the true size of government was at its smallest level since the end of the cold war. When all the numbers are added up, the true size of the federal workforce was approximately 11 million: roughly 1.8 million civil servants, 870,000 postal workers, 1.4 million military personnel, 4.4 million contractors, and 2.5 million grantees. Nevertheless, the ratio of contractors and grantees to federal employees actually increased—the civil service was shrinking much faster than the hidden workforce. By 1999, there were nearly four contractors and grantees for every federal civil servant.

Even in 1999, however, the pressure to increase the true size of government was beginning to show.[11] Nine of every ten jobs that had been cut from the true size of government between 1993 and 1999 had come from the Defense Department. These cuts were echoed, albeit in smaller numbers, at the Department of Energy and the National Aeronautics and Space Administration, both of which had experienced significant growth during the cold war.

This peace dividend gave Congress and the president the room to invest at least some of the savings in a growing domestic workforce that included 220,000 new hidden jobs at the Transportation Department, 117,000 at Justice, 90,000 at the General Services Administration, and 59,000 at Treasury. Whereas losses at the Defense and Energy Departments and the National Aeronautics and Space Administration cut the true size of government by 1.3 million jobs between 1993 and 1999, the rest of government added back more than 300,000.

All told, the end of the cold war had sliced nearly 1.6 million jobs from the true size of government, a substantial achievement, but an illusory one nonetheless. Although the decline was widely heralded among Democratic circles as proof positive that they could cut government, the hidden workforce actually grew by 100,000 over the period once Defense, Energy, and the National Aeronautics and Space Administration are removed from the totals.

Moreover, there were plenty of harbingers of increased growth across the federal government, including at Defense. The department was already preparing for another round of base closings scheduled to take effect between 2006 and 2010 when its procurement budget began increasing as the Clinton administration began to replace aging weapons systems, in 1999. Modernization spending alone accounted for a nearly $20 billion increase in procurement from 1999 to 2002, while increases in domestic departments such as Education and Health and Human Services pushed their contract- and grant-generated workforces steadily higher.

These gains did not protect the civil service, which had dropped from nearly 2.2 million employees in 1993 to 1.9 million in 1996, and dropped another 100,000 jobs by 1999. Nor did the increase in the true size of the domestic workforce prevent Bill Clinton from declaring the end of the era of big government in his 1996 State of the Union Address. Although most of the decline involved little more than post–cold war downsizing, including a total cut of nearly 400,000 jobs in the Defense Department civil service, the peace dividend created the illusion of large federal job cuts, and helped the Clinton administration eventually meet and exceed its "reinventing government" promise of a dramatic reduction in total civil-service employment.

With federal employment budgets tight, problems recruiting and retaining talented employees rising, and frustration about hyperreform and needless paperwork growing, the federal government clearly started viewing the hidden workforce as a much more pliable option for procuring labor, especially in hard-to-recruit positions such as information technology, science and engineering, program evaluation, and management analysis.

The most important question at the time was not how the true size of government got so big, but whether it had the energy to sustain high performance and meet increasing public demands. It could have been that a workforce of 12 million was still too small for the federal mission, or that a civil service of just 1.8 million employees was still too big for political comfort, or even that the federal government desperately needed more procurement workers to oversee the consolidation of contractors into megaproviders of key federal services such as the day-to-day operation of the space shuttle program.

2002. By 2002, most of my 1999 predictions about growth had proven accurate as the true size of government reached its highest level since the end of the cold war. All told, the true size of government hit 12.1 million in October 2002: roughly 1.8 million civil servants, 810,000 postal workers, 1.5 million military personnel, 5.2 million contractors, and 2.7 million grantees. With contract- and grant-generated jobs up by nearly a million since 1999, and the civil service down by just 2,000, there were more than four contractors and grantees for every civil servant.

Although the 2002 true size of government was still smaller than it had been at the end of the cold war in 1990, the era of the end of big government was clearly over. During the three short years between 1999 and 2002, the federal government added back more than half of the headcount savings produced by the end of the cold war.

At least some of this growth was sparked by new defense spending in the Clinton administration's final two budgets, but most of the 1.1 million new jobs came during the Bush administration's first two years. Although there is no way to know just how much of the money reflected the war on terrorism, the greatest growth occurred at the Defense, Health and Human Services, Justice, State, and Treasury departments, where the war was being fought.

The number of contract workers would have been even higher and the civil service cuts even deeper if the federal government had contracted out what would become 50,000 baggage and passenger screening jobs. Under pressure from the Senate, the new agency was forced to fill the jobs with civil servants. Yet, even as the new Transportation Security Agency began hiring, it created new contracts for virtually every aspect of the employment process, including hiring, training, and payroll management, which increased the number of contract-generated jobs. The agency's $554 million recruitment contract went to a consortium of California government agencies, while the $224 million pay and personnel management contract went to Accenture, a private consulting firm.

The 2002 estimates clearly showed that the true size of government was growing again. Between 1999 and 2002, the true size of government grew by 1.1 million jobs to 12.1 million in 2002. Although military and postal employment inched up during the period, almost all of the growth has occurred in two categories: contract and grant-generated jobs.

Yet, the true size of government grew across government, not just at Defense. Although some might attribute most of the 1996–2002 growth to the new war on terrorism and increased defense spending with the war in Afghanistan, the growth actually occurred in all areas of government. Except for Energy and the National Aeronautics and Space Administration, both of which continued to lose jobs as the demand for nuclear weapons and aeronautics development ebbed, and a handful of domestic agencies such as Housing and Urban Development (which clearly fell out of favor in the new Bush administration) virtually all other major departments and agencies gained jobs.

2005. Estimates of the true size of government in 2005 show continued growth, especially at the Defense Department. By the end of the federal government's fiscal year, the true size of government reached 14.6 million employees: roughly 1.9 million civil servants, 770,000 postal workers, 1.44 million military personnel, 7.6 million contractors, and 2.9 million grantees.[12] The numbers reflect a vast expansion in the contract-generated workforce, which reflected a nearly $50 billion increase in contract spending between 2004 and 2005 alone. By the end of 2005, there were five and a half contractors and grantees for every federal civil servant, up from just three and a half at the end of the cold war.

Readers are warned that these estimates reflect a shift in how the federal government tracks contract expenditures. By 2005, departments and agencies were required to use an entirely new coding system for reporting transactions, which led to mistakes in posting actual contract expenditures in 2005. Thus, $75 billion of the $425 billion in 2005 contract expenditures cannot be tracked by exact destination or purchase, which meant that the dollars could not be used in estimating contract-generated jobs without assigning them to other expenditures on a proportional basis.

Using this proportional approach to estimate the jobs created by the remaining $3.1 billion, the true size of the federal government in 2005 exceeded its 1990 mark by more than 2 million jobs, and its 1999 mark by 3.5 million. Government has been growing very fast, indeed.

This time, almost all of the growth can be attributed to the war on terrorism, which boosted Defense Department spending for both goods and services and encompassed the continued cost of the wars in Afghanistan and Iraq. There was almost nothing the Defense Department did not buy—it paid for new air bases abroad, tank treads, ammunition, meals, security, air conditioners, housing trailers in Iraq, new technologies for monitoring terrorist threats, and even writing the contracts themselves.

Between 2002 and 2005, the number of Defense Department contract employees jumped from 3.4 million to 5.2 million, with a mix of jobs in both "hard contracts" for material and "soft contracts" for services. The rest of the growth in the hidden workforce came at the Department of Energy, which moved forward on new energy and nuclear weapons programs; Health and Human Services, which bulked up its contractor workforce as part of the war on terrorism; the Department of Homeland Security, which had more than 200,000 contract employees by 2005, NASA, which increased its contract workforce following the Shuttle Columbia disaster; and the State Department, which more than doubled its contract workforce over the three years.

Twenty years after the Reagan administration's defense buildup, the true size of government had come full circle. By 2005, the post–cold war peace dividend was completely gone. As in 1984, most of the contract-generated jobs were at Defense, where the war on terrorism had replaced the cold war. But even the most optimistic forecast of the future suggests that the war on terrorism will continue far into the future, even if the war in Iraq ends.

A deeper analysis of the estimates suggests one other important trend: Most of the increases involved service jobs. Whereas manufacturing jobs remained virtually unchanged between 2002 and 2005, the number of service jobs increased by almost 2.5 million. The increase suggests that many of the jobs involve the outright purchase of labor, whether to build roads, manage parks and forests, or manage public outreach, technology services, financial systems, and personnel. Recall, for example, that the Transportation Security Administration uses contracts to manage virtually all aspects of the hiring, training, and payroll process for its baggage and passenger screeners. All of these jobs could have just as easily been filled within the civil service, which is how almost all of these services are provided in other departments and agencies.

Questions of Size

The new numbers on the true size of government raise the obvious question of whether the federal service is too small to assure safety in the executive. Although many of the contracts and grants involve perfectly legitimate transactions, some also involve the continued effort to keep the civil service small. Just as one cannot know how big the civil service would be without so many contracts and grants, one cannot know how small the hidden workforce would be if federal employment was allowed to rise to meet the growing federal mission.

But not all jobs are created equal. Although there is little hard evidence on the true cost of the hidden workforce, one can easily imagine that Congress and the president are paying a premium for their insistence on a relatively small civil service. Federal employees certainly feel the pinch in their concerns about the lack of enough employees to do their jobs well. One can also argue that the lack of hard headcounts from the hidden workforce prevents the kind of labor-cost comparisons that might drive some jobs back into the civil service.

However, increasing the size of the civil service will not replace the lost energy, especially if the new employees are placed in the same over-burdened systems and continue to be denied the resources needed to do their jobs well. In a sense, the case for an ever-expanding hidden work-force is made by federal employees themselves in their own complaints about working for government.

The case is also easily made by the thickening of government, the ap-pointments process, and the constant reform pressure. Contracts and grants may disguise the true size of government, but they also promise political comfort and a measure of responsiveness. (On the other hand, this responsiveness is often extremely difficult to monitor and some-times comes at a cost in eventual dependencies that weaken the salutary effects of what is often heralded as a competitive process.)

In turn, unfunded mandates may be the most tempting tool of all for hiding the true size of government—they simply pass the cost of imple-menting laws such as the recent No Child Left Behind Act to state and local governments, while reserving the rewards for members of Con-gress and the president. Although no one knows for sure how many hours of state and local effort are involved in the provision of services, the number is surely large and growing.

The Search for Accountability

Jefferson did not share Hamilton's belief in transparency as the sole guarantor of accountability, nor in the tight chains of command needed to assure it. Instead, he relied more on conscience. "I cannot have es-caped error," he admitted in his eighth and final annual message. "It is incident to our imperfect nature. But I may say with truth, my errors have been of the understanding, not of intention . . ."[13] He no doubt shared Hamilton's view that errors should be easy to detect, especially in a government that could be understood by the farmer.

Yet, Jefferson also believed that Hamilton's two tools for controlling the executive, censure and punishment, came too late in the process to prevent national miscarriage and misfortune. Government had to con-trol itself through conscience. Writing in 1787, he argued that con-science had to be exercised and encouraged.[14]

Absent this sense of conscience, which was less likely to be found in a government filled with "cormorants" seeking to feed, Jefferson believed in what would become codes of conduct. Indeed, the very purpose of a constitution was to "bind up the several branches of government by certain laws, which, when they transgress, their acts shall become nullities; to render unnecessary an appeal to the people, or in other words a rebellion, on every infraction of their rights, on the peril that their acquiescence shall be construed into an intention to surrender those rights."[15] Translated in a 1785 letter, "every power is dangerous which is not bound up by general rules."[16]

Indeed, Jefferson even encouraged what is now known as whistleblowing. "If any officer knows of an offense to the laws, they must declare it," he told the Virginia Board of Visitors in a harbinger of the honor code that would govern his university. "And certainly, where wrong has been done, he who knows and conceals the doer of it makes himself an accomplice, and justly censurable as such."[17]

Jefferson also understood that there might be problems monitoring the large and growing dependence on contractors who delivered services upon the young republic's behalf. Indeed, as Jerry Mashaw writes of the period, "the question of whether a particular person was an 'officer' or a 'contractor' was a much-vexed and often-litigated question, which is why Congress wrote such tight ethics laws governing the extra sources of income on which so many quasi-federal officials relied."[18]

Competition is also a device for assuring performance, though the number of contracts that are subject to competition has been falling even as the number of large, bundled contracts involving dozens if not hundreds of subcontractors has been rising. According to the *New York Times*, the number of contracts that were subject to competition fell from 79 percent in 2001 to 48 percent in 2005, even as the amount of contracting rose by almost half from $207 billion in unadjusted dollars to more than $400 million.[19]

A final way to produce accountability is through tight performance measures, which are often missing even in performance-based contracts. Under federal regulations, contractors are to prepare performance evaluations on all contracts over $100,000 and to provide past performance information in making bids. In theory, competition, not performance, provides the hoped-for effect of greater efficiency and, therefore, lower-cost performance.[20] More importantly, it is not clear that past performance is any guide to future delivery. By not setting benchmarks against which a future contract can be monitored, the federal government may be encouraging contractors to inflate their past performance.

The Market for the Hidden Workforce

Unlike the thickening of government, which appears to be driven more by bad habits and a flawed definition of leadership, the growth in the true size of government reflects clear incentives that make a contract or grant job more attractive than a civil service position.

Congress and presidents, Democrats and Republicans, and candidates for national office all view reductions in civil service employment as a measure of their commitment to smaller government. They may have tolerated small increases in the civil service over the decades, but have maintained federal employment at roughly 2 million since the 1970s. Although the Whitten amendment finally expired in 1978, its effect has been felt through one employee ceiling after another, including the one contained in the 1978 Civil Service Act, and imposed through repeated presidential orders.[21]

Federal employee unions might argue that much of the outsourcing is driven by Budget Circular A-76, which was issued in 1955. Under the circular, the federal government was prohibited from engaging in "any commercial activity to provide a service or product for its own use if such product or service can be procured from private enterprise through ordinary business procedures." Coupled with the proviso that the federal government cannot produce any product or service that is not inherently governmental, the circular has generated thousands of job competitions between federal and business employees over the decades, and became a centerpiece of the George W. Bush administration's tepid management agenda.

However, even assuming that jobs subject to the circular had been contracted out over the years, the federal workforce would not have declined by even a fraction of the increased contractor workforce. Indeed, conventional wisdom suggests that federal employees win roughly half of all A-76 competitions.

Advocates of the Hidden Workforce

The much more important explanation for the largely hidden workforce of contractors, grantees, and state and local mandate employees rests in pure political incentives. Except for federal employee unions, which seek to protect the lower-level jobs that are often subject to A-76, virtually every institution involved in the make-or-buy decision favors buying.

Contractors favor outsourcing out of obvious self-interest—the greater the outsourcing, the greater the profit. They not only lobby

Congress and the president for larger contracts, they often provide campaign contributions to friendly incumbents. In 2006 alone, the defense industry made more than $16 million in contributions to mostly Republican congressional and presidential candidates, and spent more than $100 million on lobbying.[22] These numbers have increased steadily over time, and are unlikely to decline in the future. Although federal employees and their labor unions also have friends in high places, especially within the Democratic Party, they simply cannot compete with the dollars that help contractors and grantees make their case for higher spending and the jobs it produces.

Democrats and Republicans also favor the hidden workforce, but for very different reasons. Democrats favor outsourcing largely because it insulates them from charges that they advocate bigger government. In calling for a government that works better and costs less, they can easily impose their own employment ceilings, argue for large-scale downsizing, and reduce actual civil service employment, and, in doing so, refute Republican charges that Democrats are the party of bigger government. It was precisely this reasoning that led Gore's reinventing government campaign to recommend a cut of 250,000 jobs to prove its commitment to greater efficiency.

Republicans also worry about big government—they can hardly attack the Democrats if they are just as active in promoting increased federal spending and hiring more civil servants. Indeed, as the second Bush administration discovered, increased spending alone can raise concerns among the Republican Party's core constituents that the president has lost his way. The notion that the Bush administration has favored big government was a major factor in declining public approval among Republicans starting well before the end of its first term.

But Republicans also favor outsourcing because the jobs it produces are in private industry. If the federal government has to hire someone to produce goods and services, better a business employee than a civil servant. Thus, the Republican House opposed the "federalization" of the Transportation Security Administration's workforce from the very beginning of the legislative debate. Republicans often belittled federal employees along the way, arguing that they could not be as effective as a private workforce. Members also blamed federal employees for the mistakes leading up to the 9/11 attacks, suggesting that a federal baggage and passenger screening workforce would be no more effective in preventing terrorism than federal employees had been in overseeing the private contractors who failed to prevent the airplane hijackings.

Congress and the presidency also favor the hidden workforce, again often for the same reasons. For their part, members of Congress reap campaign benefits from contractor contributions, and earn more than their share of special attention from lobbyists as part of the outsourcing process.

In turn, presidents, their top appointees, and many senior civil service executives favor outsourcing because it provides a faster, easier path to hiring employees. Although they rarely make the case publicly, presidential and civil-service executives tend to view contractors as more responsive to their direction and easier to oversee. They recognize the difficulties the federal government faces in filling hard-to-recruit positions, readily acknowledge that the federal hiring system is slow and confusing, and are just as likely as lower-level employees to criticize the disciplinary process.

Looking across the overall political economy of shifting jobs outward to contractors, grantees, and state and local government employees, it is no surprise that the true size of the hidden workforce would increase. Nor is it surprising that Congress and presidents would soon return to unfunded mandates to state and local government, in spite of the Unfunded Mandates Reform Act of 1995, which prohibited such mandates without a clear estimate of their effect. Blessed with the peace dividend created at the end of the cold war, Democrats and Republicans alike could claim enormous success in breaking the back of big government. Likewise, Congress and the president could reap the benefits of increased contributions, while senior civil service executives could cope with a sluggish hiring and disciplinary process.

Costs

The use of contracts, grants, and mandates is not without costs, however. As dollars have increased, so has vulnerability to fraud, waste, and abuse. Democrats even tried to make an issue of increased outsourcing under George W. Bush by arguing that the administration had made at least 118 "problem contracts" during the three separate contract expansions involving the Iraq war, Hurricane Katrina, and homeland security.[23]

Democrats also emphasized the increased concentration of dollars among five large contractors that collectively received more than 20 percent of all contracts awarded in 2005—Lockheed Martin, Boeing, Northrop Grumman, Raytheon, and General Dynamics—while highlighting the phenomenal growth in Halliburton's contract load. According to the Democrats, the decline in competition for many of those contracts created enormous opportunities for fraud and waste.

Noting that contracts had become the fastest growing component of federal discretionary spending, a fact confirmed in the federal budget, Democrats also argued that the growth had come at a "steep cost for federal taxpayers." "Overcharging has been frequent, and billions of dollars of taxpayer money have been squandered. There is no single reason for the rising waste, fraud, and abuse in federal outsourcing. Multiple causes—including poor planning, noncompetitive awards, abuse of contract flexibilities, inadequate oversight, and corruption—have all played a part."[24] In particular, Democrats highlighted the increasing use of noncompetitive contracting, the declining use of performance-based contracts, particularly in Iraq, and the increasing stress on purchasing offices, which experienced a rough doubling of their purchasing portfolios between 2001 and 2005 with no appreciable increase in staffing.

Democrats hardly needed to issue their own report on troubled contracts, however. Contract management has been a recurring item on the GAO "high risk" list of roughly two dozen troubled federal programs and systems for the better part of two decades. GAO put Defense, Energy, and National Aeronautics and Space Administration contract management on its very first high-risk list in 1990, and has yet to remove them.

According to GAO's 2007 update, Defense remained on the list because of wide-ranging weaknesses in initiating work before requirements were defined or understood, and "often used criteria that were not directly related to outcomes"; Energy stayed on the list because of its "record of both inadequate management and oversight of contractors and failure to hold contractors accountable"; while NASA stayed on the list because its financial management system placed "little emphasis on product performance, cost controls, and program outcomes."[25]

The problems were hardly restricted to these three agencies, however. Writing to the new Congress in November 2007, the nation's Comptroller General, David Walker, put contract management at the top of his list of targets for near-term oversight. As he wrote, Congress not only needs to make sure all agencies have "sufficient workforce capacity to monitor contractor cost, quality, and performance," it must also guarantee that the purchase of goods and services is "performance- and outcome-based, with appropriate risk-sharing contracts in place."[26]

With contracts now running more than $500 billion a year and grants approaching the $100 billion mark, the lack of accountability for results is particularly troubling. Although many federal contracts and grants are well executed, the federal service simply does not have the capacity to assure the transparency needed across the vast panoply of its purchases of goods and services. It most certainly does not have the capacity to monitor the actions of its vast and hidden workforce.

Nor, as James P. Pfiffner argues, does that vast and hidden workforce necessarily have a public service ethic. "These workers are not just making a profit and earning a living, but are also serving the public, and the consequences of success and failure are often much broader than purely private sector jobs."[27] As such, private employees are bound by Jefferson's compact of conscience as well. They, too, must share a commitment to the public good for government to assure accountability for results.

Conclusion

Even as it provides perceived political and administrative benefits, the rise of the hidden workforce carries great potential cost in lost accountability, not to mention potential increases in labor costs that remain invisible absent a hard headcount of contract- and grant-generated employment, as well as the dependency on single suppliers that is created as industries have consolidated over time. As Hamilton argued, government should be able to control its agents no matter where the point of delivery occurs. As long as contracts and grants are tight, oversight is adequate, and financial statements are clear, there should be no difference in accountability.

But these assumptions are often violated by a procurement process that is short on qualified government employees and overwhelmed by the "bundling" of large contracts into a byzantine maze of potential and interlocking conflicts. According to one recent analysis, the Defense Department's procurement budget nearly doubled between 1997 and 2004, even as its procurement workforce dropped slightly from 20,000 employees to 19,000. Although some of the decline involved higher productivity, it is hard to argue that the overall effect was salutary.[28]

These blurred lines are only part of the long-term erosion of an energetic federal service, however. They weaken action to strengthen the federal workforce by giving Congress and the president an easy option for hiring needed capacity. They also weaken the case for building strong networks between government and its contractors and grantees by letting the contractors and grantees manage the networks themselves. Finally, they undermine the federal government's institutional capacity by weakening its own ability to attract and retain talented employees. Private contractors and grantees can hardly be faulted for providing better jobs at higher pay, nor can they be criticized for giving their employees a more tangible sense of accomplishment.

This is one area where a focus on both Hamilton and Jefferson might improve accountability. Hamilton's belief in transparency deserves a special embrace in calls for a larger purchasing workforce to oversee contracts, grants, and other forms of outsourcing, while Jefferson's calls for simplification and civic duty suggest a much tighter focus on just who occupies the hidden workforce and why they are hidden. Because Hamilton and Jefferson alike believed in transparency, they would certainly call for some accounting of the true size of the federal workforce as one device for assuring a due responsibility to the public.

Bluntly put, if the hidden workforce is to provide goods and services on the federal government's behalf, it should be governed by the same rules that affect the federal service. That includes full transparency of just how that workforce is making decisions, spending money, and allocating costs, information that is not available today. Much as Jefferson favored decentralization, he certainly did not intend it to involve a large workforce of de facto federal employees.

CHAPTER EIGHT

Reversing the Decline

Neither Hamilton nor Jefferson could have known how their early opinions and decisions might affect government in the distant future. After all, they were dealing with a very small federal service, and could not have anticipated the tremendous growth that would follow decades of expansion, particularly during and after the New Deal and Great Society.

Hamilton could not have known that execution in detail would eventually create layers upon layers of management between the top and bottom of government which would obscure the president's ability to oversee the faithful execution of the laws. Although he soon discovered just how difficult it was to monitor the Treasury Department's employees, especially those located in field offices far from headquarters, he surely could not have guessed that government would eventually contain dozens of seemingly meaningless titles designed more to aggrandize than improve the faithful execution of the laws.

Similarly, Jefferson could not have known that his early attempts to create a politicized presidency through rotation in office would eventually lead to an emphasis on campaign experience and zealotry as essential ingredients of what he had described as the "merit and reputation" of an administration. Hard as he worked to remove several hundred Federalists from office, he could not have known that the political hierarchy would eventually grow to include so many layers that oversee government. After all, it was one thing to root the Federalists out, and quite another to provide a tool for future centralization of management control, especially given Jefferson's deep commitment to harmony in the executive and decentralization toward the states. Nor could Jefferson have known that his focus on a frugal government would lead to the persistent war on waste that has starved government over the past decades.

Indeed, as one works through the inventory of early administrative decisions and implied definitions of an energetic federal service, one must always remember that the early days of the republic involved great experimentation and outright chaos. Yet, even acknowledging the uncertainties surrounding the first few decades, scholars must pay more attention to the underlying structure that Hamilton and his Federalists brought to the basic operations of government.

With little guidance from the Constitution itself, they managed to construct the administrative state, setting an impressive array of precedents along the way. As Mashaw writes, working through the young institutions of their new national government, the Federalists "made enormous progress in constructing a system of political, managerial, and legal controls over administration. And they accomplished this while simultaneously building the administrative institutions necessary to run a government."

As Mashaw concludes, the first twelve years of government were "in some sense a continuation of the Constitutional Convention."[1] And many of the decisions still hold today, undermining an energetic federal service and the faithful execution of all the laws regardless of their ideological merits. Recall Hamilton's warning that all resistance must cease once a law is passed. There is simply no place for differences of opinion and the jarrings of parties that worried Hamilton in *Federalist No. 70*.

Hamilton and Jefferson Reconciled?

Before turning to possible reforms to restore the energetic federal service needed to deliver on the federal government's agenda, it is important to note that Hamilton and Jefferson were not as far apart on Hamilton's definition as it sometimes seems.

Granted, Hamilton viewed administration as a top-down process of tight control, while Jefferson viewed it as a bottom-up process designed to avoid centralization. Yet, as Lynton Caldwell wrote, "the differences which separated them seem less fundamental and more complex than either they or their more partisan interpreters would perhaps admit . . .

If the opposing assertions of Hamilton and Jefferson concerning their differences are taken at face value, Hamilton was a monarchist committed to the conversion of the Constitution of 1789 into a centralized government dominated by a plutocracy and administered by a hereditary nobility; Jefferson, a demagogue with an insatiable desire for popularity and an unreasonable jealousy of power in the hands of others."[2]

The reality is much more nuanced, with Hamilton the greatest influence on how government should work and Jefferson ever concerned about what it should do. Hence, the recurring theme in this book about the need for a bit more Jefferson in tempering the unintended consequences of Hamilton's precedents, and a bit more Hamilton in protecting government from the constant echoes of Jefferson's call for a war on federal fraud, waste, and abuse.

The challenge is to rebuild an energetic federal service as a whole, top to bottom, thereby addressing the steady erosion documented in this book. Much as one might admire current efforts to streamline the appointments process, accelerate the civil-service hiring process, and strengthen oversight of federal contracts and the hidden workforce they create, such reforms are only pieces of a comprehensive agenda for reform.

In fact, an incremental approach to reform may create more problems than it solves. Fixing the hiring process does little to eliminate the frustrations among the federal service as a whole; streamlining the presidential appointments process does little to streamline the chain of command; flattening the hierarchy demands much greater investment in the training, technology, and staffing of the career civil service; advertising federal careers does little to address the frustrations new recruits face in building a vibrant career; stopping the onslaught of reform does little to remove the sediment of past management fads; and so forth down the list.

Throughout it all, Congress and the president will no doubt continue to ask more for less, while denying the resources to convert government's greatest endeavors into achievements. Absent some sorting of the expanding mission, it is difficult to restore the sense of purpose that substantial percentages of federal employees express in a post-9/11 world. In the end, rebuilding an energetic federal service is rather like moving mercury—push it here and it moves there. Done incrementally, it is an exercise in frustration.

Only comprehensive reform and the trade-offs that might create political momentum will do. Congress and the president, as well as the federal service itself, will not come gently to reform unless they see at least some benefits for themselves. Presidents will not permit cuts in the number of political appointments without a flatter hierarchy; civil servants will not accept a flatter hierarchy without newfound resources; Congress and the president will not provide the resources for training, technology, and adequate staffing without promised cost savings and higher performance; and young Americans will not accept the call to service without career paths that acknowledge their desire to make a difference.

The following chapter will provide a sample of the kinds of comprehensive reforms that might reenergize the federal service by addressing the problems highlighted earlier in this book. At times, the reforms merely involve an injection of more Jeffersonian thinking about how the administrative state might work—for example, less execution in detail or a greater call to duty—while others involve a return to Hamilton's model—for example, less focus on the war on waste. But the following sample of reforms is intended primarily to illustrate the need to imagine action across the array of current threats to an energetic federal service, not just one facet or another of what has become a serious crisis that threatens the government's ability to faithfully execute all the laws.

The Baby-Boom Legacy

Comprehensive reform requires both an action-forcing event such as a crisis and an action-producing tool such as a fast-track legislative process. The coming baby-boom retirements from the federal workforce actually provide both elements by giving Congress and presidents the ability to reenergize the federal service without inflicting great pain.

On the one hand, if current projections hold, almost half the federal workforce will retire in the coming decade, including many who entered government during the glory days of the 1960s and 1970s when the call to service was bright and opportunities for advancement still apparent. The retirements have prompted urgent and predictable calls to fix the recruitment process, lest the federal government face an untenable rise in vacancies at all levels of the hierarchy. The retirements have also created images of hollow government even more dependent on the hidden workforce to execute the laws, not to mention new campaign rhetoric by candidates such as Rudy Giuliani, who promised not to fill half the vacancies at all.

Viewed as a problem, the coming retirements constitute a serious threat to government's ability to faithfully execute the laws. Institutional memory will decline as senior executives leave, turnover at the top and bottom of government will create gaps in service and accountability, and the thickening of government will tend to erode the chain of command. Although the baby boomers will not retire in one giant mass, their exits from both the civil service and the hidden workforce will create accelerating pressure for replacements as government, contractors, grantees, and state and local governments compete for their share of talent in a changing labor market.

On the other hand, the baby-boom retirements create the opportunity to reshape federal careers, particularly if the vacancies are not automatically filled by the next federal employee in line. Evaluating each job as the occupant leaves would create the opportunity to thin government, shift resources downward to the front lines where government services are delivered, abandon needless reform, and renew the promise of meaningful work for talented Americans. Such an effort to evaluate each job would have to meet several tests:

- It would have to be agency neutral. As already noted, all federal retirements will not occur simultaneously. Some agencies such as the Environmental Protection Agency have older workforces because they did most of their recruitment in the 1970s, while others such as the Transportation Security Administration have younger workforces because of high turnover. Thus, any methodology for evaluating jobs would have to be careful not to punish agencies simply because they happen to be older.

- It would have to be nonpartisan. Assuming that all jobs must be evaluated before they are refilled, the methodology must be absolutely insulated from political or ideological bias. Assuming that the methodology would be administered by the chief operating officers in government, who are presidential appointees, the process might require creation of a nonpartisan oversight board to review the basic guidelines and implementation of the new system.

- It would have to be fair. The evaluative criteria for assessing vacancies must be clear and fair, and they must also assure that the harvesting and backfilling does not reinforce the glass ceiling for women and people of color who may have been waiting years for their chance to advance. Thus, any methodology would have to assure maximum protection for disadvantaged groups.

- It would have to be tested. Federal personnel law currently allows waivers for experiments in hiring and supervising federal employees, which could be used to carefully but expeditiously test the methodology for evaluating jobs. The methodology might also be coupled with special programs to create incentives for early retirements in order to achieve more immediate impact.

It is impossible to know just how far the true size of government could shrink and how flat the federal hierarchy could become if all of the vacancies were captured, evaluated, and refilled, eliminated, or redistributed. Indeed, if business experience with such harvesting and backfilling methods holds true and only half the jobs prove essential, the true size of government could shrink by several million jobs, especially in the contractor community.

The civil-service jobs would not necessarily disappear from government, however. Indeed, the harvesting could produce a large redistribution of resources downward where the complaints about a lack of resources were the most intense. This in turn could actually increase the overall size of the civil service.

The retirement of the baby boomers could also produce a much more pliable government, including a new disciplinary system that involves an end to inflated annual performance ratings, room for at least some migration of inherently governmental contractor jobs back into government, and a restoration of the federal service's reputation as an employer of choice for young Americans. It could also provide the political anchor for the recommendations below.

The rest of this chapter will examine the components of comprehensive reform in greater detail. It will start with a review of the problems facing the federal service, and then turn to a problem-by-problem agenda for reform. The time for tinkering is long gone. A better disciplinary system would certainly help morale, for example, but not without gains in resources; a better pay-for-performance process would help, too, but not without a more effective call to service. Restoring the federal service involves a package of problems that cannot be addressed one at a time.

An Inventory of Erosion

The weakening of the federal service reflects a series of separate trends that come together to weaken the faithful execution of the laws as a whole. Based on the belief that government can always do more with less, these trends have created a cascade of failures that are harbingers of further, deeper distress.

Both by accident and intent, this belief has been nurtured by repeated campaigns against government, and is reflected in the seven trends embedded in the contemporary erosion, explained earlier in this book. Although each of the trends has contributed to the crisis separately, they have combined to create a desperate moment in bureaucratic time in which the lack of action can only condemn government to greater frustration and failure.

An Ever-Expanding Mission

The threat to the federal service would not be relevant if government did not have such a large list of significant missions. After all, the federal agenda includes many of the most difficult and important problems the nation faces, whether guaranteeing voting rights through decent technology and aggressive enforcement, reducing disease through continued research in modern laboratories, improving the quality of life for older Americans through Social Security and an expanded Medicare program, or protecting the environment through effective implementation of the Clean Air and Water Acts. Americans may not agree on every mission, but the federal government is given little choice but to implement them all.

This is not to argue that the mission is expanding exponentially, however. As this book shows, there has been a substantial slowdown in congressional and presidential action. Whereas the federal mission expanded dramatically during the 1960s and early 1970s, it has been slowing down ever since as Congress and presidents have pursued fewer major legislative initiatives. Starved by tax cuts, government simply has less room on its agenda. This has not prevented mission creep but it has created a downward curve in total growth.

Even a slowly expanding mission sets the stage for further erosion of an energetic federal service. The federal government can hardly be expected to convert its long list of endeavors into achievements without the leadership and resources to do so. But those resources have been difficult to find in an era of aggressive efforts to honor promises to reduce federal spending and drive total federal employment ever downward.

Democrats and Republicans alike have joined the effort to starve government. Even with the kind of aggressive sorting discussed below, the federal government cannot protect its past achievements, let alone convert its most significant disappointments into successful endeavors, unless it provides the resources to succeed. Its mission simply cannot grow and starve at the same time.

Still Thickening Government

The federal government's expanding hierarchy reflects its steadily expanding mission, as well as the constant mimicry of new titles. Both by inattention and intent, Congress and the president continue to build a towering monument to their addiction to leadership by layers.

As this book suggests, the federal government has never had more layers of management or more leaders per layer. Despite his promises of businesslike government, George W. Bush's administration now oversees sixty-four discrete titles at the top of the federal government, and almost 2,600 titleholders, up from fifty-one titles and 2,400 titleholders in the final years of the Clinton administration. Although some of the growth reflects the war on terrorism, every department has expanded. Presidents may think the titles create greater leadership, but this book suggests just the opposite—more leaders create more opportunity for delay and obfuscation.

Unfortunately, the thickening has resisted all efforts to contain it. The Reagan administration lost the battle of the bulge against middle-level supervisors, and the Clinton administration appears to have created an entirely new industry in reclassifying supervisory titles into nonsupervisory titles that are still part of the chain of command. Although the Clinton administration deserves credit for cutting the number of supervisors by at least a quarter, it also merits blame for increasing the number of senior layers at the same time. If breadth does not increase, depth will, and vice versa. Both of these trends reduce the clarity of command, while increasing the distance that information must move and the potential distortions associated with ever-lengthening reporting chains.

Innocent until Nominated

In theory, tight chains of command should increase executive control at all levels of government. However, the presidential appointments process has become so slow and cumbersome that many layers remain unoccupied for months at the start of a new presidential administration, and continue unoccupied as appointees exit with regularity after eighteen to twenty-four months on the job.

As the scrutiny has increased, the process has slowed. Whereas the Kennedy administration was up and running within three months of inauguration day, the second Bush administration waited more than eight months on average to complete its long list of cabinet and subcabinet appointments. The delays have raised the importance of the de facto subcabinet composed of appointees who serve solely at the pleasure of the president without Senate confirmation.

This book does not address the impact of zealous appointees on the erosion of an energetic federal service, though there appears to be an increase in such appointees in Democratic and Republican administrations alike, especially in the rapidly expanding public affairs offices that often seek to politicize unpleasant facts and scientific evidence. However, there is no question that the process itself increasingly discourages appointees, whatever their ideology and intensity, from accepting the call to service. Delays are common, even among highly-qualified appointees, and complaints about the Senate and White House are high. Past appointees report that neither institution acts responsibly, while potential appointees worry that the process will embarrass and confuse them.

Although potential appointees worry more about the process than the past experience of actual appointees suggests is necessary, they also see living in Washington, D.C., as a significant barrier to service, and report significant concerns about the impact of presidential service on their future careers, especially their ability to return to their previous jobs. The result is a dwindling pool of potential appointees, many of whom may be motivated more by the chance to make future contacts and increase their earning power than the chance to serve an admired president.

A Deafening Crisis

Whatever their motivation, presidential appointees oversee a federal workforce that reports serious obstacles to success, especially when compared with business and the nonprofit sector.

On full exertion for the public benefit, many federal employees said they took their jobs for the pay, benefits, and security instead of the chance to accomplish something worthwhile. Compared to nonprofit employees, who emphasize the chance to accomplish something worthwhile and the nature of the work, federal employees have taken Hamilton's model seriously, putting compensation at the top of the list for coming to work each day.

On work that matters, federal employees reported that they do not always receive the kind of work that encourages innovation and high performance. At first glance, the quality of work looks reasonably attractive, especially among employees who said they are surrounded by peers who are committed to the mission, given the chance to do the things they do best, and encouraged to take risks and try new ways of doing things. But when compared with business and nonprofit employment, the quality of federal work suffers.

On the adequate provision of support, federal employees were consistently dissatisfied with access to the tools they need, including training, technology, and enough employees to do the job. Nor did they rate their leadership and coworkers as competent as business and nonprofit employees. At least according to the 2001 and 2002 surveys, most federal employees rated their peers as not particularly competent and not getting better.

On rewards for a job well done and discipline for a job done poorly, most federal employees gave their organization's disciplinary process failing marks and blamed this poor performance in part on their organization's unwillingness to ask enough of all employees. Federal employees also gave their own organizations low ratings on basic tasks such as delivering programs and services, being fair, and spending money wisely.

Finally, on the respect of the public served, ordinary citizens are not the only ones who have come to distrust government. Federal employees themselves showed little trust in their own organizations, in no small part because the federal government has been so penurious with the basic resources they need to do their jobs well.

Ironically given the urgency of the war on terrorism, many of these indicators actually decayed following the 9/11 attacks, in part because federal employees may have become less tolerant of bureaucracy and red tape. The most surprising problems came at the Department of Defense, where employees simultaneously reported an increased sense of mission, but more layers of needless management, inadequate staffing levels, and less access to the technology and training they needed to succeed. Faced with an urgent mission, they became increasingly angry with the bureaucracy around them, and surprisingly less likely to report high morale among their colleagues.

The Spirit of Service

All of these trends have contributed to declining interest in federal service among young Americans, who rightly wonder whether the federal government can deliver on its promises of extensive and arduous enterprise without sacrificing each new generation of talent. In a very real sense, the federal government's reputation precedes it, whether on college campuses, in professional schools, or in the halls of government itself.

As this book suggests, many college seniors would not want a federal job even if they knew how to get one, too many graduates of the nation's top professional schools see government as a destination for pay, benefits, and security rather than challenging work, and too many Presidential Management Fellows are thinking that government might be a good place to begin a career, but not to stay. Having redefined the basic meaning of public service almost to the point of excluding government work, young Americans now view nonprofits as the destination of choice for making a difference and learning new skills. Asked to show them the work, the federal government too often shows young Americans the bureaucracy, including a hiring process that sends the instant message that life will be difficult at best once on the federal payroll.

These young Americans are all part of a new public service that is searching for meaningful work and the chance to accomplish something worthwhile wherever it might be in the multisector public service. This new public service is no longer only interested in government. Indeed, the federal government is running third as a destination of choice behind business and nonprofit organizations. Ready to pursue the chance to accomplish something worthwhile in any sector, this new public service is also quite willing to switch sectors in search of good work. It is also part of a seller's labor market that has many opportunities to make a difference outside the federal government.

The Tides of Reform

The onslaught of reform over the decades has contributed to the federal government's reputation for administrative inertia. Despite the congressional and presidential slowdown in passing major laws, the number of major management statutes has been increasing since the end of World War II, with a particularly rapid acceleration since Watergate. To the extent senior federal employees feel that Congress and the president act in ways that damage performance, the rising tides of management reform are partly to blame.

The level of federal reform appears to parallel the frenzy of management improvement fads in business. But as the pace of federal management reform has increased over the past thirty years, so has the mix of reforms. As Congress has become more involved in making government work, federal employees have faced one competing reform after another, leading to confusion, wasted motion, and frustration in setting priorities with fads and fashions that are now out of favor.

The reform activity speaks to profound confusion over just how to make government work, in part because past reforms have been piecemeal at best. There has been no systematic effort to assess the administrative state since the early 1950s when former President Herbert Hoover led a major reform commission. Absent a basic template for measuring the performance of government, federal employees have been bathed in constant change, often toward contradictory goals. Although there is still some hope that government will learn how to measure its success, recent experience suggests that this too shall pass.

The True Size of Government

The rising tides of reform speak to a general frustration with government's ability to perform, but much of that performance is now dependent on a hidden workforce of contractors, grantees, and state and local employees who labor under federal mandates. Although this workforce is essential to implementing the federal mission, there is cause for concern about the costs embedded in continued outsourcing, especially given the lack of an experienced cadre of federal employees to oversee the activity.

There is no question that this hidden workforce is growing. Although the true size of government dropped sharply in the years following the end of the cold war, it began rising in the late 1990s and has been growing ever since. In 1999, for example, the true size of government had reached its lowest level in more than a decade, dropping to just 11 million civil servants, postal workers, military personnel, and contract- and grant-generated employees. Six years later, in 2005, the true size of government had risen to 14.6 million, largely driven by the burgeoning war on terrorism and the Iraq War. Most of the increase did not come from the purchase of goods but from services such as computer programming, management assistance, and temporary labor.

The hidden workforce is increasingly governed by performance-based contracts that ignore labor costs entirely. But such contracts are notoriously difficult to oversee, especially when the rules are set by the contractors themselves. Having resisted every effort to get an accurate headcount of its employees, the federal government has little choice but to accept reassurances that it is actually reaping the benefits of competition among private contractors and grantees, even though recent industry consolidations suggest that the federal government is increasingly dependent on suppliers who rarely compete at all.

It is impossible to claim that the hidden workforce of contractors and grantees is not doing its job either effectively or at reasonable cost, if only because such a claim would require more information and oversight than overworked federal procurement officers now have. Nevertheless, the increasing use of contractors, grantees, and state and local employees suggests a significant substitution of hidden workers for full-time federal employees. In turn, this substitution effect creates a series of illusions, including the notion that the federal government can actually track its large and increasing number of megacontracts and the labor they purchase. The hidden workforce may be mostly invisible to the public and press, but it exists nonetheless.

An Agenda for Reform

Big problems demand big answers, which is why tinkering will no longer suffice. Although there may be benefits in taking on one problem at a time and building momentum toward government-wide action on many of the threats of further harm, such efforts have stalled repeatedly in past Congresses.

It is time, therefore, to think about how to build consensus on a package of reforms that would offer trade-offs among the three reform philosophies that hold hope for progress—scientific management toward pay for performance, liberation management toward a flattening of the hierarchy, and watchful eye toward greater public awareness of the true size of government. Congress and the president will not reach agreement, however, without a bit of Hamilton and Jefferson blended together to create needed consensus built around cuts in the total workforce and reduction in the number of presidential appointees. And cuts in the number of appointees will not produce consensus without greater presidential authority to shape the overall package, as suggested later in this section.

It is impossible to deny the great challenges in building this kind of consensus, however. As Table 8.1 suggests, the reforms are broad, indeed, and would create a long list of adversaries.

Reversing the erosion itself is no small task. It involves debate across all seven signposts of the erosion, including the mission, thickening, appointments, the workforce, hyperreform, the true size of government, and student interest. Driven by analysis of the existing government mis-

Table 8.1 Recommendations for reform

Sort the federal mission
1. Develop a sorting methodology for determining the importance, difficulty, and success of the federal government's mission, and jettison missions that are no longer relevant, while possibly combining others.

Thin government
1. Develop a clear and consistent methodology for counting the layers of government.
2. Set a target of no more than six layers between the top and bottom of each federal department and agency.
3. Substantially reduce the number of alter-ego titles that are interposed between the top and bottom of government.
4. Reduce the number of managers by half at all levels of government.

Accelerate the appointments process
1. Streamline and reconcile the major forms that govern the appointments process, including the financial disclosure form.
2. Provide modest federal funding to the major national parties for preelection transition planning by the major party candidates.
3. Reduce the number of presidential appointees by half to accelerate the process by reducing the size of the nomination pipeline, while also opening opportunities for career officers to take higher-level positions.
4. Provide transition assistance for presidential appointees who move to Washington, D.C.
5. Abolish any presidential position that cannot be nominated and confirmed within six months of a vacancy.

Rebuild vigor and expedition
1. Increase basic resources for training, and redistribute jobs toward the front lines of government.
2. Track access to basic resources through careful analysis, including line items in the federal budget.
3. Create a faster, simpler hiring process, and use it.
4. Experiment with an up-or-out promotion system for federal supervisors modeled on the military's up-or-out promotion system.
5. Streamline the disciplinary process, and experiment with the use of a "grading curve" on the number of employees who can receive high ratings through the annual performance appraisal process.
6. Create incentives for much greater movement of employees into government at the middle levels of government.
7. Talk incessantly about the important contributions federal employees make through their service.

Invite talented Americans to serve
1. Focus the call to service on making a difference, not pay, benefits, and security.

Table 8.1 (continued)

2. Reserve a quarter of all middle- and senior-level job openings for outside candidates.
3. Continue implementing a pay-for-performance system based on the pay banding concept embedded in recent departments of Defense and Homeland Security legislation.
4. Become more rigorous about performance measurement.

End hyperreform
1. Place a moratorium on reform for at least two Congresses.
2. Require sequential referral of all legislation containing any department or agency management reforms to the House and Senate government operations committees for further assessment and reporting.

Manage the true size of government
1. Systematically count the true size of government.
2. Impose the retirement-recapturing provisions recommended for government on the contract- and grant-generated workforce.
3. Strengthen oversight of contracts and grantees by rebuilding federal procurement units, and spend more energy monitoring mandates to state and local government.
4. Establish "in-sourcing" mechanisms designed to ask whether outsourced jobs should be returned to government.
5. Stop using de facto headcount ceilings to constrain federal employment.

sion, the reversal effort must first decide just how big the federal mission should be, then ask what the federal government needs to protect its past achievements and convert its past disappointments into success.

Taking the baby-boom retirements as one leverage point for action, the question is what might actually work to restore the energetic federal service that is needed to faithfully execute all the laws. As the following pages suggest, the answers add up to a very deep reform agenda. Tempting though it is to delegate the agenda to a national restructuring commission, there is more than enough evidence in this book to support a long list of recommendations, some easy, others much more difficult.

Sorting Missions

The package should include at least some effort to sort the federal mission, or at least establish some rules for starting the process. Although the sorting can involve a number of methods, including sunsets on existing programs, and efforts to build a mission-centered government by eliminating duplication and overlap, it must be driven by some methodology for determining which endeavors the federal government should keep, and which it should abandon. Congress and the president should either support the faithful execution of all the laws, abandon the lost causes, or transfer responsibilities to innovative states and localities.

There are many ways to sort the agenda, including old-fashioned logrolling and constituency pressure. But the most compelling method involves a sequential sorting of the importance, difficulty, and past success in pursuing each given endeavor. As Table 8.2 shows, this sorting technique might involve a sequential assessment of (1) the importance of solving the problem, (2) past success in doing so, and (3) the difficulty of achieving results.[3] Each question applies to a set of specific examples identified through the survey of the 450 historians and political scientists interviewed on government's greatest endeavors.

The result is a list of questions to be asked about whether and how to manage the federal government's many missions. Can government protect past achievements such as water quality? Can it produce greater success among endeavors rated important, successful, yet less difficult, such as voting rights? Can it expand its impact on endeavors rated as difficult and generally unsuccessful, such as arms control and disarmament? And what has frustrated success on endeavors rated important and difficult, such as health care for low-income Americans?

Some of these questions involve hard choices about what a society asks of itself. Perhaps it should pursue the easiest issues; perhaps it should focus only on success; perhaps it should ignore importance. But whatever the sorting mechanism, government must decide what it should keep and what it should drop.

Thinning Government

The thickening of government is much easier to address than sorting endeavors. It involves at least four discrete efforts that are easily within reach as Congress and the president confront the underlying problems moving information up the chain of command and guidance down:

1. The federal government should develop a clear and consistent methodology for determining the actual length of chains of command between the top and bottom of government. Such a methodology should start at the bottom with the front-line jobs that are most important to public confidence, and then work upward in search of opportunities for reducing distance.

Table 8.2 A methodology for sorting missions by importance and difficulty

	More important		Less important	
	More successful	Less successful	More successful	Less successful
More difficult	Greatest achievements How can the achievement be protected? • Workplace equality • Public health • Desegregation and public access • Water quality • Workplace safety	Greatest causes What will it take to succeed? • Arms control and disarmament • Air quality • Primary and secondary education • Hazardous waste • Energy • Human rights • Mass transportation	Greatest trade-offs Do the benefits justify the costs? • Federal budget deficit • Foreign trade • Space exploration	Greatest puzzles Is there another way? • Community development • Crime • International economic development • Endangered species • Welfare reform • Immigration • Campaign reform
Less difficult	Greatest opportunities Is there anything more to do? • Right to vote • Safe food and drinking water • Hunger and nutrition • Health care for older Americans	Greatest disappointments Why is government failing? • Health care for low-income Americans • Assistance for the working poor • National airways system	Greatest bargains Is there any reason to stop? • Protecting financial markets • Veterans readjustment • National highways system	Greatest failures Is there any reason to continue, and, if so, how? • Low-income housing • Health care infrastructure • Government transparency • Job training
Government performance	• Financial security for older Americans • Post-secondary education • Consumer protection • Wilderness protection	• Science and technology • Persian Gulf stability	• National defense • Home ownership	• Agricultural price supports • Deregulation • Tax reform • Devolution

2. The federal government should set a target of no more than six layers between the top and bottom of government. Such a target, which is a common goal among high-performing businesses, should drive decisions to remove layers from each organization's chain of command. Instead of focusing on the ratio of supervisors to nonsupervisors among both presidential appointees and the civil service, this effort should focus exclusively on layers.

3. The federal government should make a sustained effort to reduce the number of alter-ego titles that exist mostly to give principal officers a greater sense of importance. Such titles have spread well beyond their usefulness and should be created only in extreme cases. As such, every new alter-ego title should be subjected to close scrutiny, and every past title should be considered a prime target for abolition.

4. The federal government should use the baby-boom retirements to reduce the number and layers of managers by half at all levels of government, while preventing the conversion of managerial positions into nonmanagerial positions that still involve substantial managerial responsibilities. Such a reduction should place the burden of proof on the federal government to show that a given layer or manager is still needed in a slimmer structure, and would address the widening of government at the top of the executive hierarchy. This recommendation should also apply to the federal government's hidden workforce.

This slimming process would create winners and losers, and is clearly controversial. Tying the reductions to the baby-boom retirements would certainly make the cuts more palatable, while placing a moratorium of six months on filling the vacant jobs would give federal departments and agencies ample time to make the case for each job.

The key is to stop the automatic filling of jobs with the next federal employee in line. The federal government should have several options instead, including redistributing the jobs toward the front lines of government. Such redistribution would address complaints from lower-level staff that their organizations simply have too few employees to succeed. This redistribution would also theoretically reduce some of the pressure for outsourcing and the use of unfunded mandates to procure labor from state and local governments. As part of an overall process for evaluating each job vacated over the coming decade, redistribution could become the most important legacy of baby-boom civil servants.

Accelerating Appointments

There are many ways of accelerating the appointments process, especially by streamlining the questions that potential appointees must answer. The Senate and White House could easily work together to make sure that questions are not repeated, while a single questionnaire could be designed that would govern every position and be electronically available. They could also work together to streamline the burdensome financial disclosure forms. The public interest is well served by making sure financial conflicts are exposed, but doing so hardly requires the equivalent of a net-worth statement. At least some privacy rights can prevail without sacrificing the need to cure potential conflicts.

The process should also begin well before the end of the presidential campaigns. Under current law, the outgoing administration is required to give each presidential candidate a complete list of appointments, which certainly helps fill the pipeline of potential appointees. But major parties are not given federal funding to actually start vetting candidates. Campaigns are reluctant to engage in such preelection vetting lest they be accused of overconfidence. Moreover, even trivial funding for postelection planning is seen as a drain on essential financing for the campaign itself.

Essentially trivial funding for preelection planning was contained in the Senate's version of the 1988 revision of the Presidential Transitions Act. Such funding would have given tacit approval to preelection planning, but the bill was defeated by the House of Representatives. In theory, it would have also reduced early delays in the process. Congress should restore this provision and provide at least minimal funding for preelection planning. If the federal government can find the dollars to support the party conventions, it certainly can find the much smaller amounts required to encourage advance thought about governing.

At the same time, presidential appointees cannot be exempt from the thinning of government. The appointments process would not only move faster with a significant reduction in the number of appointments, it would likely improve lower-level confidence in the competence of leaders by increasing the attractiveness of appointments, while strengthening presidential leadership by bringing greater clarity to the chain of command.

To move toward resizing the appointments process to fit these goals, Congress and the president should cut the number of executive appointments in half. This would not diminish presidential leadership at all—to the contrary, such a cut would strengthen executive unity. Although Congress and the president would need a clear methodology for evaluating each presidential position, the number of presidential appointments could be cut in half with a net increase in government performance and presidential leadership. With a streamlined appointments process in place, the president's cabinet and subcabinet could be appointed within a few months, not nine. This recommendation would also increase the value of lower-level positions that must often go in search of talented candidates.

At the same time, the federal government should give presidential appointees the same transition package that it gives its own civil servants who change posts, including support for house-hunting trips, temporary housing, closing costs and other lease expenses, and extended storage of household goods. It should also create a placement service to help spouses and partners find new jobs, and consider consulting services to help families adjust to their new homes.

Finally, the Senate and president must address the increasing partisanship that pervades the contemporary process. No one can force the president and Senate to cooperate, consult, and ultimately reach consensus on the many controversial appointees they handle. The best recommendation I can make for breaking these kinds of delays is to abolish any appointee position that is not filled within six months of a vacancy. While such a proposal is well beyond radical, it would force the president to do more preelection planning, and push the Senate to move nominations forward or abandon them quickly. Bluntly put, any position that can stand vacant for six months or more is a position that is not needed.

Building a High-Performance Workforce

The federal workforce will not rebound without a sustained effort to overcome the key barriers to performance embedded in the current system. In a single word, the answer is "resources." Federal employees desperately need access to training, especially if they are to enter a new, thinner bureaucracy that places more responsibility in their hands. They also need state-of-the-art technology, not the patchworked systems that so many departments and agencies have purchased over the decades. And they need enough employees to do the job, which is a potential side benefit of redistributing labor down the chain of command.

The first way to rebuild the resource base is to track it. Federal departments and agencies do not know how much they spend on training, rarely have personal development plans for their employees, and only occasionally make promotions based on a portfolio of skills. In short, they only invest in their employees to the extent their employees can map their own course upward.

Federal employees also need a much faster hiring process and a disciplinary process that actually works. The former is more easily attained than the latter, if only because authority already exists for on-the-spot hiring and almost instant review of poor performance. If the federal government does not use these authorities properly, it is more through ignorance and habit than because of a lack of courage.

Building a more rigorous disciplinary process is a much more difficult challenge; it involves more aggressive training for managers on how to conduct effective performance appraisal and the use of a grading curve to keep the percentage of outstanding performers reasonably low.

Already, Congress is considering legislation to deny annual pay increases to employees with less than satisfactory ratings. But it makes little sense to deny annual pay increases to these poor performers in an inflated appraisal system that rates all but a handful of employees as satisfactory or better. Nor does it make sense to streamline the disciplinary process if supervisors do not have the training to determine just what constitutes high performance. As Congress moves forward with its pay reforms, it must always remember that such reforms can only create bitterness and anger if they are not fairly implemented.

Federal employees also need competent leadership, which speaks to the quality of presidential appointees and senior civil servants. Too many executives of the former received their posts through political connections, not demonstrated expertise, while too many of the latter moved into their current jobs by simply waiting in line. In theory, the vacancies created by the baby-boom retirements would allow departments and agencies to hold real competitions for the jobs they decide to fill.

In theory, too, the vacancies could give new breathing room to federal employees, and a greater sense that they can make a difference through their work. The greater accountability ensured by slimmer hierarchies should encourage employees to take more risks, albeit with appropriate supervision, while reigniting a passion to make a difference, not just to hold onto a secure job. Federal employees also need coworkers who are ready to give their complete attention to meeting expectations and creating a positive work environment.

Federal employees need a new federal career, one that emphasizes performance over automatic advancement, the chance to accomplish something worthwhile over pay, benefits, and security. They need to know that promotions are based on merit and need, not favoritism or the need to retain talented employees who deserve a perfectly legitimate pay increase.

Finally, acknowledging the need for comparable compensation in a highly competitive labor market, federal employees must come to work first and foremost for the chance to accomplish something worthwhile on behalf of the nation or find another job. Congress and the president can help by stopping their constant attacks on big government, while occasionally reminding federal employees that their work is essential to more than the war on terrorism. This is an essential step in rebuilding federal morale, and is part of inviting more young Americans to consider government jobs as a path to making a difference. Although mere rhetoric will not suffice, employees must occasionally be told that their work actually matters.

Inviting Talented Young Americans to Serve

Many of the reforms described above will no doubt improve government's reputation as a destination of choice. A faster hiring process will encourage talented young Americans to take a closer look at government work; using the baby-boom vacancies to rebuild vigor and expedition will create new opportunities to accomplish something worthwhile at the entry level; a stronger disciplinary process will reassure young Americans that performance, not time on the job, is the key to success; a flatter hierarchy will create better opportunities for advancement; more training will reassure new recruits that they will get the skills to succeed; and a more accurate accounting of the hidden workforce and its hierarchy may convince potential public servants that government can be a vibrant alternative to employment in business or with a nonprofit.

However, part of this effort must involve the right motivations for service. Instead of calling on the federal government to be more businesslike in its rhetoric and appeals, advocates of a healthy public service should ask it to become more nonprofitlike. The nonprofit sector, not the federal government or business, is the place where young Americans perceive the best chance to work for high-performing organizations, whether performance is measured by the ability to help people, accomplish something worthwhile, or deliver effective programs and services.

The nonprofit sector is also the destination where young Americans perceive the opportunity to find an inviting workplace, and get the trusting, innovative, and helpful environment they need to flourish. And it has a hiring process that is just as fast, as well as simpler and fairer.

Emphasizing the right motivations is only part of embracing the new public service. The federal government simply must allow much greater movement across the sector boundaries. Young Americans are no longer willing to sign with any employer for an entire career, and clearly want their employers to be flexible. Unless the federal government allows more lateral entry at all career levels, it will continue to lose the talent war with businesses and nonprofits. Toward this end, the federal government should reserve at least a quarter of its middle- and senior-level job openings for outside candidates, and learn how to reach those candidates through more aggressive advertising. Instead of denying that outsiders can be part of a renaissance of the new public service, the federal government should embrace the new energy.

Finally, young Americans need reassurance that they will be rewarded for their performance, not the amount of time spent on the job. Although it is still too early to evaluate current efforts to use pay "bands" instead of the intricate general schedule, efforts to place employees in a much simpler salary structure can only improve the government's ability to tie rewards to individual- or agency-level performance. Such efforts may also improve the perception that making a difference on missions that matter is respected, not to mention assuring that poor performers will receive the discipline they deserve.

The federal government must provide the basic resources to make such systems work, however, not the least of which is adequate funding for pay increases and managerial training. Such systems have performed particularly well in agencies such as the Government Accountability Office that have invested heavily in ongoing assessment and training. Such efforts have suppressed the tendency of pay-band systems to generate favoritism and discrimination, and must be part of implementation in the future. So, too, must efforts to work with federal employee unions to assure labor rights as such systems are implemented. Pay bands cannot be an excuse for dismantling past agreements that have generally worked well in encouraging labor-management cooperation.

Ending Hyperreform

It is difficult to know just what to do to constrain the tendency to overreform the executive branch. With 535 reformers on Capitol Hill and just one in the executive branch, the tides of reform will no doubt continue accelerating until Congress gets a chance to consider the kind of comprehensive proposals offered here.

Nevertheless, Congress could impose a moratorium on further tinkering until it completes a top-to-bottom assessment of past reforms, and could easily require supermajorities to pass legislation that does not originate in the Senate Homeland Security and Governmental Affairs Committee or the House Oversight and Government Reform Committee, which have primary jurisdiction over most, but not all, reforms. Congress could also require sequential review by these two committees on any legislation deemed by the Government Accountability Office to involve substantial management reform of the executive branch in whole or in part.

At the same time, Congress could be asked to review past reforms in search of legislative mandates and executive action that can be voided. As part of this "cleanout" function, Congress and the president could present a separate list of legislation that could be slated either for regular reauthorization or abandonment. Guided by a systematic effort to inventory the impact of past reforms, such an effort might reverse the tides of reform, while raising congressional consciousness regarding hyperreform.

This recommendation resembles the recent Bush administration proposal for a sunset commission to eliminate poorly performing programs, but deals entirely with management reform. Sunset commissions have been notoriously unsuccessful in eliminating programs at the state and local level, while sunsets on federal legislation have rarely produced the intended deliberative action. But sunsets on federal management legislation might have a more productive impact, if only because so many members of Congress have little interest in reform once a bill becomes law.

This effort to focus on essential reform must be embedded in progress toward measuring the actual outputs of government. Although performance management has been tried repeatedly over the past fifty years, starting with Lyndon Johnson's Planning, Programming, and Budgeting System, which morphed into Gerald Ford's Management by Objectives, which morphed again into Jimmy Carter's Zero Base Budgeting, and so forth, the effort to measure results is essential for judging the impact of given reforms in stimulating higher performance. It is also, incidentally, essential for assessing the actual impact of programs, whether for fine-tuning and adjustment or for the sorting described earlier in this chapter.

236 · A Government Ill Executed

Managing the True Size of Government

Congress already has enough legislation on the books to address the expanding true size of government, not the least of which is the 1995 Unfunded Mandates Reform Act. Unfortunately, Congress already has plenty of experience ignoring these statutes. There are four steps toward managing the true size of government more effectively:

1. The federal government should systematically count the true size of government. Estimates of the kind presented in this book are simply not enough to understand the actual impact of contracts, grants, and mandates on the hidden workforce. The federal government cannot calculate the labor costs of its actions without this information; nor can it compare the relative strength of its oversight without knowing just how many employees it oversees.

2. The federal government should also examine the vacancies created by baby-boom retirements in the contractor and grantee workforce. The burden of proof should be on contractors and grantees to show that all of their jobs are needed. Absent a hard headcount of the number of hidden employees and clear information on how those employees sort into their own hierarchies, however, this recapturing mechanism cannot work. Although the federal government has made several furtive efforts to generate this information, it must demand it as a condition for making contracts and grants in the first place.

3. The federal government must strengthen oversight of its contracts and grantees and spend more time worrying about the true cost of mandates to state and local governments. Federal procurement offices are often too small to perform the kind of oversight needed in this era of megacontracts that involve hundreds, even thousands, of subcontractors. This is not just a failure of "adult supervision," which is how former Defense Secretary Donald Rumsfeld explained the scandal involving the purchase of Boeing refueling tankers in 2005. It is a failure to adequately staff and train the government's own procurement officers.

4. The federal government should require "insourcing" of all inherently government jobs that have slipped out of the civil service over the past decades unless contractors can prove that they provide the activity at a significantly lower cost. Although the federal civil service may grow as a result, it will be growth easily jus-

tified by cost and the need to pull inherently governmental work back into government.

Although it is not clear just how big the civil service would be if it kept all of its inherently governmental jobs, what is clear is that it must be released from the current de facto caps. Even as it might shrink dramatically with the recapturing of baby-boom jobs, it might grow substantially with the insourcing mechanism described above. Too many federal jobs have been pushed out for the wrong reasons, not the least of which is the arbitrary limit on the total number of civil servants to roughly 2 million.

A Mechanism for Reform

Given this long list of potential reforms, the question is how to build the collective will to act. After all, Congress and the president have shown little interest at least since the 1978 Civil Service Reform Act in enacting the kind of sweeping reforms inventoried above. If the erosion itself is not enough to propel forward motion, what might help Congress and the president develop and enact the kind of comprehensive reform needed to reverse it?

One answer is the kind of national restructuring commission that Congress enacted in 1988 under the Department of Veterans Affairs Act. Convinced that the federal government needed a top-to-bottom review, Congress created the commission with four purposes:

1. To establish criteria for use by the president and Congress in evaluating proposals to change the structure of the executive branch, including criteria for establishing, altering, or overseeing the structure and organization of any executive entity.

2. To review the organization and structure of the executive branch and its entities, including the advisability of reorganizing, consolidating, or abolishing any such entity; the advisability of reorganizing, consolidating, or eliminating specific program activities; and the advisability of transferring activities to state or local governments.

3. To examine the organization and delivery of government services.

4. To promote economy, improve performance, and ensure adequate capacity of executive entities to meet and manage their public missions.[4]

There were two problems with the bill. First, under provisions nego-
tiated with the White House, the next president was given authority to
either establish or reject the commission. Unfortunately, the George
H. W. Bush administration had other priorities at the time, and refused
to establish the commission.

Second, even if Bush had triggered the commission into existence,
there was no mechanism for forwarding changes to Congress. The president's authority to submit up-or-down reorganization plans to Congress had lapsed before Bush entered office, and there was nothing in
the bill that would establish the kind of device used in the 1988 Base
Realignment and Closure Commission, which gave Congress a take-it-
or-leave-it option to accept a list of proposed military base closings prepared by an independent commission and sanctioned by the president.[5]

No matter how great the compromise, Congress simply does not
have the will to combine reforms into a single comprehensive package.
As it did with the Civil Service Reform Act of 1978, Congress would almost certainly jettison the more difficult provisions, while protecting
strong constituents such as contractors and federal employee unions,
which have thwarted most efforts to impose top-to-bottom reform.

Coupled with provisions that force accelerated legislative consideration of a single package of reforms, and provide opportunities for
single, up-or-down votes on a comprehensive reform proposal, a national commission on government restructuring just might be able to
create the will to act.

Conclusion

None of these recommendations is easy, particularly given the array of
potential opponents. Federal labor unions will almost certainly oppose
the new disciplinary process, and rightly so if it impinges on labor
rights. Contractors and grantees will absolutely oppose any effort to
count their employees or measure their hierarchies, especially if it
threatens the dependencies that assure near-permanent work. Congress
will oppose efforts to constrain its legislative activities, especially if it
has to wait for another national commission to offer up-or-down votes
on government reform. And the president will balk at any challenge to
the appointments process, especially if it leads to a reduction in the
number of leaders they think they control.

Nevertheless, the steady erosion of the federal service demands
strong action. With the baby-boom retirements looming, there is one

great opportunity to restructure the entire concept of federal employment. It is an opportunity that cannot be ignored. Tied to a serious effort to sort the federal mission, recapturing the baby-boom jobs can be the start of a renaissance in federal careers and operations. Frightening though it might be to departments, the recapturing can be done with enough care to assure that essential vacancies are filled, while restoring meaningful work and accountability to organizations that have become destinations of last resort.

This demand for reform is neither liberal nor conservative. Rather, it reflects the very real changes that federal employees say they want. Asked what they want from reform, they consistently talk about recruiting, resources, and discipline. Although they do care about pay, benefits, and security, they may have turned to compensation as a reason for work because the chance to accomplish something worthwhile is so often denied. Listen to them, and one cannot help but believe that radical reform would allow the federal government not only to faithfully execute all the laws, but also to honor the promises to extensive and arduous enterprise that Congress and the president have made.

The federal service can only achieve this goal with a bit of help from both Hamilton and Jefferson. Hamilton's commitment to an ever-growing list of missions that matter, tight chains of command, centralized appointments, and pay, benefits, and security as the backbone of the federal service cannot be sustained without the continued erosion of the energetic federal service he sought. Hence, the need to apply more of Jefferson's call for greater administrative harmony, more decentralization of control, and belief in civic duty as a tempering force.

At the same time, Jefferson's belief in a limited federal mission, starvation of the federal service, and his harsh rhetoric about wasteful government and the unnecessary expansion of government cannot be sustained, especially when confronted by staggering new missions such as rebuilding the economy. Hence, the need to emphasize Hamilton's belief in a strong national government, opposition to limited government, commitment to the adequate provision of support, and demand for safety in the executive.

The most successful reforms may emerge from blending Jefferson's effort to temper Hamilton's excesses, and Hamilton's effort to temper Jefferson's reluctance. Just as Jefferson began his first term as president by declaring, "We are all Republicans, we are all Federalists," reformers might say the same.[6]

Notes

Introduction

1. Alexander Hamilton, James Madison, and John Jay, *The Federalist,* ed. Benjamin Fletcher Wright (Cambridge, Mass.: Harvard University Press, 1961), p. 451.
2. See Peri E. Arnold, *Making the Managerial Presidency: Comprehensive Reorganization Planning, 1905–1980* (Princeton, N.J.: Princeton University Press, 1986), for a discussion of the search for an effective administrative state.
3. Although scholars have long assumed that the administrative state did not fully emerge until the creation of the Interstate Commerce Commission in 1887, recent research suggests that the contours of the new administrative state were visible almost immediately after George Washington became president. See Jerry L. Mashaw, "Recovering American Administrative Law: Federal Foundations, 1787–1801," *Yale Law Journal* 115 (2006), pp. 1256–1344, for a summary of this view and a contrary view of the early development of the administrative state.
4. See G. Calvin Mackenzie, ed., *Innocent until Nominated: The Breakdown of the Presidential Appointments Process* (Washington, D.C.: Brookings Institution Press, 2001).
5. G. Calvin Mackenzie, "Nasty & Brutish without Being Short," *Brookings Review* 19 (2001), p. 4.
6. *The Federalist,* p. 451.
7. *The Federalist,* p. 426.
8. *The Federalist,* p. 427.
9. *The Federalist,* pp. 440–441.
10. *The Federalist,* p. 440.
11. *The Federalist,* p. 452.

12. *The Federalist,* p. 443.

13. See Forrest McDonald, *Alexander Hamilton: A Biography* (New York: W. W. Norton, 1979), for a discussion of Hamilton's administrative philosophy, especially pp. 218–220.

14. *The Federalist,* p. 454.

15. Lynton K. Caldwell, *The Administrative Theories of Hamilton and Jefferson: Their Contribution to Thought on Public Administration* (Chicago: University of Chicago Press, 1944), p. 83.

16. Leonard White, *Introduction to the Study of Public Administration* (New York: Macmillan, 1926), p. 13.

17. Paul P. Van Riper, *History of the United States Civil Service* (Evanston, Ill.: Row, Peterson, and Company, 1954).

18. *The Federalist,* p. 464.

19. McDonald, *Alexander Hamilton,* p. 218.

20. Max Farrand, ed., *The Records of the Federal Convention* (New Haven, Conn.: Yale University Press, 1966), vol. 1, p. 82.

21. See Stephen Skowronek, *Building a New American State: The Expansion of National Administrative Capacities, 1877–1920* (New York: Cambridge University Press, 1982), for a discussion about how motivations changed with civil service reform in 1883.

22. *The Federalist,* p. 463.

23. *The Federalist,* p. 452.

24. Paul Leicester Ford, ed., *The Writings of Thomas Jefferson* (New York: G. Putnam and Sons, 1892–1899), vol. 7, p. 14. All other quotes from Jefferson in this book come from the Lipscomb and Bergh volumes cited immediately below and are referred to as *Writings of Thomas Jefferson.* The quotes are easily accessible at http://etext.virginia.edu/jefferson/quotations/.

25. Andrew Lipscomb and Albert E. Bergh, eds., *The Writings of Thomas Jefferson* (Washington, D.C.: Thomas Jefferson Memorial Association, 1905), vol. 3, p. 331.

26. *Writings of Thomas Jefferson,* vol. 3, p. 320.

27. *Writings of Thomas Jefferson,* vol. 15, p. 294.

28. *Writings of Thomas Jefferson,* vol. 6, p. 391.

29. *Writings of Thomas Jefferson,* vol. 15, p. 38.

30. *Writings of Thomas Jefferson,* vol. 10, p. 182.

31. Caldwell, *The Administrative Theories of Hamilton and Jefferson,* pp. 130–131.

32. *Writings of Thomas Jefferson,* vol. 12, p. 371.

33. *Writings of Thomas Jefferson,* vol. 6, p. 389.

34. *Writings of Thomas Jefferson,* vol. 1, p. 119.

35. *Writings of Thomas Jefferson,* vol. 11, p. 137.

36. *Writings of Thomas Jefferson,* vol. 3, p. 380.

37. Stephen Skowronek, *The Politics that Presidents Make: Leadership from John Adams to Bill Clinton* (Cambridge, Mass.: Harvard University Press, 1997), p. 73.

38. Skowronek, *The Politics that Presidents Make,* p. 73.
39. See Jerry L. Mashaw, "Reluctant Nationalists: Federal Administration and Administrative Law in the Republican Era, 1801–1829," *Yale Law Journal* 116 (2007), pp. 1636–1740.
40. Mashaw, "Recovering American Administrative Law," p. 1277.
41. Matthew A. Crenson, *The Federal Machine: Beginnings of Bureaucracy in Jacksonian America* (Baltimore: Johns Hopkins University Press, 1975), p. 88.
42. Martin Shefter, "Party, Bureaucracy, and Political Change in the United States," in *Political Parties: Development and Decay,* ed. Louis Maisel and Joseph Cooper (New York: Sage Publications, 1978), p. 211.
43. Mashaw, "Recovering American Administrative Law," p. 1319.
44. Mashaw, "Recovering American Administrative Law," p. 1310.
45. Mashaw, "Recovering American Administrative Law," p. 1344.
46. See Skowronek, *Building a New American State,* for a history of the civil service reform movement.
47. Donald F. Kettl and Steven Kelman, *Reflections on 21st Century Government Management* (Washington, D.C.: IBM Center for the Business of Government, 2007); Stephen Goldsmith and William D. Eggers, *Governing by Network: The New Shape of the Public Sector* (Washington, D.C.: Brookings Institution Press, 2004).
48. These views come from random-sample telephone surveys conducted in July and October 2001, May 2002, and October 2003 by Princeton Survey Research Associates on behalf of the Brookings Institution Center for Public Service, of which I was the director from 1999 to 2004.

1. For the Public Benefit

1. Alexander Hamilton, James Madison, and John Jay, *The Federalist,* ed. Benjamin Fletcher Wright (Cambridge, Mass.: Harvard University Press, 1961), p. 460.
2. *The Federalist,* p. 462.
3. *The Federalist,* p. 143.
4. The impact of 9/11 on the sense of purpose will be discussed in much greater detail in Chapter 4.
5. *The Federalist,* p. 139.
6. These opinions emerge from a series of opinion polls conducted by the Brookings Institution's Center for Public Service, which I founded in 1999. The surveys were conducted on behalf of the Center by Princeton Survey Research Associates, and involved random samples of roughly 1,000 Americans in May 2002 and October 2003; they have a margin of error of ±4 percent.
7. For studies of the "mission-building" process, see Charles Lindblom, "The Science of Muddling Through," *Public Administration Review* 29 (1958), pp. 79–88, for the classic statement on incremental adjustment in the issue agenda; James L. Sundquist, *Dynamics of the Party System: Alignment and*

Realignment of Political Parties in the United States (Washington, D.C.: Brookings Institution Press, 1983); Roy B. Flemming, B. Dan Wood, and John Bohte, "Attention to Issues in a System of Separated Powers: The Macrodynamics of American Policy Agendas," *Journal of Politics* 61 (1999), pp. 76–108, on changes in institutional attention; John Kingdon, *Agendas, Alternatives, and Public Policies* (New York: Longman, 2002), for a discussion of policy windows; and Bryan D. Jones, Tracy Sulkin, and Heather A. Larsen, "Policy Punctuations in American Political Institutions," *American Political Science Review* 97 (2003), pp. 151–169, and Bryan D. Jones, Frank R. Baumgartner, and James L. True, "Policy Punctuations: U.S. Budget Authority, 1947–1995," *Journal of Politics* 60 (1998), pp. 1–33, for two studies of the punctuated equilibrium thesis.

8. See James L. Sundquist, *Politics and Policy: The Eisenhower, Kennedy, and Johnson Years* (Washington, D.C.: Brookings Institution Press, 1968); Sarah A. Binder, "The Dynamics of Legislative Gridlock, 1947–1996," *American Political Science Review* 93 (1999), pp. 519–533; and Baumgartner, Jones, and Wilkerson's database at www.policyagendas.org.

9. Sundquist, *Politics and Policy*, pp. 9–10.

10. Paul C. Light, *Government's Great Achievements: From Civil Rights to Homeland Security* (Washington, D.C.: Brookings Institution, 2002).

11. David Mayhew, *Divided We Govern: Party Control, Lawmaking, and Investigations, 1946–2002* (New Haven, Conn.: Yale University Press, 2005).

12. Charles O. Jones, *The Presidency in a Separated System* (Washington, D.C.: Brookings Institution Press, 1994), p. 196.

13. Jones, *The Presidency in a Separated System*, p. 203.

14. Jones, *The Presidency in a Separated System*, p. 206.

15. Mayhew, *Divided We Govern*, p. 4.

16. There may be much less bipartisanship on investigations, however. See David C. W. Park and Matthew M. Dull, "Divided We Quarrel: The Changing Politics of Congressional Investigations," unpublished paper (2004), pp. 1–32.

17. Andrew Lipscomb and Albert E. Bergh, eds., *The Writings of Thomas Jefferson* (Washington, D.C.: Thomas Jefferson Memorial Association, 1903), vol. 10, p. 77.

18. *Writings of Thomas Jefferson*, vol. 3, p. 320.

19. *Writings of Thomas Jefferson*, vol. 15, p. 39.

20. Lynton K. Caldwell, *The Administrative Theories of Hamilton and Jefferson: Their Contribution to Thought on Public Administration* (Chicago: University of Chicago Press, 1944), p. 137.

21. Sarah A. Binder, "Going Nowhere: A Gridlocked Congress," *The Brookings Review* 18 (2000), p. 17; see also Sarah A. Binder, *Stalemate: Causes and Consequences of Legislative Gridlock* (Washington, D.C.: Brookings Institution Press, 2003).

22. Paul C. Light, *The President's Agenda: From Kennedy to Clinton* (Baltimore, Md.: Johns Hopkins University Press, 1999); see also Paul C. Light, "Fact Sheet on the President's Agenda" (Washington, D.C.: Brookings Institution Center for Public Service, 2004), pp. 1–7.

23. The Reagan quotes in this section are from campaign and official documents assembled by John Wolley and Gerhard Peters and are available at www .americanpresidency.org.

24. Arthur M. Schlesinger, Jr., "Historians Rate U.S. Presidents," *Life,* November 1, 1948, pp. 8–14; also see Meena Bose, "President Ratings: Lessons and Liabilities" (paper delivered at the 2001 meeting of the American Political Science Association, San Francisco, Calif., August 29–September 2), for a summary of the ratings; see also Jeffrey E. Cohen, *"The Polls:* Presidential Greatness as Seen in the Mass Public. An Extension and Application of the Simonton Model," *Presidential Studies Quarterly* 33 (2003), pp. 913–934, for an introduction to the ratings industry.

25. Douglas A. Lonnstrom and Thomas O. Kelly, "The Contemporary Presidency: Rating the Presidents. A Tracking Study," *Presidential Study Quarterly* 33 (2003), pp. 625–634.

26. The survey of 1,000 randomly selected adults was conducted on my behalf by Princeton Survey Research Association in July 2006 as a project of New York University's John Brademas Center for the Study of Congress. The survey has a margin of error of ±3 percent.

27. The survey of specific issues involved subsamples of 500 respondents each— the questionnaire would have been prohibitively long if all respondents had been asked about the eight issues. The margin of error on each half of the survey was ±5 percent, and among Democrats and Republicans ±7 percent.

28. National Commission on the Public Service, *Urgent Business for America: Revitalizing Government for the 21st Century* (Washington, D.C.: National Commission on the Public Service, 2003), p. 7.

29. *Writings of Thomas Jefferson,* vol. 10, p. 342.

2. Clarity of Command

1. For a more modern statement of the principle, see President's Committee on Administrative Management, *Report of the Committee with Studies of Administrative Management in the Federal Government* (Washington, D.C.: U.S. Government Printing Office, 1937), p. 1.

2. See Forrest McDonald, *Alexander Hamilton: A Biography* (New York: W. W. Norton, 1979), p. 340.

3. Lynton K. Caldwell, *The Administrative Theories of Hamilton and Jefferson: Their Contribution to Thought on Public Administration* (Chicago: University of Chicago Press, 1944), p. 95.

4. Luther Gulick and L. Urwick, eds., *Papers on the Science of Administration* (New York: Institute of Public Administration, 1937), p. 7.

5. Office of Personnel Management, personal communication, June 2003.

6. Richard Stillman, "The Romantic Vision in American Administrative Theory: Retrospectives and Prospectives," *International Journal of Public Administration* 7 (1985), p. 108.

7. David Osborne and Ted Gaebler, *Reinventing Government: How the Entrepreneurial Spirit Is Changing the Public Sector* (New York: Plume, 1993).

8. Al Gore, *From Red Tape to Results: Creating a Government that Works Better and Costs Less* (Washington, D.C.: Government Printing Office, 1993), p. 71.

9. Lawrence E. Lynn, Jr., "The Myth of the Bureaucratic Paradigm: What Traditional Public Administration Really Stood For," *Public Administration Review* 61 (2001), p. 154.

10. The survey is summarized in Paul C. Light, *A Workforce at Risk: The State of the Federal Public Service Revisited* (Washington, D.C.: Brookings Institution Center for Public Service, 2002). The survey of 1,051 federal employees was conducted on my behalf by Princeton Survey Research Associates from May to July 2001, and had a margin of error of ± percent. This sample included civil servants at the very bottom of government, as well as members of the prestigious Senior Executive Service near the very top. Only presidential appointees were excluded.

11. McDonald, *Alexander Hamilton*, pp. 219–220.

12. This coding was done by my colleague, Elizabeth Hubbard, using the Spring 2004 *Federal Yellow Book*, which is published quarterly. The methodology was exactly the same for my earlier coding—more detail on the method can be found in Paul C. Light, *Thickening Government: Federal Hierarchy and the Diffusion of Accountability* (Washington, D.C.: Brookings Institution Press, 1995). Readers should note that executive assistants, staff assistants, and other titles that were not directly linked to a primary title were excluded from the analysis.

13. The frontline jobs were air traffic controller, revenue agent, public housing specialist, veterans' hospital nurse, immigration inspector, Social Security claims representative, weather forecaster, food inspector, customs inspector, forest ranger, park ranger, wage and hour inspector, and international trade specialist.

14. Andrew Lipscomb and Albert E. Bergh, eds., *The Writings of Thomas Jefferson* (Washington, D.C.: Thomas Jefferson Memorial Foundation, 2003), vol. 15, p. 38.

15. *Writings of Thomas Jefferson,* vol. 10, p. 356.

16. Ron Chernow, *Alexander Hamilton* (New York: Penguin Books, 2004), p. 339.

17. *Writings of Thomas Jefferson,* vol. 10, p. 199.

18. *Writings of Thomas Jefferson,* vol. 10, p. 168.

19. *Writings of Thomas Jefferson,* vol. 11, p. 247.

20. *Writings of Thomas Jefferson,* vol. 14, p. 421.

21. Quoted in Light, *Thickening Government,* p. 3.

22. President's Committee on Administrative Management, *Report on Administrative Management,* p. 5.

23. President's Committee on Administrative Management, *Report on Administrative Management,* p. 6.

24. President's Committee on Administrative Management, *Report on Administrative Management,* p. 4.

25. Daniel Patrick Moynihan, personal communication, October 1980.

26. Paul J. DiMaggio and Walter W. Powell, "The Iron Cage Revisited: Institutional Isomorphism and Collective Rationality in Organizational Fields," in *The New Institutionalism in Organizational Analysis,* ed. Walter W. Powell and Paul J. DiMaggio (Chicago: University of Chicago Press, 1991), pp. 63–64, 67.

27. Peter Frumkin and Joseph Galaskiewicz, "Institutional Isomorphism and Public Sector Organizations," *Journal of Public Administration Research and Theory* 14 (2004), pp. 283–307.

28. Frumkin and Galaskiewicz, "Institutional Isomorphism," p. 303.

29. See Michael T. Hannan and John Freeman, "The Population Ecology of Organizations," *American Journal of Sociology* 82 (1977), pp. 929–964, for the classic discussion of why some organizations live, while others die.

30. See David E. Lewis, *Presidents and the Politics of Agency Design: Political Insulation in the United States Government Bureaucracy, 1946–1997* (Palo Alto, Calif.: Stanford University Press, 2003), for a broad discussion and proofs of this argument.

31. Terry M. Moe, "The Politics of Structural Choice: Toward a Theory of Public Bureaucracy," in *Organizational Theory: From Chester Barnard to the Present and Beyond,* ed. Oliver E. Williamson (New York: Oxford University Press, 1995), pp. 137, 138.

32. David E. Lewis, "The Adverse Consequences of the Politics of Agency Design for Presidential Management in the United States: The Relative Durability of Insulated Agencies," *British Journal of Political Science* 34 (2004), quoted at p. 378; see also William G. Howell and David E. Lewis, "Agencies by Presidential Design," *Journal of Politics* 64 (2002), pp. 1095–1114.

33. For a summary of the survey's recommendations and call to action, see J. Peter Grace, *War on Waste* (New York: Macmillan, 1984).

3. Posts of Honor

1. Alexander Hamilton, James Madison, and John Jay, *The Federalist,* ed. Benjamin Fletcher Wright (Cambridge, Mass.: Harvard University Press, 1961), p. 480.

2. *The Federalist,* p. 481.

3. Andrew Lipscomb and Albert E. Bergh, eds., *The Writings of Thomas Jefferson* (Washington, D.C.: Thomas Jefferson Memorial Association, 1903), vol. 10, p. 261.

4. The quote is attributed to C. Boyden Gray, whose appointment as Ambassador to the European Union was delayed in 2006 because of his involvement in the Committee for Justice, which he established to promote the Bush administration's judicial appointments.

5. Lynton K. Caldwell, *The Administrative Theories of Hamilton and Jefferson: Their Contribution to Thought on Public Administration* (Chicago: University of Chicago Press, 1944), p. 80.

6. *Writings of Thomas Jefferson,* vol. 10, p. 182.

7. For a much more detailed and nuanced discussion of patronage, see Scott C. James, "Patronage Regimes and American Party Development from 'The Age

of Jackson' to the Progressive Era," *British Journal of Political Science* 36 (2006), pp. 39–60.

8. *Writings of Thomas Jefferson,* vol. 11, p. 286.

9. *Writings of Thomas Jefferson,* vol. 10, p. 271.

10. See G. Calvin Mackenzie, *Obstacle Course: The Report of the Twentieth Century Fund Task Force on the Presidential Appointment Process* (New York: Twentieth Century Fund, 1996).

11. Diane E. Schmidt, "The Presidential Appointment Process, Task Environment Pressures, and Regional Office Case Processing," *Political Research Quarterly* 48 (1995), pp. 381–401; Howard W. Chappell, Jr., Thomas M. Havrilesky, and Rob Roy McGregor, "Partisan Monetary Policies: Presidential Influence through the Power of Appointment," *Quarterly Journal of Economics* 108 (1993), pp. 185–201.

12. Anthony Bertelli and Sven E. Feldmann, "Strategic Appointments," *Journal of Public Administration Research and Theory* 17 (2007), pp. 19–38.

13. B. Dan Wood and Richard W. Waterman, "The Dynamics of Political Control of the Bureaucracy," *American Political Science Review* 85 (1991), pp. 801–829.

14. G. Calvin Mackenzie, "Nasty and Brutish without Being Short," *Brookings Review* 19 (2001), p. 4.

15. "Nasty and Brutish," p. 4.

16. James P. Pfiffner, "Recruiting Executive Branch Leaders," *Brookings Review* 19 (2001), p. 42.

17. Paul C. Light, *Thickening Government: Federal Hierarchy and the Diffusion of Accountability* (Washington, D.C.: Brookings Institution Press, 1995), pp. 76–78.

18. Hugh Heclo, "The In-and-Outer System," in G. Calvin Mackenzie, *The In-and-Outers: Presidential Appointees and Transient Government in Washington,* ed. G. Calvin Mackenzie (Baltimore, Md.: Johns Hopkins University Press, 1987), pp. 207–211.

19. See Thomas J. Weko, *The Politicizing Presidency: The White House Personnel Office, 1948–1994* (Lawrence: University of Kansas Press, 1995).

20. Terry M. Moe, "The Politicized Presidency," in *The New Direction in American Politics,* ed. John E. Chubb and Paul E. Petersen (Washington, D.C.: Brookings Institution Press, 1985), p. 243.

21. Moe, "The Politicized Presidency," p. 245.

22. One need only read Hugh Heclo, *A Government of Strangers: Executive Politics in Washington* (Washington, D.C.: Brookings Institution Press, 1977).

23. Michael A. Fletcher, "Bush Keeping Cabinet Secretaries Close to Home," *Washington Post,* March 31, 2005.

24. See Weko, *The Politicizing Presidency,* for a history of the office and its staffing.

25. Terry Sullivan, "Fabulous Formless Darkness: Presidential Nominees and the Morass of Inquiry," *Brookings Review* 19 (2001), pp. 22–28.

26. See G. Calvin Mackenzie, *Scandal Proof: Do Ethics Laws Make Government Ethical?* (Washington, D.C.: Brookings Institution Press, 2002); see also G. Calvin Mackenzie, ed., *Innocent until Nominated: The Breakdown of the Presidential Appointments Process* (Washington, D.C.: Brookings Institution Press, 2001).

27. Sullivan, "Fabulous Formless Darkness"; see also Martha Joynt Kumar and Terry Sullivan, eds., *The White House World: Transitions, Organizations, and Office Operations* (College Station: Texas A&M University Press, 2003).

28. See Presidential Appointee Initiative, *Staffing a New Administration: A Guide to Personnel Appointments in a Presidential Transition* (Washington, D.C.: Brookings Institution Press, 2000), for the Kennedy-Clinton figures; the George W. Bush figures were calculated by the Presidential Appointee Initiative.

29. These findings are based on a survey of 435 randomly selected presidential appointees who served as a secretary, deputy secretary, undersecretary, or assistant secretary between 1985 and 1999. The survey was conducted between December 1999 and February 2000 on behalf of the Brookings Institution's Presidential Appointee Initiative, and is summarized in Paul C. Light and Virginia L. Thomas, *The Merit and Reputation of an Administration: Presidential Appointees on the Appointments Process* (Washington, D.C.: Brookings Institution Press 2000). The report can be found on the Brookings Institution website at www.brookings.edu.

30. The survey of 536 randomly selected presidential appointees who served as a secretary, deputy secretary, undersecretary, or assistant secretary between 1965 and 1984. The survey was conducted December 1984 through April 1985 on behalf of the National Academy of Public Administration and is described in detail in Mackenzie, *The In-and-Outers.*

31. Nolan McCarty and Rose Razaghian, "Advice and Consent: Senate Responses to Executive Branch Nominations, 1885–1996," *American Journal of Political Science* 43 (1999), pp. 1122–1444.

32. Presidential Appointee Initiative, *A Survivor's Guide for Presidential Nominees* (Washington, D.C.: Brookings Institution Press, 2000).

33. The findings are based on a telephone survey of 580 randomly selected leaders in business, academia, the nonprofit sector and government: 100 *Fortune 500* executives, 100 university presidents, 85 nonprofit CEOs, 95 think tank scholars, 100 lobbyists, and 100 state and local government officials. The survey was conducted on behalf of the Brookings Institution's Presidential Appointee Initiative, and is summarized in Paul C. Light and Virginia L. Thomas, *Posts of Honor: How America's Corporate and Civic Leaders View Presidential Appointments* (Washington, D.C.: Brookings Institution Presidential Appointee Initiative, 2001). The report can be found on the Brookings Institution website at www.brookings.edu.

34. Carole M. Plowfield and Paul C. Light, *Problems on the Potomac: How Relocation Policies for Presidential Appointees Can Help Win the Talent War*

(Washington, D.C.: Brookings Institution Presidential Appointee Initiative, 2002).

35. The following conclusions are drawn from regressions of the past and potential appointee surveys. The past appointees analysis involved a regression against their willingness to recommend a post to a friend, and had an adjusted R^2 of .113, which was significant at the .000 level, while the potential appointees analysis involved a regression against their favorability toward taking an appointment, and had an adjusted R^2 of .353, which was significant at the .000 level.

36. Government Accountability Office, *Human Capital: Trends in Executive and Judicial Pay*, GAO-06-708 (Washington, D.C.: Government Accountability Office, 2006), p. 3.

37. Congressional Budget Office, *Comparing the Pay of Federal and Nonprofit Executives: An Update* (Washington, D.C.: Congressional Budget Office, 2003), p. 9.

38. John B. Gilmour and David E. Lewis, "Political Appointees and the Competence of Federal Program Management," *American Politics Research* 34 (2006), p. 41.

39. See Robert Maranto, "Praising Civil Service but Not Bureaucracy: A Brief against Tenure in the U.S. Civil Service," *Review of Public Personnel Administration* 22 (2002), pp. 11–25.

40. Jeff Gill and Richard W. Waterman, "Solidary and Functional Costs: Explaining the Presidential Appointment Contradiction," *Journal of Public Administration Research and Theory* 14 (2004), pp. 547–559.

41. Joel D. Aberbach and Bert A. Rockman, *In the Web of Politics: Three Decades of the U.S. Federal Executive* (Washington, D.C.: Brookings Institution Press, 2000).

42. Robert Maranto and Karen Marie Hult, "Right Turn? Political Ideology and the Higher Civil Service, 1987–1994," *American Review of Public Administration* 34 (2004), pp. 199–221. Both of the studies cited here have their problems: Aberbach and Rockman did not have enough respondents to compare attitudes across agencies, while Maranto and Hult did not interview any presidential appointees. However, regardless of one's view of the research, cooperation is a very poor measure of appointee quality. After all, the politicized presidency thrives in part on putting contrarians into positions at hostile agencies. The fact that career executives do *not* trust their appointees may be a sign that their appointees are particularly talented in pursuing the president's agenda.

43. This summary assumes that participating actively in important historical events is a neutral measure of individual motivation to serve. But shifting the appointees who said they served to participate actively in important historical events from the "we" to "me" column does not change the general pattern: the percentage of self-interest motivation rises from 38 percent to 50 percent for the 1985–2000 appointees, and from just 11 percent to 19 percent for the 1964–1985 appointees; the difference in motivations for the two

sets of appointees remains significant. Recent appointees are simply drawn to service by a new, more self-interested set of motivations rather than a more traditional focus on affecting policy.

44. See Gene A. Brewer and Robert A. Maranto, "Comparing the Roles of Political Appointees and Career Executives in the U.S. Federal Executive Branch," *American Review of Public Administration* 30 (2000), pp. 69–86; see also Anthony Downs, *Inside Bureaucracy* (Santa Monica, Calif.: RAND Corporation, 1967).

4. Vigor and Expedition

1. Alexander Hamilton, James Madison, and John Jay, *The Federalist,* ed. Benjamin Fletcher Wright (Cambridge, Mass.: Harvard University Press, 1961), p. 443.

2. *The Federalist,* p. 73.

3. *The Federalist,* p. 200.

4. John D. Donahue makes a similar argument in *The Warping of Government Work* (Cambridge, Mass: Harvard University Press, 2007).

5. Gordon S. Wood, *The Radicalism of the American Revolution* (New York: Vintage, 1991), pp. 291, 294.

6. Lloyd G. Nigro and William D. Richardson, "The Founders' Unsentimental View of Public Service in the American Regime," in *Agenda for Excellence: Public Service in America,* ed. Patricia Ingraham and Donald F. Kettl (Chatham, N.J.: Chatham House, 1992), p. 3.

7. Lynton K. Caldwell, *The Administrative Theories of Hamilton and Jefferson: Their Contribution to Thought on Public Administration* (Chicago: University of Chicago Press, 1944), p. 85.

8. Caldwell, *The Administrative Theories of Hamilton and Jefferson,* p. 87.

9. Caldwell, *The Administrative Theories of Hamilton and Jefferson,* p. 91.

10. See Leonard D. White, *The Federalists: A Study in Administrative History, 1789–1801* (New York: Free Press, 1948), for further details on the early design.

11. See Jerry L. Mashaw, "Recovering American Administrative Law: Federal Foundations, 1787–1801," *Yale Law Journal* 115 (2006), pp. 1256–1344, for a discussion of the early civil service.

12. Andrew Lipscomb and Albert E. Bergh, eds., *The Writings of Thomas Jefferson* (Washington, D.C.: Thomas Jefferson Memorial Association, 1903), vol. 7, p. 381.

13. *Writings of Thomas Jefferson,* vol. 7, p. 287.

14. *Writings of Thomas Jefferson,* vol. 2, p. 298.

15. *Writings of Thomas Jefferson,* vol. 9, p. 118.

16. See Donald F. Kettl, Patricia W. Ingraham, Ronald P. Sanders, and Constance Horner, *Civil Service Reform: Building a Government that Works* (Washington, D.C.: Brookings Institution Press, 1996), for a list of threats.

17. National Commission on the Public Service, *Leadership for America: Rebuilding the Public Service* (Washington, D.C.: National Commission on the Public Service, 1989), p. 1.

18. Al Gore, *From Red Tape to Results: Creating a Government that Works Better and Costs Less* (Washington, D.C.: Government Printing Office, 1993), p. 22.

19. General Accounting Office, *Human Capital: Managing Human Capital in the 21st Century* (Washington, D.C.: General Accounting Office, 2000), p. 2.

20. National Commission on the Public Service, *Urgent Business for America: Revitalizing the Federal Government for the 21st Century* (Washington, D.C.: National Commission on the Public Service, 2003), p. 1.

21. Larry M. Lane, James F. Wolf, and Colleen Woodard, "Reassessing the Human Resource Crisis in the Public Service, 1987–2002," *American Journal of Public Administration* 33 (2003), p. 124.

22. See Gregory B. Lewis, "Turnover and the Quiet Crisis in the Federal Civil Service," *Public Administration Review* 51 (1991), pp. 145–155; Joel D. Aberbach and Bert A. Rockman, "Public Service and Administrative Reform in the United States: The Volcker Commission and the Bush Administration," *International Journal of Administrative Sciences* 57 (1991), pp. 403–419.

23. Robert E. Cleary and Kimberly Nelson, "The Volcker Commission Fades Away: A Case Study in Non-Implementation," *Policy Studies Review* 12 (1993), pp. 55–73.

24. Lane, Wolf, and Woodward, "Reassessing the Human Resource Crisis," p. 140.

25. See Haksoo Lee, N. Joseph Cayer, and G. Zhiyong Lan, "Changing Federal Employee Attitudes since the Civil Service Reform Act of 1978," *Review of Public Personnel Administration* 26 (2006), pp. 1–21, for a discussion of patterns in the seven federal employee surveys conducted between 1979 and 2002.

26. As the federal government's own surveys show, the federal service has doubts about its work. According to its 2006 survey of 220,000 federal employees, the U.S. Office of Personnel Management found evidence of both energy and discouragement. In a sentence, federal employees remained committed to their work and satisfied with their benefits, but disquieted by the lack of recognition for doing a good job, problems disciplining poor performance, and doubts about the leadership of their agencies. See Office of Personnel Management, *Federal Human Capital Survey, 2006* (Washington, D.C.: Office of Personnel Management, 2006).

The following discussion shows some of the same patterns, but with a multisector focus. Whereas the Office of Personnel Management asks federal employees about working for government, my surveys asked matched samples of federal government, business, and nonprofit employees about their work without reference to any particular sector. Respondents were not asked about working for government until late in the survey, and only then if they were employed at the senior level of the organization.

The following discussion also involved a completely independent assessment of employee attitudes. Whereas the Office of Personnel Management contacts employees through e-mails from inside government and directs employees to a government website, my survey resembles the proverbial search for needles in a haystack by using random-digit dialing to locate federal, business, and nonprofit employees. My sample of federal employees was the product of more than 100,000 random-digit calls.

This is not to argue that these various surveys conflict. To the contrary, many of my findings follow the broad contours of the Office of Personnel Management's findings, and actually fit well with other federal surveys conducted over the past two decades.

27. The following chapter draws upon separate surveys of federal, business, and nonprofit employees conducted on my behalf by Princeton Survey Research Associates in 2001. The survey of 1,051 federal employees was conducted from February to April 2001; the survey of 1,005 business employees was conducted in May and June 2001, and early January 2002; the survey of 1,140 nonprofit employees was conducted from October 2001 to January 2002. All three surveys have a margin of error of ±3 percent. All three surveys asked respondents to participate in "a survey about work" without reference to being employed by a federal, business, or nonprofit organization. Questions did not make reference to the type of organization, either.

28. My surveys provide at least three different ways to assess vigor and expedition to execute. First, the results of my federal survey can be compared with comparable business and nonprofit surveys to see if there are major differences in how the three groups of employees assess their jobs. All three surveys asked respondents to focus on their organization, not their sector, and were not told that the survey was about working for government.

Second, my federal survey contained separate samples of senior executives and new recruits, thereby allowing comparisons of attitudes at different levels of the hierarchy. The sample of senior executives will be used in this chapter to compare attitudes at the senior, middle, and lower levels of government, while the survey of new recruits will be used in the next chapter to assess the relative attractiveness of federal service among a critically important group of future leaders.

Finally, my results contain information from two different surveys, one before 9/11 and another nine months later. Although the second "panel survey" only included two-thirds of the original 2001 sample, the fact that it reached so many of the same employees increases the statistical power of the 9/11 effect discussed later in this chapter. The comparison is not between two snapshots of the federal workforce, but between many of the same respondents at two different points in time. When weighted to represent the 2001 group as a whole, the second survey provides a unique glimpse of how 9/11 changed employees' views of their work.

These comparisons should give readers greater confidence that the federal employees' perceptions do represent a significant cause for concern. To the extent these perceptions affect productivity, employee satisfaction, and overall performance, they are serious indicators of the capacity crisis, and cannot be ignored. But they are still perceptions, and should be viewed as such.

29. *The Federalist*, p. 436.

30. See Paul C. Light, "The Content of Their Character: A Survey of the Non-profit Workforce," *Nonprofit Quarterly* 2 (2002), pp. 11–20. See Patricia W. Ingraham, *The Foundation of Merit: Public Service in American Democracy* (Baltimore, Md.: Johns Hopkins University Press, 1995), for a discussion of the purpose of a merit system.

31. See James L. Perry, "Antecedents of Public Service Motivation," *Journal of Public Administration Research and Theory* 7 (1997), pp. 181–198.

32. Paul C. Light, *Sustaining Nonprofit Performance: The Case for Capacity Building and the Evidence to Support It* (Washington, D.C.: Brookings Institution Press, 2005).

33. For an alternative view, see U.S. Office of Personnel Management, *Poor Performers in Government: A Quest for the True Story* (Washington, D.C.: U.S. Office of Personnel Management, 1999). Using a tiny survey of federal employees, the Office estimated the percentage of poor performers at just 3.7 percent.

34. G. Calvin Mackenzie and Judith Labiner, *Opportunity Lost: The Rise and Fall of Trust and Confidence in Government after September 11* (Washington, D.C.: Brookings Institution Press, 2002).

35. Mackenzie and Labiner, *Opportunity Lost*, p. 2.

36. The Defense sample included 174 employees, while the non-Defense sample involved 499. Although not large in absolute terms, the two samples are large enough to allow statistical comparisons. Only statistically significant comparisons are provided here.

37. These results reflect a regression of poor performance against a long list of variables and had an adjusted R^2 of .324, which was significant at the .000 level.

38. The following results are based on sector-by-sector regressions of job satisfaction. The regression for federal employees had an adjusted R^2 of .574, which was significant at the .000 level.

39. For a summary of this history, see Charles H. Levine and Rossyln S. Kleeman, "The Quiet Crisis in the American Public Service," in Ingraham and Kettl, *Agenda for Excellence*, pp. 208–273.

40. Patricia W. Ingraham and David H. Rosenbloom, "Political Foundations of the American Federal Service: Rebuilding a Crumbling Base," *Public Administration Review* 50 (1990), p. 212. The article is part of a very strong compendium of basic works on the public service edited by Mark Holzer, *Public Service: Callings, Commitments, and Contributions* (Boulder, Colo.: Westview Press, 2000).

41. Charles H. Levine, "The Federal Government in the Year 2000: Administrative Legacies of the Reagan Years," *Public Administration Review* 46 (1986), p. 200.

42. Jimmy Carter, *A Government as Good as Its People* (New York: Simon & Schuster, 1977), p. 86.
43. See the papers collected and published by James P. Pfiffner and Douglas A. Brook, *The Future of Merit: Twenty Years after the Civil Service Reform Act* (Baltimore, Md.: Johns Hopkins University Press, 2000), for a much deeper discussion of the act and its consequences.
44. The quote is from Bush's acceptance speech at the Republican National Convention in New Orleans, August 18, 1988; it can be found along with other presidential documents at www.presidency.ucsb.edu/index.php.
45. Only the human services workforce has a longer list of complaints. See Paul C. Light, *The Health of the Human Services Workforce* (Washington, D.C.: Brookings Institution Press, 2003).

5. A Spirit of Service

1. Leonard D. White, *The Federalists: A Study in Administrative History, 1789–1801* (New York: Free Press, 1948), p. 303.
2. See Frederick C. Mosher, *Democracy and the Public Service* (New York: Oxford University Press, 1968), p. 57. Mosher refers to the 1789–1829 period as "government by gentlemen: the guardian period."
3. White, *The Federalists,* p. 317.
4. White, *The Federalists,* p. 320.
5. Zachary A. Goldfarb and Christopher Lee, "Civil Service Steps Up Recruitment," *Washington Post,* May 2, 2006, p. A19.
6. Congressional Budget Office, *Characteristics and Pay of Federal Civilian Employees* (Washington, D.C.: Congressional Budget Office, 2007); also quoted in Steven Barr, "Increasingly Qualified Federal Employees Receive Bigger Paychecks," *Washington Post,* April 9, 2007.
7. Lynton K. Caldwell, *The Administrative Theories of Hamilton and Jefferson: Their Contribution to Thought on Public Administration* (Chicago: University of Chicago Press, 1944), p. 73.
8. Quoted in Michael J. Rosano, "Liberty, Nobility, Philanthropy, and Power in Alexander Hamilton's Conception of Power," *American Journal of Political Science* 47 (2003), p. 68.
9. Partnership for Public Service, *Federal Brain Drain* (Washington, D.C.: Partnership for Public Service, 2005), p. 1.
10. Council for Excellence in Government, *Within Reach . . . but out of Synch: The Possibilities and Challenges of Shaping Tomorrow's Government Workforce and the Gallup Organization* (Washington, D.C.: Council for Excellence in Government, 2006), p. 1.
11. Peter Cappelli, "Will There *Really* Be a Labor Shortage?" *Organizational Dynamics* 32 (2003), p. 221.
12. Patricia W. Ingraham, *The Foundation of Merit: Public Service in American Democracy* (Baltimore, Md.: Johns Hopkins University Press, 1995), p. 118.

13. See Norma M. Riccucci, "Managing Diversity: Redux," in *Public Personnel Management: Current Concerns, Future Challenges,* ed. Norma M. Riccucci, 4th ed. (Upper Saddle River, N.J.: Pearson Education, 2006), p. 59.

14. University of California, Los Angeles, Cooperative Institutional Research Program, Higher Education Research Institute, Graduate School of Education and Information Studies, *The American Freshman: National Norms for Fall 2006* (Los Angeles: University of California, Los Angeles, 2006), p. 10.

15. Sue A. Frank and Gregory B. Lewis, "Government Employees: Working Hard or Hardly Working?" *American Review of Public Administration* 34 (2002), pp. 46–47.

16. See Edward N. Wolff, *Top Heavy: The Increasing Inequality of Wealth in America and What Can Be Done about It* (New York: New Press, 2002), for a short introduction to the basic issues embedded in income inequality.

17. Cooperative Institutional Research Program, "Today's College Freshmen Have Family Income 60% above National Average, UCLA Survey Reveals," press release, April 9, 2007.

18. Cooperative Institutional Research Project, "Today's College Freshmen."

19. See Partnership for Public Service, *Student Loan Repayment* (Washington, D.C.: Partnership for Public Service, 2005).

20. See Partnership for Public Service, *A New Call to Service for an Age of Savvy Altruism: Public Attitudes About Government and Government Workers* (Washington, D.C.: Partnership for Public Service, 2004).

21. See Jack K. Ito, "Career Mobility and Branding in the Civil Service: An Empirical Study," *Public Personnel Management* 32 (2003), pp. 1–21.

22. See Robert J. Lavigna and Steven W. Hays, "Recruitment and Selection of Public Workers: An International Compendium of Modern Trends and Practices," *Public Personnel Management* 33 (2004), pp. 237–254.

23. R. Sam Garrett, James A. Thurber, A. Lee Fritschler, and David H. Rosenbloom, "Assessing the Impact of Bureaucracy Bashing by Electoral Campaigns," *Public Administration Review* 66 (2006), pp. 228–240.

24. See Sanjay K. Pandey and Hal G. Rainey, "Public Managers' Perceptions of Organizational Goal Ambiguity: Analyzing Alternative Models," *Internal Public Management Journal* 9 (2006), pp. 85–112.

25. Donald P. Moynihan and Sanjay K. Pandey, "The Role of Organizations in Fostering Public Service Motivation," *Public Administration Review* 67 (2007), pp. 40–53.

26. Mary Ann Feldman, "Public Sector Downsizing and Employee Trust," *International Journal of Public Administration* 30 (2007), pp. 251–272.

27. Feldman, "Public Sector Downsizing," p. 265.

28. Cappelli, "Will There *Really* Be a Labor Shortage?" p. 221.

29. Carolyn Ban, "Hiring in the Federal Government: Political and Technological Sources of Reform," in Riccucci, *Public Personnel Management,* pp. 144–162.

30. Hal G. Rainey and J. Edward Kellough, "Civil Service Reform and Incentives in the Public Service," in James P. Pfiffner and Douglas A. Brook, eds., *The*

Future of Merit: Twenty Years after the Civil Service Reform Act (Baltimore, Md.: Johns Hopkins University Press, 2000), pp. 127–145.

31. Gregory B. Lewis and Sue A. Frank, "Who Wants to Work for Government?" *Public Administration Review* 2 (2002), p. 402.

32. The 2002 survey of 1,015 college seniors was conducted on my behalf by Princeton Survey Research Associates in April 2002; the 2003 survey of 1,002 seniors was conducted by Princeton Survey Research Associates in April 2003. The two surveys have a margin of error of ±3 percent.

33. The decision to shift the comparison from business in general to businesses that work for government was intended to see how students viewed such businesses as an alternative destination for public service.

34. These results reflect a regression of preference for government against a long list of variables and had an adjusted R^2 of .35, which was significant at the .000 level.

35. Paul C. Light, *The New Public Service* (Washington, D.C.: Brookings Institution Press, 1999).

36. The survey of 1,000 randomly selected members of the five classes was conducted on my behalf by Princeton Survey Research Associates from February through May 1999. The survey has a margin of error of ±3 percent.

37. The program was called the Presidential Management Internship Program until 2002, when it became the Presidential Management Fellows Program.

38. See Judith M. Labiner, *Looking for the Future Leaders of Government: Don't Count on Presidential Management Interns* (Washington, D.C.: Brookings Institution Press, 2003).

39. The random-sample telephone survey of 986 adults was conducted in May 2002 by Princeton Survey Research Associates on behalf of my Brookings Institution Center for Public Service. The margin of error in the sample was ±4 percent.

40. For a recent summary of the trust issue, see Joseph S. Nye, Jr., Philip D. Zelikow, and David C. King, eds., *Why People Don't Trust Government* (Cambridge, Mass.: Harvard University Press, 1997).

41. Arthur H. Miller and Stephen A. Borrelli, "Confidence in Government during the 1980s," *American Politics Quarterly* 19 (1991), p. 148.

42. Jack Citrin and Donald Philip Green, "Presidential Leadership and the Resurgence of Trust in Government," *British Journal of Political Science* 16 (1991), p. 438.

43. The July 2001 random-sample telephone survey involved 1,003 adults, while the October 2001 survey involved 1,033 adults. The margin of error in both surveys was ±4 percent. The 2006 data come from a sample of 1,229 adults interviewed by the CBS News/New York Times Poll in January 2006. The margin of error in that poll was ±3.

44. Council for Excellence in Government, *Changing Channels: Entertainment Television, Civic Attitudes, and Actions* (Washington, D.C.: Council for Excellence in Government, 2004).

6. Steadiness in Administration

1. Alexander Hamilton, James Madison, and John Jay, *The Federalist,* ed. Benjamin Fletcher Wright (Cambridge, Mass.: Harvard University Press, 1961), p. 463.
2. *The Federalist,* p. 463.
3. See George W. Downs and Patrick D. Larkey, *The Search for Government Efficiency: From Hubris to Helplessness* (Philadelphia, Pa.: Temple University Press, 1986).
4. See Douglas A. Brook, "Administrative Reform in the Federal Government: Understanding the Search for Private Sector Management Models," *Public Administration and Management* 7 (2002), pp. 117–167, for a bibliography of articles on the use of business models. The list appears to be increasing as an important component of what I label as liberation management.
5. Lynton K. Caldwell, *The Administrative Theories of Hamilton and Jefferson: Their Contribution to Thought on Public Administration* (Chicago: University of Chicago Press, 1944), p. 135.
6. Andrew Lipscomb and Albert E. Bergh, eds., *The Writings of Thomas Jefferson* (Washington, D.C.: Thomas Jefferson Memorial Association, 1903), vol. 15, p. 278.
7. *Writings of Thomas Jefferson,* vol. 12, p. 15.
8. *Writings of Thomas Jefferson,* vol. 15, p. 294.
9. Laurence J. O'Toole, Jr., and Kenneth J. Meier, "Plus ça Change: Public Management, Personnel Stability, and Organizational Performance," *Journal of Public Administration Research and Theory* 13 (2003), pp. 43–64, quoted at p. 43.
10. Stephen Skowronek, *Building a New Administrative State: The Expansion of National Administrative Capacities, 1877–1920* (Cambridge: Cambridge University Press, 1982).
11. Peri E. Arnold, *Making the Managerial Presidency: Comprehensive Reorganization Planning, 1905–1980* (Princeton, N.J.: Princeton University Press, 1986).
12. Paul C. Light, *The Tides of Reform: Making Government Work, 1945–1995* (New Haven, Conn.: Yale University Press, 1997); see also Paul C. Light, "The Tides of Reform Revisited: Patterns in Making Government Work, 1945–2002," *Public Administration Review* 66 (2006), pp. 27–54, on which much of this chapter is based.
13. For analysis of the reform traditions embedded in reinventing government, see Donald Kettl, "The Global Revolution in Public Management," *Journal of Policy Analysis and Management* 16 (1997), pp. 446–462; Larry D. Terry, "Administrative Leadership, Neo-Managerialism and the Public Management Movement," *Public Administration Review* 58 (1998), pp. 194–220; Lawrence E. Lynn, Jr., "The New Public Management: How to Transform a Theme into a Legacy," *Public Administration Review* 58 (1998), pp. 231–238; and David H. Rosenbloom, "History Lessons for Reinventors," *Public Administration Review* 61 (2001), pp. 161–166.

14. Lynn, "The New Public Management," p. 231.
15. See David Osborne and Ted Gaebler, *Reinventing Government: How the Entrepreneurial Spirit Is Transforming the Public Sector* (New York: Plume, 1993), for the basic tenets of these Clinton-era reforms.
16. See Ronald C. Moe, "Traditional Organizational Principles and the Managerial Presidency: From Phoenix to Ashes," *Public Administration Review* 50 (1990), pp. 129–141.
17. See David Osborne, "Can This Presidency Be Saved?" *Washington Post Magazine,* January 8, 1995, for a discussion of how he pushed for personnel cuts and budget savings as essential to selling the Clinton administration's "reinventing government" package to Congress and the public. Having been turned down for one proposed cut after another by political director, George Stephanopoulos, Osborne made a personal plea to Vice President Gore to include a recommendation to eliminate 250,000 jobs over six years, through attrition. "Without it, we argued, NPR's report would not pass the smell test. Gore was persuaded, and the report passed the test" (p. 23).
18. Herbert Kaufman, "Administrative Decentralization and Political Power," *Public Administration Review* 29 (1969), p. 4.
19. Lois Recascino Wise, "Public Management Reform: Competing Drivers of Change," *Public Administration Review* 62 (2002), p. 564.
20. These results reflect a regression of preference for scientific management and had an adjusted R^2 of .265, which was significant at the .000 level.
21. These results reflect a regression of preference for watchful eye and had an adjusted R^2 of .192, which was significant at the .000 level.
22. This result reflects a regression of preference for war on waste, and had an adjusted R^2 of .043, which was barely significant at the .048 level.
23. Peri E. Arnold, "Reform's Changing Role," *Public Administration Review* 55 (1995), p. 408.
24. See James R. Thompson and Patricia W. Ingraham, "The Reinvention Game," *Public Administration Review* 56 (1996), pp. 291–298; see also H. George Frederickson, "Comparing the Reinventing Government Movement with the New Public Administration," *Public Administration Review* 56 (1996), pp. 263–270.
25. Ronald C. Moe, "Office of Management Act of 1999," prepared statement before the House Government Reform Committee, Information and Technology Subcommittee, March, 1999, p. 9.
26. See Steven Kelman, *Unleashing Change: A Study of Organizational Renewal in Government* (Washington, D.C.: Brookings Institution Press, 2005), for a discussion of the administration's procurement reforms.
27. Personal conversation, January 2007.
28. Terry M. Moe, "Toward a Theory of Public Bureaucracy," in *Organization Theory: From Chester Barnard to the President and Beyond,* ed. O. E. Williamson (New York: Oxford University Press, 1990).
29. The total sample was 1,051 federal employees. The statistical results presented here reflect a regression of overall organizational performance against

a long list of variables and had an adjusted R² of .579, which was significant at the .000 level.

30. Paul C. Light, *What Federal Employees Want from Reform* (Washington, D.C.: Brookings Institution Press, 2002).

31. Sample size was 310 senior executives and General Schedule 13–15 employees with at least five years of government service.

32. These open-ended responses came from the 873 federal employees who said their organizations needed some reform or major reform. Employees who said their organizations did not need any reform at all were not asked what reforms were needed.

33. Haksoo Lee, N. Joseph Cayer, and G. Zhiyong Lan, "Changing Federal Employee Attitudes since the Civil Service Reform Act of 1978," *Review of Public Personnel Administration* 26 (2006), pp. 1–21.

34. Lee, Cayer, and Lan, "Changing Federal Government Employee Attitudes," p. 42.

35. Downs and Larkey, *The Search for Government Efficiency*, p. 3.

36. The random-sample telephone survey of 986 adults was conducted in May 2002 by Princeton Survey Research Associates on behalf of my Brookings Institution Center for Public Service. The margin of error in the sample was ±4 percent.

37. See Pew Research Center for the People and the Press, *Performance and Purpose: Constituents Rate Government Agencies* (Washington, D.C.: Pew Research Center, 2000).

38. Patricia W. Ingraham, "Performance: Promises to Keep and Miles to Go," *Public Administration Review* 65 (2005), p. 391.

7. Safety in the Executive

1. Alexander Hamilton, James Madison, and John Jay, *The Federalist,* ed. Benjamin Fletcher Wright (Cambridge, Mass.: Harvard University Press, 1961), p. 452.

2. *The Federalist,* p. 455.

3. Paul C. Light, *The True Size of Government* (Washington, D.C.: Brookings Institution Press, 1999).

4. Light, *The True Size of Government,* p. 37.

5. See Stephen Minicucci and John D. Donahue, "A Simple Estimation Method for Aggregate Government Outsourcing," *Journal of Policy Analysis and Management* 23 (2004), pp. 489–507 for a discussion of estimating methodologies.

6. The federal Standard Industrial Codes were replaced in the early 2000s with North American Industry Classification codes, which offer an even more precise estimate of labor burdens.

7. See E. V. Savas, *Privatization and Public-Private Partnerships* (Washington, D.C.: CQ Press 1999), for the strongest statement on sorting jobs between the private and public sectors.

8. Minicucci and Donahue, "A Simple Estimation Method," p. 400.

9. David H. Rosenbloom and Suzanne J. Piotrowski, "Outsourcing the Constitution and Administrative Law Norms," *American Review of Public Administration* 35 (2005), pp. 103–121.

10. The following discussion reflects a reanalysis of my past work on the true size of government, which contained several mathematical errors that overstated the initial impact of the end of the cold war.

11. Most of this discussion is from Paul C. Light, "Pressure to Grow," *Government Executive* (October 1, 2000), pp. 34–40.

12. Because the 2005 Federal Awards Data System had only nine months of data when this analysis was completed in mid-2006, the grant figures come from 2004.

13. Andrew Lipscomb and Albert E. Bergh, eds., *The Writings of Thomas Jefferson* (Washington, D.C.: Thomas Jefferson Memorial Association, 1903), vol. 3, p. 485.

14. *Writings of Thomas Jefferson,* vol. 6, p. 257.

15. *Writings of Thomas Jefferson,* vol. 2, p. 178.

16. *Writings of Thomas Jefferson,* vol. 4, p. 116.

17. *Writings of Thomas Jefferson,* vol. 19, p. 469.

18. Jerry L. Mashaw, "Recovering American Administrative Law: Federal Foundations, 1787–1801," *Yale Law Journal* 115 (2006), pp. 1308, 1310.

19. Scott Shane and Ron Nixon, "In Washington, Contractors Take on Biggest Role Ever," *New York Times,* February 4, 2007.

20. See Ronald L Straight, "Measuring Contractors' Performance," *Journal of Supply Chain Management* 35 (1999), p. 19.

21. The Whitten amendment was in effect during the national state of emergency that finally ended in 1978. For a short history of the amendment, see *Federal Register,* (January 10, 1995), pp. 2546–2549.

22. These figures come from the Center for Responsive Politics and are easily available through www.opensecrets.org.

23. House Committee on Government Reform, Minority Staff, *Dollars, Not Sense: Government Contracting under the Bush Administration* (committee print, 2006).

24. House Committee on Government Reform, *Dollars, Not Sense,* pp. ii–iii.

25. Government Accountability Office, *High-Risk Series: An Update* (Washington, D.C.: Government Accountability Office, 2007), pp. 71, 73, 75.

26. Comptroller General of the United States, *Suggested Areas for Oversight for the 110th Congress* (Washington, D.C.: Government Accountability Office, 2006), p. 8.

27. James P. Pfiffner, "The Public Service Ethic in New Public Personnel Systems," *Public Personnel Management* 28 (1999), p. 551.

28. See Sandra O. Sieber and Ronald L. Smith, "A Lot to Learn," *Government Executive,* www.govexec.com (June 5, 2006).

8. Reversing the Decline

1. Jerry L. Mashaw, "Recovering American Administrative Law: Federal Foundations, 1787–1801," *Yale Law Journal* 115 (2006), p. 1266.
2. Lynton K. Caldwell, *The Administrative Theories of Hamilton and Jefferson: Their Contribution to Thought on Public Administration* (Chicago: University of Chicago Press, 1944), pp. 211–212.
3. The table was created by using the mean scores of importance, difficulty, and success to develop the cells.
4. Department of Veterans Affairs Act of 1988, Public Law 100-527, 100th Cong., 2d sess. (Oct. 25, 1988), p. 107.
5. See Ronald C. Moe, "Traditional Organization Principles and the Managerial Presidency," *Public Administration Review* 50 (1990), pp. 129–141. See also General Accounting Office, *Executive Reorganization Authority: Balancing Executive and Congressional Roles in Shaping the Federal Government's Structure* (Washington, D.C.: General Accounting Office, 2003), for a history of the president's reorganization authority.
6. The quote can be found at www.presidency.ucsb.edu.

Acknowledgments

I could not have written this book without the help of dozens of mentors, funders, and fellow researchers over the past twenty-five years. Indeed, this book is the capstone of a research agenda that has involved a host of colleagues who helped design the research, conduct the analyses, interpret the results, and correct my mistakes. It has also involved the support of my family and friends, all of whom offered their support as I slowly came to the conclusion that the federal service was in sharp decline.

I might not be so worried about the decline or believe that it amounts to a crisis if I had not spent the past decade watching the trends worsen. Although I did not start studying the federal establishment in earnest until the 1980s, even my earliest encounters were troubling. I wrote my first *Minneapolis Tribune* story in 1974 on the role of the Bureau of Indian Affairs in sparking the Wounded Knee crisis, and spent the first year of graduate school in 1976 studying trust in government, which had been plummeting for the better part of a decade.

My confrontation with the decline of the federal service began in 1984 when I became director of research at the National Academy of Public Administration, which is a distant relative of the National Academy of Sciences. My projects allowed me to study every aspect of the erosion of the federal service. I was involved in studies of the presidential appointments process, morale at the Environmental Protection Agency, the politics of assumptions in the 1983 Amendments to Social Security, and the Space Shuttle Challenger accident. I also oversaw an agenda covering everything from continued management problems at the U.S. Postal Service, new rules on leaking underground storage tanks, and addressing what my friends Charles H. Levine and Rosalyn Kleeman labeled the "quiet crisis" in the civil service.

I witnessed even further erosion after joining the U.S. Senate Committee on Governmental Affairs staff in 1987. My legislative assignments focused on

264 · Acknowledgments

funding and regulating presidential transitions, lifting the Veterans Administration to cabinet status, requiring financial statements from federal departments and agencies, overseeing the growing number of chiefs of staff at the top of government, monitoring the increase in presidential appointees across government, and reauthorizing the 1978 Paperwork Reduction Act. I also worked on financial reform, results measurement, pay comparability between federal employees and their business peers, and contract fraud.

In other words, I saw the federal service at its best and worst, in agencies such as the National Aeronautics and Space Administration, still a destination of choice even after Challenger, and in agencies such as the Defense Department that could not pay their bills on time. The problems still seemed solvable at the time, even though my research showed that they were all getting worse as the federal government lost ground in the effort to build modern systems, recruit and retain talented employees, and manage an increasingly cumbersome hierarchy.

The quiet crisis became even clearer to me when I returned to university life in the 1990s and began work on studies of the federal inspectors general, the thickening of the executive hierarchy, the federal government's hidden and mostly unaccountable workforce of contractors, grantees, and state and local employees, declining trust in government, the rising cost of campaigns, and the changing nature of public service among graduates of the top schools of public affairs. As part of my work for the first National Commission on the Public Service, which was chaired by former Federal Reserve Board chairman Paul A. Volcker, I also learned that most young Americans would not know how to find a federal job even if they wanted one.

This book began to take shape a decade later after the Brookings Institution created the Center for Public Service in 1999 with a project on improving the presidential appointments process. With nearly $10 million in research funding, the Center produced a long list of studies that also examined the federal government's greatest legislative achievements, student interest in government careers, the attitudes of federal government, business, and nonprofit employees, federal contracting, and nonprofit management.

As I learned, the most interesting jobs in government were migrating to the private and nonprofit sectors, while many of the most important problems were moving toward new forms of public engagement between nonprofits and government. I then moved to New York University, where my work has been drifting further away from the federal government toward social entrepreneurs and organizational preparedness for disasters.

My research continued at New York University's Robert F. Wagner School of Public Service. New surveys and updates showed that the federal service was still in trouble and getting worse. The more I looked back to Alexander Hamilton's description of an energetic federal service, the less I could see it in the federal government today. Much as I wish I could rate the state of the federal service as healthy and strong, the evidence continues to show the crisis.

Whether or not my journey affected government, government's journey affected me. It changed the very definition of public service, not to mention what my students wanted from my courses. It also deflected my research agenda as government created new offices, added new layers, drafted new statutes, and outsourced more jobs. It obviously increased my frustration as candidates promised yet another effort to create a government that "works better and costs less," as Vice President Al Gore promised in launching his "reinventing government" campaign. And it strengthened my voice about the problems discussed in this book.

As with all books, the conclusions that follow are mine and mine alone. Much as I appreciate all the help I have received over the years, I own the mistakes and errors in interpretation readers will find in this book. Nevertheless, I would be remiss if I did not thank Robert A. Katzmann, Barbara Kibbe, G. Calvin Mackenzie, Mary McIntosh, and Pietro Nivola for their encouragement, and did not acknowledge the enormous support of my colleagues at Brookings and New York University. I would be especially careless if I did not thank my dean at NYU, Ellen Schall, as well as the many funders who made this book possible, most notably Rebecca Rimel at the Pew Charitable Trusts, Douglas Dillon at the Dillon Fund, Carol S. Larson at the David and Lucile Packard Foundation, Michael Lipsky at the Ford Foundation, Geri P. Manion at the Carnegie Corporation, and Mark Steinmeyer at the Smith Richardson Foundation, all of whom had the faith to invest in the projects leading to this final book. Finally, I would be overwhelmingly selfish if I did not thank the many research assistants who made this project a success, including Todd Ely, Elizabeth Hubbard, Judith Labiner, Carole Plowfield, Carmen Marie Rogers, and Sara Wheeler-Smith, as well as Michael Aronson and Barbara Goodhouse, who made this book a reality through their careful editing and patience on behalf of Harvard University Press.

Index

Accountability: definition of, 9; in thickening hierarchy, 76; GAO and, 80, 102, 106, 209, 234–235; of executive, 189–190; Hamilton on, 189–190, 211; transparency providing, 190–192, 210–211; in outsourcing, 191–192, 204–205, 210, 223–224; conscience providing, 204–205; Jefferson on, 204–205, 211; codes of conduct providing, 205; competition providing, 205; performance measures producing, 205; increase in, 232

Adaptability in administration, 164–165

Adequate support: energy from, 4–5, 11, 102, 107–108, 113–114, 120–121; for missions that matter, 102; vigor and expedition from, 107–108, 113–114, 120–121; Presidential Management Fellows on, 155; obstacles facing, 221

Administration. *See* Executive branch; Steadiness in administration

Administrative class, 131

Administrative Procedure Act of 1946, 166–167

Agenda, of federal service: size of, 2, 7, 22–23, 50; studies on, 22; for reform, 224–237

Agriculture, price stabilization in, 27, 40–43

Air quality, improvement of, 25, 40–43

Airways system, strengthening of, 27, 40–43

Appointees: federal service led by, 3; nomination of, 3, 7–8, 57, 78–88, 98, 219–220; of Washington, 8, 13; importance of, 80–81; of Bush, George W., 81, 83–84, 86–87, 98, 220, 243n7; Congress confirming, 81; of Roosevelt, Franklin D., 81; hierarchy thickened by, 81–83, 99–100; creeping appointeeism and, 82; discontinuity among, 82; short-term rationale among, 82; loyalty in, 83; of Nixon, 83, 87, 98; of Reagan, 83, 86–87, 98; recruitment of, 83, 94–95; of Eisenhower, 85; entry cost of, 85; of Carter, 86–87; of Clinton, 86–87; of Bush, George H.W., 87; of Johnson, Lyndon B., 87; of Kennedy, 87, 219; on appointments process, 88–94; costs *v.* benefits for, 91–95; transition costs for, 93, 231; previous employers of, 95; salaries of, 95–96; qualifications of, 96–100, 250n42; civil service *v.*, 101; dwindling pool of, 220; zealous, 220; preelection vetting of, 230; reduction in, 230–231; placement service for, 231. *See also* Qualifications, of appointees; Thickening of hierarchy

Appointments process: partisanship in, 7, 231; intrusiveness of, 15, 79, 85–87, 219–220; Hamilton on, 78–80, 100;

civil service reforms of, 127; impeachment trial of, 159; Government Performance and Results Act of, 167
Cold war, 196–199, 223
College seniors: interested in federal service, 138–149, 222; job goals and expectations of, 139–140, 143–146; motivation of, 139–149; public service defined by, 140–143; sector destinations of, 140–143, 145; school loans of, 145; confused about finding work, 145–148; parents influencing, 158–159; distrust of, in government, 158–160
Commissions on the Organization of the Executive Branch of Government, 168–169, 223
Committee for Justice, 247n6
Communism: containment of, 24, 40–43; cold war and, 196–199, 223
Competent powers, 4–6, 11
Conflict-of-interest prohibitions, 13
Congress: party conflict in, 6; energetic government and, 12–13; missions expanded by, 21–22, 33, 50–51; agenda of, 31–32; government expanded by, 31–33; worry/attention gap and, 48; appointees confirmed by, 81; reforms instigated by, 173–175, 184, 214–215; hidden workforce favored by, 208
Congressional Quarterly, 22–23
Constitution: president's role described in, 2, 213; convention for, 134, 213; reform tides described in, 167; purpose of, 205
Constitutional Convention, 134, 213
Consumer protection, 24, 40–43
Contractors, 190–192, 202, 205–211
Creeping appointeeism, 82
Crime: Omnibus Crime Control and Safe Streets Act of 1968 and, 26, 28; reduction of, 26, 28, 40–43
Customer service ratings, of government, 1

Democratic Party, 207–209
Department of Defense: expansion of, 61, 65, 72, 196–203; Department of Veterans Affairs *v.,* 66; workforce of, 122–123, 196–203, 210, 221; personnel systems of, 174; downsizing of, 198–199; modernization spending in, 200; procurement budget of, 210. *See also* Military; National defense
Department of Homeland Security, 177,

208; hierarchy of, 70; creation of, 173; Homeland Security Act establishing, 174; personnel systems of, 174
Department of Veterans Affairs: Department of Defense *v.,* 66; expansion of, 72; Department of Veterans Affairs Act for, 237–238. *See also* Veterans
Department of Veterans Affairs Act, 237–238
Disarmament. *See* Arms control and disarmament
Discipline. *See* Rewards and discipline
Disease, reduction of, 26, 40–43, 46–49
Downsizing: of federal workforce, 55, 137–138, 198–199, 200, 203–204, 217; motivation influenced by, 137–138; of Department of Defense, 198–199; of civil service, 200, 203–204; of hidden workforce, 217

"Echo" generation, 135
Economic development: missions that matter influencing, 21; of impoverished communities, 24, 40–43; international, 25, 40–43
Education: schools for, vii, 8, 133; improvement of, 25, 40–43; postsecondary, 25; No Child Left Behind Act for, 46, 204; Hamilton supporting, 133–134; financing of, 136, 145
Eisenhower, Dwight D., 85, 193
Elections: of president, 5; preelection planning and, 230
Endangered species, protection of, 26, 40–43
Energetic government, 2–4, 6–14; Hamilton's vision of, 1–14, 212–213; in executive branch, 2, 4–6; definition of, 4; from adequate support, 4–5, 11, 102, 107–108, 113–114, 120–121; from duration in office, 4–5, 11; from unity in executive, 4–5, 11; from competent powers, 4–6, 11; from missions that matter, 7, 15, 20–51; from clarity of command, 7–8, 13, 15, 52–77; from posts of honor, 8, 78–101; from spirit of service, 8, 131–162; from vigor and expedition, 8, 102–130; from steadiness in administration, 8–9, 16, 163–188; from safety in executive, 9, 189–211; bureaucracy created by, 10; Congress and, 12–13; rebuilding of, 16–19, 212–239; erosion of, 217–224